LAOS

Marxist Regimes Series

Series editor: Bogdan Szajkowski,
Department of Sociology, University College,
Cardiff

Further Titles

LAOS

Politics, Economics and Society

Martin Stuart-Fox

Frances Pinter (Publishers), London
Lynne Rienner Publishers, Inc., Boulder

First published in Great Britain in 1986 by
Frances Pinter (Publishers) Limited
25 Floral Street, London WC2E 9DS

First published in the United States of America by
Lynne Rienner Publishers Inc.
948 North Street
Boulder, Colorado 80302

British Library Cataloguing in Publication Data

Stuart-Fox, Martin
    Laos: politics, economics and society.——
    (Marxist regimes series)
    1. Laos——Social conditions
    I. Title   II. Series
    959.4 ′04   HN700.4.A8
    ISBN 0-86187-426-9
    ISBN 0-86187-427-7 Pbk

Library of Congress Cataloging in Publication Data

Stuart-Fox, Martin, 1939–
    Laos: politics, economics, and society.
    (Marxist regimes series)
    Bibliography: p.
    Includes index.
    1. Laos—History 1975–   . I. Title.
II. Series.
DS555.84.S78   1986   959.4 ′04   86-17810
ISBN 1-55587-004-X (lib. bdg.)

Typeset by Joshua Associates Limited, Oxford
Printed by SRP Ltd, Exeter

Editor's Preface

The interaction between the traditional values of Theravada Buddhism and Marxism in contemporary Laos is unique in the world-wide context of Marxist adaptations. This, the first full analysis of politics, economics and society in Laos since the communist victories in Indo-China in April 1975, provides the reader with a comprehensive assessment of both the background and current socialist developments in that country.

This book is based on material gathered primarily during the author's field trips to Laos which also involved conducting extensive interviews with government and party officials, among others. First-hand experience with Laotian socialism has allowed the author to give a lucid account of the evolution of social and political structures in Laos as well as a rare insight into the complexities of current developments in one of the most under-developed, secretive and unknown contemporary Marxist regimes. The publication of this book coincides with the thirtieth anniversary of the founding of the Lao People's Revolutionary Party and the passing of the first decade of its coming to power. This work should prove indispensible for an understanding of the future course of events in one of the most strategically important countries of South-east Asia.

In addi:.ion this work also raises a number of very important questions about the appraisal of Marxist adaptations in the developing countries. The study of Marxist regimes has commonly been equated with the study of communist political systems. There were several historical and methodo-logical reasons for this.

For many years it was not difficult to distinguish the eight regimes in Eastern Europe and four in Asia which resoundingly claimed adherence to the tenets of Marxism and more particularly to their Soviet interpretation—Marxism–Leninism. These regimes, variously called 'People's Republic', 'People's Democratic Republic', or 'Democratic Republic', claimed to have derived their inspiration from the Soviet Union to which, indeed, in the overwhelming number of cases they owed their establishment.

To many scholars and analysts these regimes represented a multiplication of and geographical extension of the 'Soviet model' and consequently of the Soviet sphere of influence. Although there were clearly substantial similari-ties between the Soviet Union and the people's democracies, especially in the initial phases of their development, these were often overstressed at the expense of noticing the differences between these political systems.

It took a few years for scholars to realize that generalizing the particular, i.e. applying the Soviet experience to other states ruled by elites which claimed to be guided by 'scientific socialism', was not good enough. The relative simplicity of the assumption of a cohesive communist bloc was questioned after the expulsion of Yugoslavia from the Communist Information Bureau in 1948 and in particular after the workers' riots in Poznań in 1956 and the Hungarian revolution of the same year. By the mid-1960s, the totalitarian model of communist politics, which until then had been very much in force, began to crumble. As some of these regimes articulated demands for a distinctive path of socialist development, many specialists studying these systems began to notice that the cohesiveness of the communist bloc was less apparent than had been claimed before.

Also by the mid-1960s, in the newly independent African states 'democratic' multi-party states were turning into one-party states or military dictatorships, thus questioning the inherent superiority of liberal democracy, capitalism and the values that went with it. Scholars now began to ponder on the simple contrast between multi-party democracy and a one-party totalitarian rule that had satisfied an earlier generation.

More importantly, however, by the beginning of that decade Cuba had a revolution without Soviet help, a revolution which subsequently became to many political elites in the Third World not only an inspiration but a clear military, political and ideological example to follow. Apart from its romantic appeal, to many nationalist movements the Cuban revolution also demonstrated a novel way of conducting and winning a nationalist, anti-imperialist war and accepting Marxism as the state ideology without a vanguard communist party. The Cuban precedent was subsequently followed in one respect or another by scores of regimes in the Third World who used the adoption of 'scientific socialism' tied to the tradition of Marxist thought as a· form of mobilization, legitimation or association with the prestigious symbols and powerful high-status regimes such as the Soviet Union, China, Cuba and Vietnam.

Despite all these changes the study of Marxist regimes remains in its infancy and continues to be hampered by constant and not always pertinent comparison with the Soviet Union, thus somewhat blurring the important underlying common theme—the 'scientific theory' of the laws of development of human society and human history. This doctrine is claimed by the leadership of these regimes to consist of the discovery of objective causal relationships; it is used to analyse the contradictions which arise between goals and actuality in the pursuit of a common destiny. Thus the political elites of these countries have been and continue to be influenced in both their ideology and their political practice by Marxism more than any other current of social thought and political practice.

The growth in the number and global significance, as well as the ideological political and economic impact, of Marxist regimes has presented scholars and students with an increasing challenge. In meeting this challenge, social scientists on both sides of the political divide have put forward a dazzling profusion of terms, models, programmes and varieties of interpretation. It is against the background of this profusion that the present comprehensive series on Marxist regimes is offered.

This collection of monographs is envisaged as a series of multi-disciplinary textbooks on the governments, politics, economics and society of these countries. Each of the monographs was prepared by a specialist on the country concerned. Thus, over fifty scholars from all over the world have contributed monographs which were based on first-hand knowledge. The geographical diversity of the authors, combined with the fact that as a group they represent many disciplines of social science, gives their individual analyses and the series as a whole an additional dimension.

Each of the scholars who contributed to this series was asked to analyse such topics as the political culture, the governmental structure, the ruling party, other mass organizations, party-state relations, the policy process, the economy, domestic and foreign relations together with any features peculiar to the country under discussion.

This series does not aim at assigning authenticity or authority to any single one of the political systems included in it. It shows that depending on a variety of historical, cultural, ethnic and political factors, the pursuit of goals derived from the tenets of Marxism has produced different political forms at different times and in different places. It also illustrates the rich diversity among these societies, where attempts to achieve a synthesis between goals derived from Marxism on the one hand, and national realities on the other, have often meant distinctive approaches and solutions to the problems of social, political and economic development.

University College   *Bogdan Szajkowski*
Cardiff

Contents

List of Illustrations and Tables

Map

Figures

Tables

Acknowledgements

I would like to express my thanks to all those who aided me in obtaining the information which made it possible for me to write this book. Many of these people cannot be named, for fear that they may be held accountable for what I have written. Their assistance was given at all times in the sincere belief that in doing so they contributed to furthering international understanding of and sympathy for the Lao People's Democratic Republic through making its political system, economic problems and social structure more widely known. One who can be named who assisted me throughout both the research and writing of this book is Elisabeth Stuart-Fox. Were it not for her linguistic skills, part at least of the field research would not have been completed. Were it not for her continuous support, the writing would have been far more of a burden.

On the production side, I would like first to thank Mary Kooyman for her always cheerful expertise in transforming my all but illegible manuscript into the finished product of the word processor. The series General Editor Bogdan Szajkowski and Heather Bliss, editor for Frances Pinter (Publishers), have both been most understanding over unavoidable delays in meeting my manuscript submission deadline. To both I extend my thanks for their helpful suggestions for improvement of the final presentation of this book, and for enabling it to appear in this valuable series.

Preface

Much information that is readily available in most other countries is surprisingly difficult to come by in Laos. Many policy documents are circulated only within the still semi-secret Lao People's Revolutionary Party, and are never made public. No official notification is given of administrative changes, even of such major significance as a rearrangement and increase in the number of provinces. Changes of personnel, even at ministerial or vice-ministerial level, are not gazetted. As a result, one of the games played by Western embassies in Laos is to try to determine who holds what position in what ministry. The only way to discover who has been reappointed, demoted, sent for ideological education in Vietnam, or purged for some reason, is either to note some change in designation or surprise omission in the list of dignatories welcoming a visiting delegation or to ask innocent questions at diplomatic gatherings.

Even apparently non-political factual information can be all but impossible to obtain. For example, ever since its inception in 1975, the government of the Lao People's Democratic Republic has proclaimed itself the representative of all sixty-eight 'nationalities', or ethnic groups, in the country. The number 'sixty-eight' has been repeated time and again as an official figure; yet it is quite impossible to discover what these 'nationalities' are. No list of sixty-eight ethnic groups is available in Vientiane, either from the Nationalities Commission charged with supervising ethnic affairs, or from the Ministry of Culture, which has a special ethnological research unit. In an interview with the Chairman of the Nationalities Committee, it was revealed that the magic number 'sixty-eight' did not include such ethnic groups as resident Vietnamese, Chinese, Indians or Thais, many of whom have Lao nationality. Nor apparently does it include the most primitive of all ethnic minorities, the extremely shy nomadic, jungle-dwelling Phi Tong Luong, known to inhabit certain remote parts of Sayaboury province. Further probing did, however, reveal a possible reason for the secrecy surrounding the number 'sixty-eight': the basis of classification—linguistic or cultural—is in question: there may not be sixty-eight 'nationalities' after all. In the meantime, there seems to be no one with either the competence or the authority to decide one way or the other.

This kind of difficulty and consequent frustration meets the researcher at every turn. Information officers have no information—every question has to be referred to some higher authority. Even a question on which foreign languages were currently being taught at the Dong Dok Teachers Training College was referred to a member of the Politburo to answer. 'Delicate' questions are not even asked in the LPDR, let alone answered. For example, nobody asks questions about the Lao People's Army. After some hesitation the author was eventually accorded the first interview in the ten years the regime has been in power with a spokesman for the Ministry of Defence. Written questions were submitted, with embarrassing ones omitted. Replies and the interview itself remained at the level of propaganda and generalities. Questions as to structure and personnel were artfully parried; questions as to troop levels and deployment were not even asked.

So extraordinary is the degree of unavailability of often even the most basic information in Laos that the phenomenon itself needs explaining. It is, of course, a characteristic of communist regimes to control information as a means of maintaining the Party's monopoly of political power. In Laos, information is restricted on a need-to-know basis. No encouragement is given to any kind of intellectual curiosity, or to the pursuit of knowledge as a means of improving the quality of life. The National Library is not open to the public; the country's two bookshops contain nothing but Eastern bloc magazines, the works of Marx and Lenin and a few 'acceptable' novels translated into Lao. Rare indeed is it to see anyone reading, and intellectual discussion (at least with foreigners) is definitely discouraged. Nothing that might lead to a questioning of the Party line is permitted; the Chinese embassy is as isolated as is the American.

In restricting information, of course, the Lao authorities are acting in accordance with communist example to protect their own power and authority. They have undoubtedly learned much from the Soviets and Vietnamese. The Lao Planning Commission, where Soviet influence is strongest, has consistently refused to make the country's first five-year plan available to officials of the United Nations Development Programme in Laos. How dozens of UNDP projects fit into the overall plan remains unclear. A confidential World Bank Report admitted that not only did Bank officers have no contact with top decision-makers in Laos, they could not even obtain information on the process by which decisions were made. Bank officers did not know the departmental responsibilities of the vice-ministers of finance or the vice-chairmen of the State Bank Committee. They did not even know the names of the three directors of the Bank for External Trade. The same secrecy surrounds Vietnamese and Soviet activities in Laos. The Vietnamese embassy's information officer was unwilling to name even one important

Vietnamese aid programme in Laos, let alone confirm or deny any cost estimate of total Vietnamese assistance broadcast over Radio Vientiane. In fact no cost estimate of any Soviet or Vietnamese aid project in Laos has been revealed to any competent authority.

What, however, apart from communist example, are the reasons for the obsessive secrecy and control of information in Laos? One is simply the shortage of trained personnel. So great has been the loss of educated refugees fleeing Laos that the government does not have the necessary cadres to obtain the information it needs. Statistics are inaccurate because there is no adequate systematic collection of data. This does not prevent the Lao authorities from providing whatever figures foreign governments and international organizations might want, even though such 'statistics' often amount to little more than informed guesses.

Another reason for the reluctance to provide information is that lower level cadres and civil servants are fearful even of being seen talking to a foreigner, let alone taking the decision to provide information. So politicized has Lao society become, so concerned are most Lao to keep their political noses clean through adhering to the line of the Party, that few take the risk of communicating what could possibly be considered 'sensitive information'.

A further reason for the regime's reluctance to provide information has to do with its continuing, almost paranoic, concern over security. Thirty years of revolutionary war has induced a fear of betrayal, an obsession with possible enemies, that has resulted in far too many arrests for no good reason. Differences of opinion are treated as indictable offences against the security of the state. Anyone seeking information is suspect because he, or she, could possibly use it to undermine the confidence of the masses in the regime, by criticizing the Party line or by 'sabotaging' Party directives.

The present study is based on available written sources, plus research and interviews conducted in Laos over a five-week period during July and August 1985. Ten interviews were conducted with ministers, vice-ministers or ministerial spokesmen. Two sets of answers to written questions were also provided. Four other interviews requested on agriculture and cooperatives, the Lao People's Revolutionary Party, government and local government and reorganization of the Prefecture of Vientiane were regrettably not forthcoming. This study can only be the poorer as a result. Whatever strengths it has are due to assistance provided by friends and acquaintances, officials and representatives, both inside and outside Laos, with whom I have discussed various aspects of contemporary Lao politics and society. Its weaknesses are due to my own shortcomings—and to the scarcity of information available in the Lao People's Democratic Republic.

Laos

Basic Data

Official name	Lao People's Democratic Republic (Sathalanalat Pasathipatay Pasason Lao)
Population	3,584,804 (1985 census) (47% below the age of 15; 47% aged 15–60; 6% over 60)
Population density	15 inhabitants per sq. km.
Population growth (% p.a)	2.9 (birth rate 46 per 1,000; death rate 17 per 1,000)
Urban population (%)	15
Total labour force	1.5 million
Life expectancy	46 years
Infant death rate (per 1,000)	118 (1985)
Ethnic groups	Approximate percentages: Lao Loum (includes Hill Tai as well as lowland Lao, 56%; Lao Theung, 34%; Lao Soung, 9%; others, 1% (Vietnamese, Chinese, Indians, etc.)
Capital	Vientiane
Land area	236,800 sq. km. (91,100 sq. miles) of which 4% is cultivated; 4% grassland, 47% thick forests, 17% open savannah and woodland; much of the remaining area is covered by secondary growth after being used for slash-and-burn agriculture
Official language	Lao
Other main languages	Tai dialects, Hmong, Lao Theung dialects
Administrative division	16 provinces, plus the autonomous prefecture of Vientiane; 112 districts (*muong*); 950 sub-districts (*tasseng*); 11,424 villages (*ban*).
Membership of international organizations	UN since 1952; IMF since 1961; World Bank and ADB; Conference of Non-aligned Nations

Foreign relations	Diplomatic relations with 52 states; 27 diplomatic missions represented in Vientiane.

Political structure
Constitution	Not yet drafted (as of January 1986)
Highest legislative body	Supreme People's Assembly
Highest executive body	Council of government
Prime Minister	Kaysone Phomvihane
President	Souphanouvong
Ruling party	Lao People's Revolutionary Party
Secretary General of the Party	Kaysone Phomvihane
Party membership	43,000 (1985) (less than 3% of adult population)

Growth indicators (% p.a.)
National income	(GDP) 1980–1, +6.6%; 1981–2, +1.9%; 1982–3, −3.3%; 1983–4, +8.1%

Industry
Heavy	none
Consumer	14% (1981–4) last production still below 1974 level
agriculture	(rice) 11% (1977–84)
food production per capita	350 kg

Trade and Balance of Payments
Exports	US$42.8 million (1983)
Imports	US$135.1 million (1983)
Exports as % of GNP	7.45 (1983)
Main exports	Electricity, timber, forest products (benzoin, sticklac, etc.)
Main imports	Fuel, vehicles and spare parts, machinery and equipment, consumer goods
Destination of exports	Vietnam, Thailand, Soviet Union
Main trading partners	Vietnam, Soviet Union, Thailand, Japan
Foreign debt	US$400 million (of which US$140 million to convertible area and balance to Socialist Bloc)

Main natural resources	Hydroelectricity, timber, tin, gypsum (plus unexploited iron ore and other minerals)

Food self-sufficiency	Self-sufficient in food production. Paddy production 1.3 million tonnes (1985)
Armed forces	53,700 (Army 50,000; River Navy 1,700; Air Force 2,000)

Education and health
    School system — 11 years (ages 6–17): 5 years primary; 3 years 1st cycle secondary; 3 years 2nd cycle secondary

Primary school enrolment	85%
Secondary school enrolment	23%
Higher education	2.5% (more than half studying abroad)
Adult literacy	85% (UN estimate, 1985; regime claims 100%)
Population per hospital bed	400 (1985)
Population per physician	8,576 (1985)

Economy
GNP	26,580 million kip (1984)
GNP per capita	US$184 (IMF estimate January 1985); other estimates run as low as $98
State budget: expenditure	8.0 billion kip (1984)
: receipts	4.5 billion kip (1984) (balance from foreign aid)
Monetary unit	Kip

Main crops	Rice, maize, cassava, coffee, tobacco, cotton
Land tenure	No land redistribution carried out, so where land not collectivized, private holdings vary from 0.5 to 10 hectares, but average 1.5 hectares per family
Main religions	Theravada Buddhism, Animism
Rail network	Nil
Road network	Approximately 1,300 km. asphalted; 5.300 gravelled; 3.900 dirt (1982)

Population Forecasting

The following data are projections produced by Poptran, University College Cardiff Population Centre, from United Nations Assessment Data published in 1980, and are reproduced here to provide some basis of comparison with other countries covered by the Marxist Regimes Series.

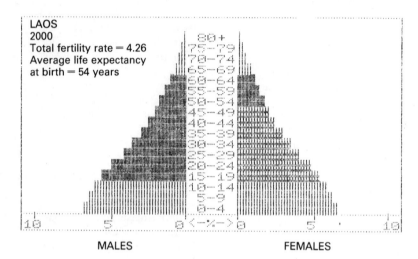

MALES   FEMALES

Projected Data for Laos 2000

Total population ('000)	5,728
Males ('000)	2,878
Females ('000)	2,850
Total fertility rate	4.26
Life expectancy (male)	52.0 years
Life expectancy (female)	55.1 years
Crude birth rate	31.8
Crude death rate	12.6
Annual growth rate	1.92%
Under 15s	37.89%
Over 65s	3.44%
Women aged 15–49	24.97%
Doubling time	36 years
Population density	24 per sq. km.
Urban population	25.1%

Glossary

Administrative divisions

ban	village
tasseng	sub-district; groups five to ten villages
muong	district of canton
khoueng	province

Educational institutions

pathom	primary school covering the first five years
mathanyom	junior high school, years 6 to 8
udom	senior high school, years 9 to 11
mahavitanyalay	university

Ethnic groups

Hmong	name by which the opium-growing Lao Soung tribe of northern Laos, often called Meo, call themselves; means 'free'
Khmer	dominant ethnic group in Cambodia/Kampuchea
Lao Loum	inclusive term for all peoples of Tai stock living in Laos, including lowland Lao and upland Tai peoples
Lao Phuan, Lao Yuan	Laoized Tai groups
Lao Soung	Lao of the mountain peaks; ethnic groups speaking Tibeto-Burman languages, traditionally living at high altitudes in northern Laos
Lao Theung	Lao of the mountain slopes; ethnic groups speaking Austronesian languages, traditionally living at medium altitudes, farming by slash-and-burn methods
Lu (or Tai-Lu)	Tai peoples inhabiting the Sip Song Panna area of southern China and northern Laos
Tai	generic term for all ethnic groups speaking T'ai languages
T'ai	the language group spoken by Tai peoples
Tai Dam	Black Tai (upland Tai tribe)

Tai Deng	Red Tai (upland Tai tribe)
Tai Khao	White Tai (upland Tai tribe)
Tai Neua (or Lao Neua)	people inhabiting Houa Phan province; closely similar to lowland Lao
Tai Syam	Siamese, Tai of central and lower Menan valley
Thai	people of modern Thailand

Political terms

Cambodia/ Kampuchea	Cambodia was the name used until 1975, thereafter known as Kampuchea
Pathet Lao	literally 'Land of the Lao'; used since 1954 by Western writers to refer to the Lao Communist movement as a whole
Siam	former name for Thailand

Religious terms

baci	semi-secular ceremony of welcome or farewell to honoured guests
boun	pagoda fair or festival
karma	the moral effect, either positive or negative, of deeds or intentions performed at some earlier stage during this lifetime or in previous lifetimes
Sangha	the Buddhist order of monks and nuns
wat	Buddhist temple, or pagoda

Abbreviations

ADB	Asian Development Bank
ASEAN	Association of Southeast Asian Nations
BN	Bulletin de Nouvelles, Ministry of Foreign Affairs of LPDR
CC	Central Committee
CIA	Central Intelligence Agency
CPC	Central Propaganda Committee
DRV	Democratic Republic of Vietnam
FAO	Food and Agriculturel Organization
FBIS	Foreign Broadcasts Information Service
FEER	Far Eastern Economic Review
FLTU	Federation of Lao Trade Unions
GDP	Gross Domestic Product
ICC	International Control Commission
ICP	Indochinese Communist Party
IDA	International Development Association
IMF	International Monetary Fund
JPRS	Joint Publications Research Service
KPL/BQ	Khaosan Pathet Lao/Bulletin Quotidien (Summary in French)
KPL/NB	Khaosan Pathet Lao/News Bulletin (Summary in English)
LDC	Least Developed Country
LFNC	Lao Front for National Construction (Neo Lao Sang Sat)
LPA	Lao People's Army
LPDR	Lao People's Democratic Republic
LPLA	Lao People's Liberation Army
LPF	Lao Patriotic Front
LPP	Lao People's Party
LPRP	Lao People's Revolutionary Party
LPRY	Lao People's Revolutionary Youth
LUBA	Lao United Buddhists Association
MIA	Missing in action
NL	Nouvelles du Laos (published by LPDR Embassy in Paris)
NLHS	Neo Lao Hak Sat (Lao Patriotic Front)

NPCC	National Political Consultative Council
PGNU	Provisional Government of National Union
PL	Pathet Lao
PRC	People's Republic of China
RLA	Royal Lao Army
RLG	Royal Lao Government
SPA	Supreme People's Assembly
SPC	Supreme People's Court
SRV	Socialist Republic of Vietnam
ULW	Union of Lao Women
UN	United Nations
UNDP	United Nations Development Programme
UNHCR	United Nations High Commission for Refugees
UNICEF	United Nations International Children's Emergency Fund
USAID	United States Agency for International Development
VNA	Vietnam News Agency
WHO	World Health Organization

1   Political History of the Lao State

The Geographical Setting

Laos is the least populated and militarily and economically the least powerful state in mainland Southeast Asia. It covers an area of 236,800 square kilometres (approximately 91,000 square miles) stretching a distance of roughly 1,000 kilometres from north to south, and between 200 and 400 kilometres from east to west. Laos is bordered to the north by the Chinese province of Yunnan (424 kilometres), to the northwest by Burma (238 kilometres), to the northeast and east by Vietnam (1,650 kilometres), to the south by Kampuchea (540 kilometres), and to the west by Thailand (1,754 kilometres). The Lao state is thus entirely landlocked. Access to the sea via a neighbouring country is virtually impossible through Burma or across the mountains of southern China. To the east, the Annamite Cordillera presents a formidable barrier, traversable only at half a dozen mountain passes. To the south, the cataracts of Khone and the Dangrek Ranges prevent easy communication via Kampuchea. Only to the west does the Korat Plateau of northeastern Thailand provide relatively easy access to the Gulf of Siam.

The present borders of the Lao state are the product of historical expediency: all cut across geographical features and divide ethnic groups. Although the western frontier follows the crests of the Annamite Chain, it divides closely related tribal peoples who have little in common with either the Vietnamese or the lowland Lao. In the northwest and north, the Lao frontier divides two regions, both of which have a well-defined historical and ethno-geographical identity—the Sip Song Chau Tai stretching into north-western Vietnam, and the Sip Song Panna including parts of northwestern Burma and southern China. To the west, the northern sector of the border between Thailand and Laos follows the watershed between the Menam and the Mekong river systems, only to loop back to follow the Mekong itself for a distance of some 800 kilometres. By so doing, it effectively divides the Lao-speaking people of the Mekong valley in present day Laos from the far more numerous ethnically and culturally all-but-identical Lao-speaking people of the northeastern, or Isan, region of Thailand.

Geographically Laos is dominated by two features: the mountains of the north and east, and the Mekong river and its east-bank tributaries. Northern

Laos is almost entirely mountainous, an extension of range upon range of peaks and valleys stretching southeast from Tibet. The steep mountain slopes are covered with dense jungle descending to narrow valleys. The high annual rainfall drains off into a series of major rivers running west and south to the Mekong: the Nam Tha in the north, the Nam Ou, the Nam Suong and the Nam Ngum watering the Vientiane plain. The other major feature of northern Laos is the high plateau of Xieng Khouang, known colloquially as the Plain of Jars, an area of undulating hills at an average altitude of over 1,000 metres. Just to the south rises the Phou Bia massif with peaks above 2,800 metres.

In central and southern Laos the land falls away from the Annamite Cordillera in the east to the Mekong in the west, drained by another series of fast flowing rivers—the Nam Ca Dinh, Sé Bang Fai, Sé Bang Hieng, Sé Done, Sé Khong. Like the rivers of the north, those of the south hold considerable hydro-electrical potential. In central Laos, the rice plains east of the Mekong are more extensive. Further south, the Bolovens Plateau rises to an altitude of 1,000 metres. The forests of central and southern Laos are sparser, more easily exploitable than those of the north, giving way in places to savannah country.

The mountain valleys and rivers of Laos run for the most part east–west or northeast–southwest, cutting across the northwest–southeast axis of the country. Only the Mekong provides a means of communication running the length of the country. For most of the more than 1,600 kilometres over which the Mekong either borders or flows through Lao territory the river is navigable. However, four series of rapids divide this length into three reaches, and effectively close off communications either to the north or to the south. North of Ban Houei Sai the river increasingly takes on the character of a Himalayan torrent. The reach from Ban Houei Sai to south of Luang Prabang forms the first large navigable stretch, but a series of rapids prevents larger vessels reaching Vientiane except during the rainy season when the river is high. The second navigable reach extends from west of Vientiane to south of Savannakhet, and terminates in the rocks and rapids of Khemmarat. South of Khemmarat, the third navigable reach extends through the province of Champassak to the impassable thirteen-kilometre cataracts of Khone which divide the Lao and Kampuchean stretches of the Mekong.

These three navigable stretches of the Mekong correspond to three naturally separate and historically important areas of population and political influence: in the north Luang Prabang extending across to the west bank of the river to take in the province of Sayaboury; in the centre Vientiane-Savannakhet now confined to the east bank only but previously taking in the Khorat Plateau; and in the south Champassak with a truncated west bank extension. Only during periods of strong central government were the three regions united to form a single state. Once that central power weakened, a restive regionalism exerted itself, reinforced by the lack of natural means of communication. Thus has geography shaped the history of the Lao state—and continues to hamper its economic integration.

Early History: The Buddhist Heritage

In view of the ethnic diversity of the people of Laos, and the geographical extension of the Lao as an ethnic group, it would be a mistake to confuse the history of the Lao state with the history of the Lao race. Nevertheless, as the ethnic Lao have constituted the dominant political and cultural group in the country throughout at least the last six hundred years, any history of Laos must take this into account. The political institutions of the traditional Lao state were created by ethnic Lao, albeit under the influence of a borrowed system of beliefs (Theravada Buddhism) and in interaction with indigenous ethnic groups.

The origins of the Lao race should probably be sought in the region of Kwangsi in southern China (Wyatt, 1984, but cf. Terwiel, 1978). Under the pressure of Han Chinese expansion, proto-Tai peoples from this area appear to have moved south and west into Yunnan and the Sip Song Chau Tai area of what is now northwestern Vietnam, eventually establishing in the eighth century the powerful Tai kingdom of Nan Chao (Coedès, 1968). The gradual movement of Tai peoples continued between the eighth and thirteenth centuries, as far west as Assam, but principally southwest and south down the tributaries and valleys of the Mekong and Menam. There they came under the political domination of the Khmer empire with its capital at Angkor. The Tai inter-married with local inhabitants, accepted Khmer administration and served in the Khmer army. they also came into contact, for the first time, with Theravada Buddhism, spread by Mon monks from the former kingdom of Dvaravati situated in the lower Menam valley, an area by then also incorporated into the Khmer empire. The earliest Buddhist remains discovered in Laos date from the seventh or eighth century, and are of Mon provenance (Lévy, 1974), but Buddhism may well have been known to the Lao even earlier.

By the beginning of the thirteenth century Tai peoples were well established within the nominal confines or just beyond the fringes of the Khmer empire: the Tai Syam in northern Thailand; the Tai Lu further north in the Sip Song Panna; the upland Tai peoples—Tai Deng (Red Tai), Tai Dam (Black Tai), etc.—in the Sip Song Chau Tai; the Tai Neua in parts of northern

Laos and the Tai Lao along the upper Mekong. The thirteenth century was a period of considerable ferment. Establishment of the new Mongol (Yuan) dynasty in China coincided with the gradual decline of the Khmer empire following the death of Jayavarman VII. The Mongol conquest of Nan Chao in the mid-thirteenth century accelerated the movement of Tai peoples south, and stimulated the foundation of new independent Tai principalities centred on Chiang Mai, Sukhothai and Luang Prabang (then known as Muong Swa).

Lao legend traces the origins of the Lao people to a ruler of Muong Tèng, meaning the principality of the gourd, the Tai name for Dien Bien Phu. This ruler, Khun Borom, was the son of the spirit of heaven sent to earth to exercise authority over three groups of people who spilled out of three broken gourds: Lao aristocrats, Lao commoners, and the indigenous hill tribes (Lao Theung, known pejoratively as Kha or slaves) who inhabited Laos before the Lao arrived. Khun Borom had seven sons whom he sent out to found seven principalities of their own. The eldest son, Khun Lo, was sent to Luang Prabang where he became the first of a shadowy line of twenty-one princes. The change of title of the rulers of Luang Prabang from Khun to Thao ('prince') to Panya ('he who upholds') may signify three separate dynasties for it seems likely that this line of early rulers has some historical reality (cf. Dommen, 1985).

In 1316 occurred the first recorded event in Lao history, the birth to Phi Fa, heir apparent of the principality of Luang Prabang, of a son named Fa Ngum. When Phi Fa was banished for having seduced one of his father's wives, he journeyed south, taking his young son with him, and sought asylum at the Khmer court at Angkor. There Fa Ngum was brought up, married a Khmer princess and from there he set out at the head of a Khmer army to reconquer his ancestral domains. In so doing, he took advantage of the relative weakness of the Khmer empire to carve out for himself a kingdom including the Sip Song Panna in the north, Xieng Khouang and the Sip Song Chau Tai in the northeast, Champassak in the south and most of the Korat Plateau in the west. Thus was established the Kingdom of Lan Xang ('a million elephants'), a state able to hold its own against other fourteenth-century kingdoms—Burma, Vietnam, Champa, Cambodia and the newly founded Tai Syam state of Ayuthia.

Fa Ngum declared himself king of Lan Xang in 1353, with his seat of government at Luang Prabang. For all its remoteness, Luang Prabang remained the capital of the Lao state for the next two centuries. It was there that the institutions, ceremonies and beliefs which were to shape the traditional Lao-Buddhist state for the next six hundred years were established.

Annual reenactment of a series of myth-enforcing rituals effectively reiterated the claims of the royal clan to the office of king, of the Lao nobility to its monopoly of social authority, and of the Lao to their right to dominate all other ethnic groups (cf. Stuart-Fox, 1983, from which this section is largely drawn). But the legitimacy of the Lao social order and the bases of Lao political culture rested on more than the courtly ceremonial reiteration of myth and legend. For the Lao peasantry scattered throughout hundreds of virtually autonomous and self-sufficient village communities, the king's right to rule and the nobility's right to exercise local power depended primarily on the support provided for the conception of kingship and social status by the popular form of Buddhism which constituted the axiological framework of the traditional Lao world view. Theravada Buddhism provided the broader context within which a whole range of mythic folk beliefs and borrowed Indian notions of statecraft could be integrated (cf. Reynolds, 1969; Aijmer, 1979).

The legitimizing role of Buddhism in reinforcing the authority of the king goes back to the reforms instituted by Fa Ngum. The mission he despatched to Angkor returned with the Phra Bang, a sacred Buddha image which became the palladium of the kingdom and centre of ceremonies symbolizing the superiority of the *Dhamma* (Buddhist Truth) over both gods and men. In New Year rituals, both the king and masked dancers representing the ancestral guardian spirits of the kingdom performed acts of lustration signifying submission to Buddha, *Dhamma*, and *Sangha* (the order of monks). This was followed by an oath of loyalty taken by nobles to the king. Thus the hierarchical ordering of the temporal realm was confirmed by placing it within a wider legitimizing religious context which re-emphasized the primacy of the king and status of the nobility. The king was the means by which, through support for the *Sangha*, the *Dhamma* was made known to his people, for their spiritual benefit (cf. Archaimbault, 1973).

The right of the king to fulfil this function was reinforced in the eyes of his subjects by the notions of *karma* and merit. Lao Buddhism teaches that the accumulation of religious merit leads to rebirth under conditions favouring advancement towards enlightenment, or Buddhahood. It is but a step from this to the popular belief that accumulation of merit must lead to a 'better' rebirth in terms of social status and/or material affluence. Thus it was widely believed that a king must have accumulated considerable religious merit in previous existences. He was king, therefore, by spiritual as well as hereditary right. In other words, he owed his exalted position primarily to the workings of the immutable law of *karma*, which holds that personal circumstances are the cumulative effect of individual moral actions and intentions. Similar beliefs explained the status of the nobility. Buddhism thus effectively reinforced the established social order.

However, the relationship between the king and nobility on the one hand and the *Sangha* on the other was reciprocal. The king was expected to demonstrate his religious commitment by generously endowing Buddhist pagodas and actively encouraging propagation of the *Dhamma*. By its presence in almost every Lao village, and through its missionizing activities among other ethnic groups, the *Sangha* acted as an important unifying force within the state. The monopoly exercised by the *Sangha* over education ensured continued legitimacy for the Lao social order, while at the same time the *Sangha* hierarchy provided an avenue for social advancement for those frustrated by class distinctions.

Elsewhere I have summed up the Lao-Buddhist world view as follows:

At one level, the king owed his right to rule to his inheritance, as descendant of the guardians of the Lao state and of the great kings of the past. But a higher legitimation was provided by his relationship to a higher truth—the *Dhamma* of the Buddha and his *Sangha*, of which the monarch was both conduit and embodiment. Position within the social hierarchy was equally the result of merit gained through the action of *karma*, with additional support provided for the aristocracy by the myth of an origin distinct from that of the mass of the Lao people. The crucial factor in determining the social hierarchy was thus not birth alone, but birth as a result of possession of merit, and thus of fulfilment of *Dhamma*. Below the aristocracy came the Lao peasantry, whose rank above the *Kha* was determined both by origin, and by the fact that the Lao sought merit while the *Kha*, as non-Buddhists, did not. This ordering of society legitimized the right of the aristocracy, with the king at its head, to wield temporal power—except over the *Sangha*, which, as an independent hierarchy apart from and yet part of society, served as the guardian of Truth (*Dhamma*). The *Sangha* thus enjoyed a mutually supportive relationship with the government of the state: it provided legitimation in return for a monopoly over religious office and orthodoxy. [Stuart-Fox, 1983, p. 433.]

In the traditional Lao-Buddhist state, the above world view legitimized the existing social order and the exercise of political authority, but it could not guarantee the continued exercise of political authority by any particular ruler. The structure of traditional Lao society contained certain inherent weaknesses since it constituted what has been termed a 'galactic polity' (Tambiah, 1976)—that is, one in which the political unit consists of a hierarchy of dependent territorial units, each the quasi-feudal domain of a subordinate ruler bound to the king only by ritually reinforced oaths of allegiance. As a result, authority was decentralized, not delegated by the king but exercised nominally on his behalf only as long as his semi-divine status translated into the realities of central state power—military, administrative, socioeconomic. This meant that the strength of allegiance of peripheral domains was purely a function of the power of the centre; and that the boundaries of adjacent power centres fluctuated in accordance with the relative military and economic strength of each. No centrally appointed bureaucracy tied outlying provinces to the centre; no rigid feudal relationships defined the extent of territorial holdings. Every princeling saw himself as potentially having the *karma* to become a *cakravartin*—a universal ruler, or 'world conqueror'—or at least to obtain a degree of autonomy by playing off one centre of power against another. Thus a rationale for ambition always existed which posed a potential threat to the stability of the state. Shifting allegiances were seen as a natural accommodation to changing political circumstances and therefore as essentially temporary. In this 'mandala' system of relations between princely states, the enemy of one's enemy was a friend—but only until one's enemy was overcome.

The Kingdom of Lan Xang was a loose conglomeration of tributary principalities, or *muong*, held together by the power of the king and fear of his enemies. Relations with other states were assured through marriage contracts. Fa Ngum's son contracted marriages with the daughters of the kings of both Ayuthia and Chiang Mai. Whilst the central power was sufficiently strong, the state held together. Once that power began to wane, the personal ambitions of petty princelings made disintegration ever more likely and opened the way for a transfer of allegiance of constituent principalities to neighbouring states. In Laos difficulties of north–south communication reinforced these tendencies. For almost 350 years, however, the Lao state held firm as a major power in southeast Asia, capable of defending its interests against Siamese, Vietnamese and Burmese alike. Its decline since the beginning of the eighteenth century has been of major importance in shaping the modern political map of the region.

Fa Ngum, through his military exploits, civil administration and reform of Buddhism, laid the basis for a powerful Lao state. His work was continued by his son who took the name Samsenthai, meaning ruler of 300,000 Tai. He was a pacific ruler, devoted to Buddhism, who prudently established relations with the new and powerful Ming dynasty in China. This did not, however, prevent the Lao state from becoming embroiled in the recurrent warfare of the region. Samsenthai defeated a Burmese invasion; his son inadvertently attracted Vietnamese reprisals when the Lao army he sent to help the Vietnamese expel Chinese forces from their territory defected to the enemy. Half a century later, in 1479, a Vietnamese army ravaged Xieng Khouang and captured Luang Prabang before finally being forced to withdraw.

During the sixteenth century the kingdom of Lan Xang was invaded first by the Siamese then by the Burmese. In 1563, King Setthathirat transferred his capital from Luang Prabang to Vientiane, a site both more centrally situated with respect to the Lao territories and more easily defensible against Burmese attack. The new capital was embellished with a series of fine Buddhist monuments, among which were Wat Phra Keo, erected to house the Emerald Buddha, and the stupa of That Luang.

The seventeenth century saw the Lao state at the apogee of its power, under the long rule of King Souligna Vongsa (1637–94). During this period, the kingdom was visited by the Dutch merchant Geritt van Wuysthoff, who has left a valuable account of the splendour of its capital and the customs of its people (Lévy, in de Berval, 1959). The state Souligna Vongsa ruled covered an area of more than 400,000 square kilometres stretching from the Sip Song Panna in the north to Champassak in the south, including Lao territories on both banks of the Mekong. The capital of Vientiane was a renowned centre of Buddhist learning where Thai, Cambodian and even Burmese monks came to pursue their studies.

Two events during the reign of Souligna Vongsa were to have serious implications for the future of the kingdom. One was the forced marriage of the daughter of the prince of Xieng Khouang to the king which earned the undying hatred of this princely family for the dynasty of Vientiane. The other was the execution for adultery of the king's only son which left the succession of the kingdom in dispute. Upon the death of Souligna Vongsa a nephew of the king succeeded, with the support of a Vietnamese army, in conquering the throne of Vientiane. In response, his cousin gathered an army in northern Laos, took Luang Prabang and declared his independence. Four years later the prince of Champassak also proclaimed himself king and renounced his allegiance to Vientiane. As none of the three Lao states was sufficiently powerful to exert its suzerainty over either of the other two, all three fell prey to the intrigues and pressures of their powerful neighbours: the Vietnamese to the east, the Siamese to the west.

Both Vietnam and Siam had certain advantages denied the Lao principalities. The power of both states was based upon rich alluvial, irrigated rice plains of far greater extent than those of the middle reaches of the Mekong, and able to support far larger concentrations of population. The basin of the Menam and the Red River delta gave the Siamese and Vietnamese a primary economic and political focus which, after the seventeenth century, the Lao lacked. In addition, lack of access to the sea deprived the Lao states of valuable contact with European military technology and new sources of wealth through trade. By the beginning of the nineteenth century, the contrast between the powerful and unified states of Siam and Vietnam and the weak and divided Lao states was striking.

The Burmese had been the first to take advantage of Lao weakness to involve themselves in Lao affairs. Twice, in 1753 and in 1771, Burmese armies took and sacked Luang Prabang—the second time with the connivance of Vientiane, an act which left a permanent bitterness between the two Lao states. When the Siamese attacked Vientiane in 1778, no help was forthcoming from Luang Prabang. The Siamese carried off the Phra Bang, which was later returned, and the Emerald Buddha, which has since become the palladium of the ruling Thai dynasty.

In 1791, Vientiane found an excuse to invade Luang Prabang, capture and sack the capital and annex the area of Houa Phan. This gave the Siamese an excuse to interfere again in Lao affairs. The king of Vientiane was punished by being deposed in favour of his younger brother, and Siamese hegemony was effectively established over both states. As Champassak was by then already tributary to Bangkok, this brought all three Lao states under Siamese suzerainty.

In 1805, Chao Anou mounted the throne of Vientiane. As a vassal of Bangkok, he assisted Siamese forces in suppressing a revolt among the Lao Theung tribes on the Bolovens Plateau. In return, the Siamese accepted the nomination of Chou Anou's son as prince of Champassak. On the basis of this extension of his power, Chou Anou attempted to recreate something of the former splendour of the kingdom of Lan Xang by embellishing his capital, Vientiane, with new buildings. Wat Sisakhet was constructed at this time, the only monastery to escape the eventual destruction of the city by the Siamese in 1827.

Chou Anou seems to have had the intention of reunifying the Lao principalities and of freeing them from Siamese hegemony. He could make no move against the semi-independent principalities of Luang Prabang and Xieng Khouang, however, without laying central and southern Laos open to Siamese attack. On hearing a rumour to the effect that an English fleet was about to attack Bangkok, Chou Anou sent his armies against the Siamese. The venture, however, was ill-prepared, lacked co-ordination and made little use of possible allies, such as the Vietnamese. The king of Luang Prabang refused all overtures from Chou Anou to join him against the Siamese, and even sent a contingent of 3,000 troops to fight on the Siamese side.

The Siamese reacted with despatch. The main body of the Lao army was defeated southwest of Udom, and Vientiane was taken and sacked. Six thousand families were deported to the west bank of the Mekong. Chou Anou fled his capital before its capture and took refuge in Vietnam. Neither of the Lao princes of Luang Prabang and Xieng Khouang, nor the ruler of Chiang Mai further west was prepared to risk the wrath of the Siamese to help Chou Anou regain his throne. Eventually he returned to Vientiane with a small contingent of Vietnamese, drove out the Siamese garrison and reoccupied the city. Siamese reaction was again swift. Chou Anou was forced to flee in the face of another Siamese army. He took refuge in Xieng Khouang, but was handed over to the Siamese by the ruler of that state. Chou Anou died in captivity in Bangkok in 1835; the principality of Vientiane was reduced to an appendage of the Siamese state.

The importance of the revolt of Chou Anou lies in the way it has coloured subsequent Lao–Thai perceptions of their mutual relationship. For the Lao, Chou Anou has always been seen as a hero who fought to free his people from the burden of Siamese suzerainty. For the Thai, Chou Anou was a rebel who was justly punished for breaking his vows of allegiance (Wyatt, 1984). (Modern Lao Marxist interpretations of Chou Anou as a hero of the anti-imperialist struggle, who marched on Bangkok only to assist the Siamese to defeat a rumoured British attack, can be dismissed as an historical fiction.)

The Vietnamese took advantage of the destruction of the kingdom of Vientiane to seize other parts of Laos. Xieng Khouang was forced to acknowledge Vietnamese suzerainty; its ruler was executed for having handed Chou Anou, whom the Vietnamese considered their vassal, over to the Siamese. Most of the province of Khammouane was also claimed by Vietnam. Of the former Kingdom of Lan Xang only the principality of Luang Prabang retained a tenuous independence by maintaining relations with both Bangkok and Hué. Champassak was a Siamese tributary state entirely dependent on Bangkok.

By the mid-nineteenth century the French were preparing to extend their control over Vietnam. Cochinchina was invaded in 1859, and a French protectorate established over Cambodia in 1863. The preoccupation of the court of Hué with the incursions of the French permitted the Siamese to extend their influence in Laos at the expense of Vietnam. All south and central Laos fell under *de facto* Siamese control. In northern Laos the situation was confused by the presence of bands of Chinese outlaws, but these provided an excuse to extend Siamese influence even beyond Luang Prabang.

In 1883, Bangkok despatched troops to northern Laos to drive off a new invasion by armed bands of Chinese marauders. This Siamese force, with British encouragement, penetrated as far as the Sip Song Chau Tai, the region at the headwaters of the Red River inhabited by mountain Tai tribes. This provoked a French reaction. Having completed, by 1885, the colonization of Vietnam, the French saw themselves as inheriting all Vietnamese territorial claims to parts of Laos, including tributary rights over the kingdom of Luang Prabang. On this basis, they secured Siamese agreement to establish a French vice-consulate in Luang Prabang itself.

The first vice-consul was Auguste Pavie, who arrived in the city early in the fateful year of 1887. Soon after his arrival the Siamese column withdrew from northern Laos, taking with it a number of hostages to ensure the proper behaviour of the mountain tribes. In June, a mixed force of mountain Tai and Chinese, led by the White Tai chieftain Deo Van Tri, captured and sacked Luang Prabang in revenge for this Siamese action. The small remaining Siamese garrison fled, and it was only at the last moment that Pavie and his interpreters managed to get the old king into a boat and escape downstream. Overcome with gratitude, King Oun-Kham asked for, and was swiftly accorded, French protection. The first step in the imposition of a French protectorate over Laos had been accomplished.

The French Colonial Interlude

Not until 1893, after six years of mounting pressure culminating in a blockade of Bangkok by French warships, was the Franco-Siamese treaty establishing French control over Laos eventually signed. The treaty ceded all Lao territories to the east of the Mekong, and all islands in the river itself, to France, and established a demilitarized zone twenty-five kilometres wide the length of the west bank in which French representatives had the right to circulate freely, and in which French consulates and commercial posts might be established. This treaty, based as it was upon the European notion of fixed and formal frontiers, effectively divided the Lao people. Even though for many Frenchmen, if not for the government of the time, the twenty-five kilometre demilitarized zone was only a first step in the extension of French influence over Siam leading to eventual annexation of the Siamese state, the treaty recognized, at least for the interim, Siamese jurisdiction over all ethnic Lao living more than twenty-five kilometres west of the Mekong. No attempt was made to determine either the historical claims of the kingdom of Luang Prabang to the ancient territories of Lan Xang, or the extent of settlement of ethnic Lao on the Korat Plateau, either of which might have formed the basis for French support for the reestablishment of a viable Lao state. As it was, French interests were an extension of those of Vietnam—division of the Lao principalities in such a way that the Siamese share of the spoils was minimized and the French share maximized—for the benefit of French Indochina, centred on Vietnam. The Franco-Siamese treaties and conventions of 1902, 1904 and 1907 extended the Lao territories to include Sayaboury and part of Champassak situated to the west of the Mekong. This left in Siamese hands all the Korat Plateau, with a Lao population more than three times that of French Laos. The Franco-Siamese treaties of 1925 and 1926 finally excluded the possibility of further French territorial gains at the expense of Bangkok.

In 1900, the French chose Vientiane as their administrative capital, and began the restoration of the monuments left in ruins after the Siamese sack of 1827. A skeleton administration was established consisting of representatives or 'residents' in each of nine provinces in south, central and northwestern Laos, excluding Luang Prabang. As of 1916, the northeastern region (later Phongsaly province) was constituted as the 'Vè territorire militaire', an extension of four similar territories covering equally mountainous and sensitive areas along the Chinese border in northern Vietnam. The territory of the kingdom of Luang Prabang including Sayaboury, Oudomsay and much of Houaphan province became a French protectorate. There the place of the *résident* was taken by a commissioner of the colonial government, responsible to the Résident Supérieur in Vientiane. Both in Luang Prabang and in the directly administered provinces a small French administration was installed, consisting of a deputy resident, commander of the local detachment of the 'native guard' (*garde indigène*), a paymaster representing the Treasury, a postmaster, schoolteacher and doctor. Later a director of public works and a veterinary officer were added. Together with local missionaries, representatives of French companies, and an occasional French *colon* or settler, these made up the small French community in Laos. In 1904 no more than seventy-two French officials all told administered the entire country (McCoy, in Adams and McCoy, 1970).

From the beginning, the French looked upon Laos as a region that needed to be developed as rapidly as possible. Like Cambodia, Laos formed part of the Indochinese Union, dominated by the three Vietnamese regions of Tongking, Annam and Cochinchina. French policy in Laos was to develop the country not for the benefit of Laos as a separate entity in itself, but rather for the benefit of French Indochina as a whole, and thus of metropolitan France. For this purpose, public works and communications were a first priority. Work was undertaken on a system of roads and telegraph lines. Navigation was improved over difficult stretches of the Mekong. A short railway was constructed for the portage of goods to avoid the rapids of Khone. Administrative buildings, housing, barracks, prisons, and later dispensaries and schools were gradually constructed.

The costs of French administration and public works were borne for the most part by the local inhabitants. However the small population in Laos, large distances and difficult terrain meant that the local budget regularly ran a deficit which had to be met from the general budget for Indochina in the form of annual subvention. Taxes were nevertheless high for a population consisting mostly of subsistence farmers. All ethnic Lao males between the ages of eighteen and sixty had to pay an annual head tax equivalent to five gold francs and perform ten to twenty days of unpaid corvée labour, which could be redeemed only by payment of a further five francs. Other ethnic groups paid half as much tax and performed ten days' corvée. Vietnamese paid five francs with no corvée; Chinese and other Asians 12.5 francs. Only Buddhist monks, local officials, members of the *garde indigène* or former members who had served for at least four years, the sick and former slaves were exempt (Lévy, 1974). Other sources of revenue derived from the issuing of passports and permits to carry arms, duties on the export of commodities and livestock, and later a tax on draught animals—buffalo, oxen and elephants. An increasing amount of revenue came from the purchase of opium which the French enforced as a state monopoly by controlling the activities of Chinese merchants entering Laos from Yunnan. The monopolistic sale of opium throughout Indochina contributed a major portion of the general revenue of Indochina as a whole.

The slow economic development of Laos was a constant source of disappointment to French administrators. The Lao were disinclined to take advantage of the French presence to produce more. Commerce was minimal, and Chinese merchants preferred to trade through Thailand rather than through Vietnam. Consumer goods sold in Laos were thus more often of British or German than of French manufacture. Two conditions, it was concluded, were necessary for the development of Laos: construction of a railway line from coastal Vietnam to the Mekong at Thakhek and large-scale Vietnamese settlement. Although preliminary studies for the railway were completed, and its construction agreed upon, the line was never built. It remains an option for the present regime. As for the anticipated migration of Vietnamese into Laos, this never occurred on the scale hoped for by the French, a scale which would eventually have reduced the Lao to a minority in their own country. The French envisaged an influx into Laos of Vietnamese peasant farmers; the Vietnamese who arrived settled rather in the towns where they formed their own quarters. Many set up shop as tailors or hairdressers, jewellers or bicycle repairers, restaurateurs or general merchants. Many Vietnamese held positions in the French administration. Vietnamese were preferred to Lao as everything from clerks and teachers to construction foremen and hospital attendants. Vietnamese also comprised a large proportion of both the *garde indigène* and of the police force. The great majority of all positions of intermediate responsibility in the French administration in Laos were held by Vietnamese, many recruited in Vietnam. Lao labourers, clerks and guards usually found themselves receiving orders from Vietnamese, a situation which frequently caused resentment. Even in Luang Prabang, where the façade of a traditional Lao administration remained in place, Vietnamese held important posts in the parallel French administration (cf. Toye, 1968, p. 44–5). By 1943, Vietnamese accounted for more than half the population of Vientiane, and as much as 85 per cent of Laos' second largest city, Thakhek (McCoy, in Adams and McCoy, 1970, p. 84).

It is not without point to speculate what might have happened had French designs for Laos been realized. After dividing the former Lao territories between Siam and Indochina, the French saw Laos merely as the resource-rich hinterland to Vietnam, an area which could absorb excess Vietnamese population, and in so doing become profitable in the sense (a) that it would no longer be a drain on the general Indochina budget; (b) that it would contribute through the exploitation of its resources to the developing economy of French Indochina; and (c) that it would provide a' market for French goods. Had the railway been built, had Vietnamese settlement been more actively encouraged as a result, had the Second World War not cut short French plans, Laos might well have been effectively absorbed within a greater Vietnam.

Opposition to the establishment of French rule in Laos was scattered and took a number of different forms. The ethnic Lao of southeastern Laos sullenly refused to cooperate with the French because their Lao Theung slaves had been freed and they were forced to cultivate their own rice paddies. In addition, they were no longer permitted to collect the traditional tribute they demanded from more remote Lao Theung tribes. Some resentment was also expressed by the Lao aristocracy in Luang Prabang, jealous of their former prerogatives which they saw progressively eroded by the French presence. In general, however, the ethnic Lao accepted the imposition of French rule with remarkably little opposition—a fact frequently commented upon by early French administrators.

The principal opposition to the French presence came rather from the mountain tribes, both Lao Theung and Lao Soung. In southern Laos on the Bolovens Plateau a major rebellion broke out in 1901 led by traditional sorcerers known as *Pho-mi-boun.* The leaders of the revolt, Bak-mi of the Alak tribe and Kommadan and his brother of the Loven tribe of Lao Theung, found considerable popular support for their call to expel the foreign invaders. Apart from abolishing the institution of slavery, the French presence had brought few benefits to the Lao Theung. French taxes, levied individually, were higher than the traditional tribute of gold dust paid communally by the villages to their Lao overlords (a portion of which was passed on as tribute to the Siamese). Corvée labour was particularly resented, especially as most Lao Theung did not have the means to redeem their corvée through payment. The revolt quickly gained widespread popular support, not only from Lao Theung tribes, but also from many ethnic Lao. By the end of the year it had spilled over into both the Central Highlands of southern Vietnam and across the Mekong to the region of Ubon in Siam. On 19 April 1902, the French administrative post of Savannakhet was surrounded by hundreds of chanting Lao. The *garde indigène* opened fire; 150 people were killed and a similar number wounded (Le Boulanger, 1931, p. 346).

French military action against the rebels was hampered by lack of intelligence and by the guerrilla tactics of the rebels. Not until 1907 was Bakmi killed and his band dispersed. Not until 1910 did peace come to the Bolovens. Kommadan retreated deep into the mountains only to provoke a further uprising in 1934, again calling for expulsion of the French. The military column sent to suppress his followers carried out a scorched earth policy, destroying crops and villages and forcibly relocating the population. Despite, or rather because of, these actions the Bolovens remained a centre of anti-French activity throughout and after the Second World War.

In northern Laos a revolt broke out in Phongsaly in 1899 which was only finally brought under control with the death of the Tai Lu chieftain Vannaphoum in 1910. In 1914, a major revolt engulfed much of northeastern Laos from Phongsaly to Houaphan when local Tai dissidents joined with Chinese marauders to threaten French control of the region. The major cause of the revolt seems to have been resentment over heavy French taxation and demands for corvée labour, and interference in traditional trading patterns—including particularly the opium trade. In November 1914 the post of Sam Neua was captured by the rebels and the French representative killed. Extensive military operations involving up to two-and-a-half thousand troops continued in the region until 1917, by which time most of the Chinese had been driven back across the border and peace restored. Two years later, however, another serious revolt broke out among the Hmong of Xieng Khouang. Again the causes were resentment over taxation, failure to pay for requisitioned pack horses and interference in the opium trade in order to enforce the French monopoly. The leader of the revolt was a Hmong chieftain named Ba-Chay, originally from northern Vietnam, who preached a messianic cult calling for the establishment of a Hmong kingdom centred on Dien Bien Phu. It took two years of military operations and the death of Ba-chay before Hmong resistance was broken.

The period between the two world wars was for the most part a peaceful one in Laos—except for Kommadan's call for renewed resistance on the part of the Lao Theung tribes of the Bolovens. French interest in Laos was slight compared with Vietnam. Vietnamese nationalist movements had their followers among the Vietnamese communities in Laos, but the Lao themselves took little interest in these developments. Only a handful of Lao students who went to pursue their higher studies in Vietnam were influenced by their Vietnamese friends and began to think in nationalist terms. It was not until the early 1940s, however, that a Lao nationalist movement developed in Laos.

Marxist ideas were equally slow to take root in Laos. During the 1930s Marxism was almost entirely limited to members of the Vietnamese community. Even after the Indochinese Communist Party was formed in 1930, little effort was made to recruit ethnic Lao. Prior to 1940 the communist movement in Laos consisted of a harried band of Vietnamese adherents relentlessly pursued by the French *Sûreté* (Brown & Zasloff, 1986). Attempts to recruit Lao members met with little success. After reorganization of the ICP in Laos early in 1935, the executive reportedly included one ethnic Lao. This was probably Kham Sen, since officially honoured as the first Lao communist. The following year a Committee for Laos was set up with the aim of recruiting Lao members. However, Marxism only gained a following in Laos after the resurgence of nationalist sentiment during the Second World War, and in response to French attempts to reimpose colonial rule over Indochina.

The balance sheet after half a century of French presence in Laos was not impressive. Apart from constructing 5,000 kilometres of mediocre roads with corvée labour, France did virtually nothing either to encourage economic development or to improve social welfare. Ninety per cent of the population remained subsistence farmers; there was no industry and a small tin-mining venture benefited only the French company involved and its Vietnamese workers. Health care was confined to a few urban centres and consequently failed either to decrease the consistently high rate of child mortality in the rural areas, or to increase life expectancy. Primary education was left to the Buddhist pagoda schools. Secondary education in French was confined to a tiny minority, and went no further than middle school. No high school (*lycée*) was ever built. French policy in Laos was limited to administering the colony at minimal cost.

This pattern of benign neglect was interrupted by the Second World War.

The Japanese presence in Indochina from 1940 to 1945, together with Vichy French weakness in the face of Bangkok's militant pan-Thaïism, led to an awakening of Lao nationalism. In January 1941, Thai and French forces fought a number of inconclusive engagements which led the Japanese to impose an armistice. As part of this agreement, France ceded all Lao territories on the west bank of the Mekong (all Sayaboury and part of Champassak province) to Thailand. The Lao reaction was one of impotent anger. Only rapid French compensation of Luang Prabang for loss of territory prevented the abdication of King Sisavang Vong. In addition, in order to counter pan-Thai propaganda, French administrators deliberately began stimulating a sense of Lao nationalism. Vichy-style youth groups were created to instill into the younger Lao elite both pride in Lao history and culture and a sense of discipline and patriotism. Under the auspices of the National Renovation Movement, meetings were held, plays were performed and the first Lao language newspaper began publication. In 1943, the first Lao light infantry battalion was formed. The movement as a whole gave rise to a Lao cultural renaissance. Young Lao rediscovered their own literature, music and dance forms. Through communal projects such as building schools and first-aid centres they learned techniques of organization and self-help. Irredentist pan-Lao aspirations even began to appear, seeking the re-establishment of a Lao state stretching across the Mekong to include the Lao of northeastern Thailand. Such notions were further stimulated by the Free Lao movement organized in Thailand in support of the Allies. This new Lao sense of racial and national pride, though mobilized to resist pan-Thai blandishments, increasingly sought to free Laos from French tutelage. Such sentiments, once roused, were not to be suppressed.

The Thirty Year Struggle

On 9 March 1945, Japanese forces seized power from the Vichy French administration in Indochina. In Laos, Crown Prince Savang Vatthana responded by calling in the name of the king for a popular uprising against the Japanese. Under Japanese pressure, however, the king was forced to repudiate all ties with France: he declared the independence of Laos on 8 April. With the defeat of Japan Prince Phetsarath, as viceroy and prime minister, reaffirmed Lao independence and proclaimed in Vientiane the fusion of all Lao territories in a unitary kingdom of Laos. By this time, however, French agents had reached Luang Prabang, and the king responded by reaffirming the protectorate and dismissing his prime minister—whereupon a Provisional People's

Assembly meeting in Vientiane voted to depose the king. A provisional constitution was promulgated, and a government formed known as the Lao Issara (Free Laos).

For six months, from October 1945 to April 1946, the Lao Issara government attempted to exercise its authority. A defence force was established under the command of Phetsarath's younger half-brother Souphanouvong, with the assistance of the Viet Minh government of Ho Chi Minh; fruitless negotiations were entered into with French authorities; and relations were eventually patched up with the king, who agreed to be reinstated as a constitutional monarch. Despite initial American sympathy and some assistance from Chinese forces which had accepted the surrender of Japanese troops in northern and central Laos, the Lao Issara government was unable to prevent the return of the French, who were determined to re-establish their Indochinese empire. French forces began their thrust north in March 1946 from bases in southern Laos following withdrawal of the Chinese. Outnumbered Lao Issara forces, aided by local Vietnamese, made a stand at Thakhek, but were soundly defeated. Souphanouvong himself was wounded. By May, Laos was in French hands, and the Lao Issara government was in exile in Thailand. Under French tutelage, Laos became a nominally independent Associated State within the French Union, with a constitutional monarchy and an elected National Assembly. In January 1947 Thailand officially restored to Laos those territories on the west bank of the Mekong (Sayaboury and Champassak) that it had annexed with Japanese support in 1941.

The semblance of independence which the French permitted in 1947 was quite unacceptable to the Lao Issara leaders in Thailand. Nevertheless, they were divided as to how to respond. The government-in-exile was unable to obtain international recognition or assistance from any state other than Thailand. Negotiations with French authorities through intermediaries led nowhere. Guerrilla raids across the Mekong caused the French some annoyance during 1946 and 1947, but caused little concern thereafter. More effective were Viet Minh directed activities along the Lao-Vietnamese border, especially in southern Laos where a 'Committee of Lao Resistance in the East' was formed to carry on anti-French resistance. The core of this resistance was an alliance between Lao (Nouhak Phoumsavan) or Lao-Vietnamese (Kaysone Phomvihane) cadres acting under ICP direction and traditional, strongly anti-French tribal chiefs, notably Sithon Kommadan, leader of the southern Lao Theung tribes and the Hmong chieftain Faydang Lobliayao. Lowland Lao members of the Resistance Committee had been recruited into the ICP in the mid 1940s as a result of contacts, through birth, language, marriage or business dealings with the Vietnamese. They were to form the most significant strand in the leadership of the Lao communist movement. Revolutionary activist members of the traditional Lao elite (Souphanouvong, Souk Vongsak, Phoumi Vongvichit) formed the other principal strand (Stuart-Fox, 1977a). Over the next few years resistance leaders kept up sporadic guerrilla activity against the French but emphasis was placed more on propaganda, organization and recruitment. Not until January 1949 did Kaysone found the first regular unit (the 'Latsavong' brigade) in the 'Army of Free Laos', forerunner of the Lao People's Liberation Army (LPLA).

As pressure for a political solution to the Indochina problem mounted with continued French failure to defeat the Viet Minh militarily, negotiations for a greater degree of independence for Laos began to bear fruit. In July 1949 a Franco-Lao General Convention was signed which gave the Lao government greater say in its foreign relations, and created a separate Lao National Army, albeit still under French command. The majority of Lao Issara leaders remaining in Bangkok thereupon agreed to accept a proferred amnesty and returned to Laos to take part in the political process. The Lao Issara government in exile was formally dissolved in October 1949. Prior to this, however, the Lao Issara government had split over the question of cooperation with either the French or the Viet Minh. As minister of both defence and foreign affairs in the Lao Issara government and commander-in-chief of its guerrilla forces, Souphanouvong had maintained continuous contact with Viet Minh leaders through his Vietnamese advisers. His independent and haughty attitude was resented by other members of the government. When in March 1949 certain of his decisions were questioned by his colleagues, Souphanouvong angrily resigned his Lao Issara portfolios. In August he announced he was forming a 'Lao Liberation Committee' dedicated to continuing anti-French resistance. When other Lao Issara leaders returned to Laos, Souphanouvong made his way to the Viet Minh headquarters at Tuyen Quang in northwestern Vietnam. There on 13 August 1950, after consulting with Ho Chi Minh and Vo Nguyen Giap, Souphanouvong presided over the first Congress of People's Representatives of the 'Lao Resistance Front'.

The Congress appointed a Lao resistance government (of the Land of the Lao, or *Pathet Lao* (PL), the name by which the Lao communist movement became known) with Souphanouvong as prime minister and minister of foreign affairs, and Kaysone Phomvihane as minister of defence. Nouhak was named minister of economy and finance, and Phoumi Vongvichit interior minister. Following Vietnamese precedent, the Congress established a broad resistance front, the Neo Lao Issara (Free Laos Front), with a nineteen-member Central Committee, and drew up a twelve-point political action programme (Zasloff, 1973).

In February 1951 the Indochinese Communist Party, which had been officially dissolved at the end of 1945 but which had continued to operate clandestinely, was reconstituted in the form of separate national parties for the three states of Indochina. The Lao People's Party (Phak Pasason Lao) was not officially founded, however, until the 22 March 1955. What happened in the intervening four years has never been revealed. It seems probable that no formal Lao party existed. Former Lao members of the ICP, such as Kaysone and Nouhak, may actually have transferred their membership to the Vietnamese Worker's Party (cf. Summers, in Szajkowski, 1981). This would be all the more probable if, as seems likely, Souphanouvong and his former Lao Issara colleagues, such as Phoumi Vongvichit and Souk Vongsak, were not then members of the ICP, or for that matter committed communists. Only six months had elapsed since the first Lao Resistance Congress. It could be that the Vietnamese counselled against forming a party without participation of former Lao Issara leaders for fear of alienating them and were not sufficiently convinced of their commitment and credentials to include them at that time. When the Lao People's Party was eventually formed, it comprised all leading resistance figures by then tempered by years of political activism and guerrilla struggle. If former Lao members of the ICP had indeed joined the Vietnamese Worker's Party, this would explain subsequent reluctance to discuss this period. Any Lao subservience to Vietnamese designs remains a delicate issue.

In March 1951, following the dissolution of the ICP, a conference of representatives from the three countries of Indochina set up a Laos–Vietnam–Cambodia Alliance Front to coordinate the military struggle against the French. This was only the cover for Viet Minh direction of the war effort throughout Indochina. Resistance units in Laos were supplied and advised by Viet Minh cadres. By 1953, twenty-seven major zones of operation had been established throughout Laos, mainly in frontier areas inhabited by tribal minority peoples, among whom Pathet Lao recruitment was particularly effective (Deuve, 1984).

The return of moderate Lao Issara leaders to Vientiane in November 1949, and their integration into the political life of the country, was rewarded by recognition of the Lao government in February 1950 by the United States and the United Kingdom. This followed recognition of the Viet Minh government by the newly created People's Republic of China. The second phase of the First Indochina War had begun. All was relatively quiet in Laos, however, during the years 1950–2. The Pathet Lao were busy building their revolutionary organization, while the government in Vientiane progressively consolidated its administrative capacities. Services covering everything from customs to the preservation of historic monuments, from a Royal Police Force to a national airline, were set up. In November 1951, Souvanna Phouma, elder half-brother of Souphanouvong, formed his first government with the avowed aim of working towards national reconciliation. To this end, he pressed hard for full independence through the transfer of all remaining French powers to the Lao government. Aided by American pressure, his efforts bore fruit in the Franco-Lao treaty signed 22 October 1953. But by then Laos was more deeply embroiled than ever in the Franco–Viet Minh struggle.

In April 1953 three Viet Minh divisions with the assistance of Pathet Lao units penetrated deeply into northern Laos. Only a gallant defence by Lao troops enabled French reinforcements to be flown in and prevented the capture of Luang Prabang. A Lao infantry battalion at Muong Khoua held off the 316th Viet Minh division for thirty-six days: there were three survivors (Fall, 1969). The early onset of the monsoons persuaded the Viet Minh to withdraw, leaving the Pathet Lao in control of large areas of northern Laos, including the town of Sam Neua, capital of Houa Phan province. Then in December a Viet Minh regiment thrust towards the Mekong, briefly occupying the town of Thakhek. In January 1954, with French forces already blockaded in the doomed stronghold of Dien Bien Phu, another Viet Minh feint into northern Laos again drew off French reserves for the defence of Luang Prabang, and left Phong Saly province in the hands of the Pathet Lao. On 7 May 1954 the French garrison at Dien Bien Phu surrendered. The following day the 1954 Conference on Indochina opened in Geneva.

The first contentious issue faced by the conference concerned the question of representation. Democratic Republic of Vietnam (DRV) Prime Minister Pham Van Dong demanded in his opening speech the seating of a separate Pathet Lao delegation on an equal footing with Royal Lao Government (RLG) representatives. This was vigorously resisted by the RLG delegation under the leadership of Phoui Sananikone, who argued forcibly first that Laos was already a sovereign independent state, a member of the French Union, and also of the United Nations; second, that Lao national sentiment was overwhelmingly focused upon the person of the king; and third, that military operations in Laos were the work of foreign Viet Minh forces, rather than the indigenous Pathet Lao with whom a political solution could be worked out.

In the end, the DRV delegation abandoned its demand for formal Pathet Lao participation at the conference, and suggested instead the regrouping of opposing military forces into separately administered zones in all three countries of Indochina. This plan was eventually adopted, and led to the partitioning of Vietnam at the seventeenth parallel into the DRV in the north and the Republic of Viet Nam (RVN) in the south. The government of Prince Sihanouk successfully argued against any division of Cambodia, but Phoui failed to prevent the designation of Phong Saly and Houa Phan provinces (joined by a narrow corridor) as Pathet Lao administered regroupment areas in Laos. Nevertheless Laos did come out of the conference intact. RLG administration, albeit with Pathet Lao participation, was to be re-established in the two regroupment provinces, and the way was open for a political solution which would reintegrate the Pathet Lao into the political life of the country. The DRV agreed to withdraw all Vietnamese 'volunteers' from Laos, a process to be verified by an International Control Commission (ICC) composed of Indian, Canadian and Polish representatives.

Lao communist historians now represent the formation of the first and both subsequent coalition governments in Laos as part of a long-term plan intended eventually to seize political power. However, the first coalition government was formed only after long and patient negotiations on the part of Royal Lao governments led by Souvanna Phouma and Katay Don Sasorith aimed at overcoming Pathet Lao suspicion and reluctance to permit re-integration of 'their' provinces and armed forces in the national polity and the Royal Lao Army (RLA). It took three years of almost continuous negotiations backed by moral and political suasion from friendly powers, and in the face of inflexible American cold war attitudes and policies, before the first coalition was formed. It lasted less than eight months.

By the end of 1954, Pathet Lao fighting units had been regrouped in Phong Saly and Houa Phan provinces and negotiations between the two sides had begun. Their respective positions, however, were far apart. Whereas RLG negotiators wanted simply to reintegrate the Pathet Lao into the political life of a functioning state, PL negotiators wanted to reshape the political institutions of the state itself. They sought to modify both the Constitution and the existing electoral laws so as to enable the Pathet Lao as a political movement to compete more effectively for political power. By the end of 1955, little progress had been achieved and the Pathet Lao boycotted elections for the National Assembly.

The Pathet Lao leadership made good use of this period of extended negotiation to consolidate political and administrative control over 'their' provinces, and to lay the institutional basis for the revolutionary struggle ahead. Following formation of the clandestine Lao People's Party, and acting in accordance with a decision made at the Party's founding congress, a broad political front organization was formed and its statutes submitted to the RLG Ministry of the Interior for registration as a political party. Thus was founded the Lao Patriotic Front (Neo Lao Hak Sat) whose forty-member Central Committee presided over by Souphanouvong was at all times secretly guided by the LPP.

In February 1956, Souvanna again became prime minister. The previous month the ICC, while proving generally ineffective in policing the cease-fire, had ruled that the RLG had the right to reintegrate the two PL provinces into the kingdom. Souvanna further strengthened his hand by appealing for support to both China and the DRV. Both agreed that reintegration of the Pathet Lao was an internal affair for Laos alone. Opposition to any compromise with the Pathet Lao came mainly from the political right, backed by Thailand, and from the United States which was adamantly opposed to any coalition government which included communist ministers (Brown & Zasloff, 1986). Nevertheless, in August 1956, preliminary agreements were signed between the two sides providing for an end to hostilities, administrative integration of the two PL provinces, inclusion of PL troops in the Royal Lao Army and of civilian representatives in the RLG administration and government and the holding of supplementary elections which the LPF would contest. By dint of further protracted negotiations, a final agreement was eventually arrived at in November 1957 establishing the first coalition government. This included Souphanouvong as Minister of Planning, Reconstruction and Urbanization and Phoumi Vongvichit as Minister of Religion and Fine Arts. The two PL provinces were formally returned to the authority of the king in a symbolic ceremony in Vientiane, and the two ministers took up their duties.

Among the major powers, only the United States expressed dissatisfaction over formation of the new government. In Laos it received the unanimous approval of the National Assembly. In May 1958, supplementary elections were held for twenty-one new seats in the National Assembly. The major political issue during the campaign was alleged corruption in connection with the burgeoning American economic and military aid programme and interference in Laos' internal affairs. The Pathet Lao contested the election under the banner of the Lao Patriotic Front. LPF candidates won nine seats and their allies in the left-wing Santiphap (Peace) Party another four. Right-wing parties suffered a severe defeat.

The right, with insistent American backing, responded by hardening its political opposition to the LPF. June 1958 saw the formation of the Committee for Defence of National Interests (CDNI) by a group of ambitious younger civil servants and military officers whose principal political goal was to form an anti-communist front. In the political manœuvring which followed, and in face of a calculated suspension of American aid, Souvanna Phouma's government fell, to be replaced by the staunchly anti-communist government of Phoui Sananikone. Both PL ministers lost their portfolios. Harrassment of LPF cadres increased, as did military interference in political affairs. The American embassy pressed for inclusion of military officers in the government. In January 1959, upon receiving falsified reports of DRV troop concentrations on the frontier with Laos (Toye, 1968; Deuve, 1984), Phoui obtained emergency powers from the National Assembly to rule by decree for one year—an action which denied the LPF deputies any further political role. Phoui's reshuffled cabinet formed to deal with the 'crisis' contained three army officers.

In the early part of 1959, Royal Lao Army directed repression against the LPF was stepped up. The Front's newspaper was banned. At the same time the government determined to complete the integration of PL military units into the RLA, as agreed under the 1957 accords. The two PL battalions were stationed one in the vicinity of Luang Prabang, the other near the Plain of Jars. The commanders of both battalions had been ordered to accept integration only in the presence of representatives of the LPF Central Committee. When permission for LPF representatives to attend the integration ceremony was denied, both battalions refused to participate. Thereupon each was surrounded by RLA forces and an ultimatum was issued for the surrender of their arms. In Vientiane all LPF deputies to the National Assembly were placed under house arrest. The First PL battalion near Luang Prabang surrendered, but the Second skilfully slipped past RLA forces and escaped. The LPF deputies were thereupon imprisoned, leaving command of the PL movement in the hands of its clandestine organization in revolutionary bases in the Lao-Vietnamese northeastern border region. As of July 1959, guerrilla warfare resumed throughout the country.

These events have been recounted in some detail because of their significance for the modern history of Laos (cf. Deuve, 1984). There is some reason to believe that at this time the DRV, and almost certainly also the Soviet Union and China, were prepared to accept a neutral coalition government in Laos in which communist ministers would participate. That the DRV had already decided on a course of armed insurgency against the government of Ngo Dinh Diem in South Vietnam does not necessarily mean it was determined to pursue a similar policy in Laos. All the DRV needed was what Sihanouk was prepared to give them in Cambodia—access routes into South Vietnam. The quid pro quo for Sihanouk was DRV tacit agreement *not* to support Khmer communist insurgents. It was an agreement Hanoi kept until Sihanouk's overthrow, and the final abandonment of Cambodian neutrality in 1970. What happened in Cambodia then had already been played out in Laos in 1959. Once the powerful families of the political right in Laos had, with the active encouragement of the United States and Thailand, effectively destroyed the painstaking efforts of Souvanna Phouma to reintegrate the Pathet Lao into the political life of a neutral Laos, the DRV believed it had no option but to protect both its vulnerable western frontier and its essential access routes to South Vietnam (later known as the Ho Chi Minh trail) by carving out 'liberated areas' in Laos with the assistance of its PL allies. Group 959 was accordingly set up as the command structure for Vietnamese forces in Laos (JPRS 80968, 1982). What appears to have been a genuine opportunity to insulate a neutral Laos from the gathering clouds of war in South Vietnam was thus lost, partly through the myopic veniality of the political right in Laos, partly through the ideologically motivated opposition of the United States.

The renewal of fighting between combined PL-DRV forces and the RLA led to a rapid increase in American military aid to Laos. American military equipment and personnel, including Special Forces troops in civilian dress, poured into Laos, in contravention, like the actions of the DRV, of the provisions of the Geneva Agreements. In December yet another political crisis developed when the four-year mandate of the National Assembly expired. An attempt to extend parliament and reshuffle the government was opposed by the CDNI, who forced the resignation of Phoui Sananikone. On the pretext of maintaining order, the high command of the RLA then announced that the army would ensure the functioning of the administration of the country until a new government could be named. These actions amounted to a military *coup d'état* and seizure of power by the CDNI. Their success was frustrated, however, by pressure from the ambassadors of the major Western powers, for once acting in concert, who convinced the king not to hand over power to the coup leader, General Phoumi Nosavan. Instead, an interim government was appointed until new National Assembly elections could be held.

These took place in April 1960 but were blatantly rigged. Electoral rules were altered to disadvantage opposition candidates, votes were bought with American Central Intelligence Agency funds, ballot boxes were stuffed. The LPF was prevented from participating since its leaders were in prison. Not surprisingly the CDNI won a resounding victory, and formed the new government. The new prime minister was Tiao Somsanith, but power lay in the hands of the American-backed military 'strongman', Phoumi Nosavan, the Minister of Defence. At last, after continuous American interference, a government of the extreme right was in power in Laos. All possibility of compromise with the Pathet Lao was at an end; the outlook was for civil war.

These events provoked two dramatic responses. All sixteen PL leaders in prison in Vientiane put into effect a joint escape plan with the assistance of their guards and rejoined the maquis. And a young paratroop captain named Kong Le decided he must prevent the CDNI from pursuing policies which could only lead to continuing pointless bloodshed. On the evening of 8 August 1960, the Second Paratroop Battalion took up positions in Vientiane. The next morning Radio Vientiane announced in the name of the 'High Command of the Revolution' the seizure of all civil and military power. The coup came as a complete surprise: no one had heard of Kong Le. The announced programme of restoration of neutrality and suppression of corruption met, however, with an enthusiastic popular response. Souvanna Phouma, concerned as he was over the drift towards civil war, agreed to become Prime Minister of the new government.

Reaction to these events was varied. For his part, Souphanouvong immediately despatched two trusted agents to Vientiane to monitor events. Members of the Somsanith government had been caught unawares in audience with the king in Luang Prabang where they remained irresolute—all but General Phoumi who flew to Savannakhet where with Thai backing he issued a call to arms. The United States was, like everyone else, caught off balance. While the State Department, advised by the American ambassador in Vientiane, responded cautiously, the CIA suffered no such qualms. Phoumi was ensured 'an unending stream of dollars, material and encouragement' (Dommen, 1985, p. 66) as he built up his military and political forces for a showdown with Kong Le.

Once again Souvanna Phouma attempted to negotiate a compromise political solution which would end civil dissension. Phoumi was offered the post of Deputy Prime Minister and Minister of the Interior in Souvanna's new government, but refused to take up his duties—at American urging (Toye, 1968). In September PL and DRV forces reoccupied San Neua town. The following month Souvanna reopened talks with the PL, much to the chagrin of the United States. Washington thereupon suspended the financial aid programme used to pay military salaries, those of Kong Le's troops as well as Phoumi's forces. When payments were resumed, so was military aid to Phoumi. In order to circumvent a Thai economic blockade, Souvanna turned for assistance to the Soviet Union which promised to airlift essential supplies to Vientiane. In November he met with Souphanouvong who agreed in principle to the formation of a new coalition government.

Phoumi in the meantime was marching on Vientiane, where convenient across Thai territory, with the open support of the United States (Dommen, 1971). At Phoumi's approach, Souvanna and most of his ministers flew to Phnom Penh, while in Hanoi Information Minister Quinim Pholsena negotiated an agreement for Soviet military aid to Kong Le's neutralist forces. When on 13 December 1960 Phoumi finally attacked Vientiane, Kong Le withdrew north and seized the Plain of Jars. There he was eventually joined by Souvanna and members of his government. Laos henceforth had two governments—one in Vientiane with Boun Oum na Champassak as Prime Minister but with power in the hands of Phoumi Nosavan and the military; and the other on the Plain of Jars. The Boun Oum government was recognized by the United States, Britain and France; the Souvanna Phouma government was recognized by the communist bloc together with neutralist states such as India, Burma and Cambodia.

As allies of a legally established internationally recognized government, the PL took advantage of the situation to extend the area under their control. Joint PL–DRV forces mounted a series of attacks on rightist positions in the early part of 1961. When a combined Neutralist–PL thrust sent rightist forces fleeing south towards Vientiane from Vang Vieng, the new Kennedy administration in the United States was forced to recognize that a right-wing military victory in Laos was unrealistic. The only alternative was a new round of negotiations towards formation of a new coalition government.

Meetings took place in Laos between the three princely leaders of the three political factions—Souvanna Phouma for the neutralists, Boun Oum for the right, and Souphanouvong for the PL—and in Geneva between representatives of fourteen powers interested in the future of Laos. Negotiations dragged on inconclusively for the rest of 1961 and into 1962, with Phoumi Nosavan seeking by all possible means to prevent formation of a tripartite coalition. At the end of March 1962, the United States finally suspended aid to the Boun Oum government in order to force its cooperation. Phoumi responded by staging a military operation in northern Laos designed to demonstrate the reality of the communist threat and so convince the United States to alter its policy. On 5 May, a column of rightist troops was ambushed by neutralist and PL forces. Two thousand soldiers and quantities of military equipment were captured (Deuve, 1984). Surviving rightist forces retreated in disorder to, and even across, the Mekong to Thailand. Kennedy sent American Marines to the Thai–Lao border, but the incident only confirmed his belief that a military solution was not possible in Laos. In June the three princes met again on the Plain of Jars and agreed to formation of a tripartite coalition Government of National Union. In Geneva, later in the month this government joined other participants in signing the international agreement on the neutralization of Laos.

The second Lao coalition government foundered on the geo-military realities of the Second Indochina War and on the differing conceptions of neutrality entertained by the protagonists in that war. By 1962, the Second Indochina War was rapidly assuming major proportions. American military aid to the government of South Vietnam was steadily increasing, a build up which could only be matched by the DRV by correspondingly increasing its own flow of personnel and material in support of the southern insurgency down the Ho Chi Minh trail. For the United States, therefore, an agreement on the neutrality of Laos which committed all parties not to introduce any foreign troops or military personnel of any kind in any form into Laos would have had the benefit of eliminating all use of the trail. The DRV conception of neutrality was somewhat different. Vietnamese communist forces attached to the Pathet Lao would be withdrawn and the DRV would not interfere in Lao affairs. For the DRV, this commitment did not prevent the movement of cadres, both military and political, down the Ho Chi Minh trail for these were bound for South Vietnam and constituted no threat to Laos. Even the commitment not to use the territory of the kingdom of Laos for interference in the internal affairs of another country did not prevent use of the trail, since for the DRV South and North Vietnam were but different regions of the temporarily divided Vietnamese state.

The tragedy for Laos was that neither the United States nor the DRV had any intention of permitting the neutrality of Laos to interfere with their prosecution of the war in South Vietnam. The DRV was prepared to accept the neutrality of Laos only in so far as it conformed to the pattern of neutrality in Cambodia until the overthrow of Sihanouk—and that for the Americans was not neutrality at all. As a result, both sides ended up by disregarding their commitments to the neutrality of Laos. Instead both sides carried the war onto Lao territory, each using its own Lao allies as more or less willing proxies. The polarization which resulted had the effect of destroying the neutralists as a political force in Laos within two years of the signing of the 1962 Geneva Agreements (Deuve, 1985). Souvanna Phouma remained a symbol of what might have been, retained as a figurehead of use to both sides as a cover behind which to pursue their own aims and ambitions.

The neutralists in Laos were in an impossible position, for alone of the three factions they could depend upon no powerful foreign backer. Communist, particularly DRV, military supplies went primarily to the PL; American supplies went to the rightist RLA. Politically too the neutralists were under pressure from both sides. Neutralist village propaganda teams were the targets for repression both by the PL and by rightist police. Both the PL and right-wing politicians in Vientiane worked relentlessly to draw the neutralists into a political alliance against the other. Perhaps inevitably the neutralists eventually split into a minority pro-PL 'patriotic neutralist' faction entirely dependent on DRV supplies after termination of the Soviet airlift, and a majority faction led by Kong Le forced by circumstances into a *de facto* alliance with the RLA and thus equally dependent on the United States.

Early in 1963 these political struggles came to a head. A number of neutralist officers and politicians were assassinated, including the coalition Foreign Minister Quinim Pholsena. Tensions ran high and fighting broke out on the Plain of Jars between PL and neutralist units. In April both PL ministers in the government left Vientiane for reasons of security and took up residence at Khang Khay in the Pathet Lao zone, to be followed later by the two PL secretaries of state. Although their portfolios were held vacant, they never returned to Vientiane. Attempts by Souvanna to reconstitute the coalition failed. The second coalition had lasted no longer than the first.

As fighting between PL and neutralist forces continued into 1964, Souvanna made yet another attempt to re-form the coalition. By then, however, neither the DRV nor the United States was prepared to relinquish positions in Laos which each considered essential to its war effort in South Vietnam. Souvanna's failure to gain agreement at a meeting between himself, Souphanouvong and Phoumi in April led him to announce his intention to resign. This immediately sparked an attempted military coup by younger generals determined to deny Phoumi the perquisites of power in the absence of Souvanna. Political pressure by Western ambassadors obtained Souvanna's freedom, and continuation as Prime Minister, but increasingly he became a prisoner of the right, beholden to the United States for his political survival. The Pathet Lao moved to strengthen their own position in accordance with the ten-point political programme adopted at the Second Congress of the Lao Patriotic Front held in Sam Neua in April. Joint PL-'patriotic neutralist' forces drove Kong Le's troops off the Plain of Jars. In reply the United States began low-level reconnaissance flights over the area, and Lao Air Force T-28 warplanes bombed PL headquarters on the plain at Kang Khay. The air war over Laos had begun.

In 1965 the tempo of war increased in South Vietnam as American combat troops were committed in ground fighting. In response, the DRV stepped up the supply of arms, munitions and personnel flowing south down the Ho Chi Minh trail. At the same time, the Vietnamese communist leadership moved to unify the anti-American struggle. An Indochinese Peoples Conference attended by DRV, South Vietnamese National Liberation Front, LPF and 'patriotic neutralist' delegations was hosted by the Cambodian leader Prince Sihanouk in Phnom Penh in February 1965 to denounce American intervention in the region. Although nominal PL representation was retained in Vientiane, the LPF labelled the RLG an 'illegal regime' and a 'US puppet', and set about consolidating political and administrative control over the 'liberated zone'. PL forces were officially designated the Lao People's Liberation Army, and in 1967 a three-year economic plan was announced for PL-controlled areas.

DRV military assistance to the Pathet Lao steadily increased during the next few years, including commitment of substantial Vietnamese ground forces in Laos. The United States for its part stepped up the regular secret bombing of communist areas in Laos begun in October 1964. At the same time increased aid was channelled to the RLA and to expanding guerrilla forces in northern Laos, recruited from the Hmong and Yao ethnic minorities (Dommen, 1971; Branfman, in Adams and McCoy, 1970; and Branfman, in Borosage and Marks, 1976). For the eight years from 1965 until the cease-fire and political settlement of 1973, the PL and the RLA fought a seasonal war of attrition with relatively little territory changing hands. LPLA forces concentrated their military pressure especially on Vang Pao's guerrillas operating in the vicinity of the Plain of Jars, and on the RLA in southeastern Laos. PL recruitment steadily continued and LPLA forces more than doubled between 1962 and 1970 to number around 48,000. American bombing reached saturation levels during these years, forcing the PL high command in Houa Phan province literally to go underground into vast limestone caverns. By the time the bombing was finally terminated, more than two million tons of bombs had been dropped on Laos alone—more than the total tonnage dropped by American aircraft throughout the Second World War (Dommen, 1985, p. 90)—and some 750,000 people, fully 25 per cent of the country's population, had been forced to flee their homes. At no time, however, did bombing close the Ho Chi Minh trail; the only attempt by South Vietnamese ground forces to cut the trail, in February 1971, ended in defeat.

By 1972, the United States was preparing to withdraw from Vietnam. At its Second Congress in February, the Lao People's Party concluded that the time was ripe for a new political initiative. As the outline of a military cease-fire and political settlement in Vietnam emerged from negotiations in Paris between the DRV and the United States, the PL stepped up pressure for a parallel settlement in Laos by offering to engage in negotiations with the RLG without preconditions. The offer was accepted by Souvanna, and negotiations began in Vientiane in October. These led to the signing in Vientiane on 21 February 1973, less than a month after conclusion of the Paris Agreement on Vietnam, of an Agreement on the Restoration of Peace and Reconciliation in Laos. The Agreement called for strict application of the 1962 Geneva Agreements, cessation of all military activity by foreign powers in Laos, and withdrawal of all military personnel within sixty days of the formation of a Provisional Government of National Union (PGNU) together with a policy-making National Political Consultative Council (NPCC). Until the Protocol to the Agreement was signed spelling out in detail the joint political institutions, the neutralization of Vientiane and Luang Prabang and the means of investigation of alleged violations, each side was responsible for the administration of its respective zone. The settlement reflected the greatly enhanced political and military position achieved by the PL in the decade following the collapse of the second coalition government. By then some four-fifths of the national territory and two-fifths of the population were under Pathet Lao control.

The Protocol establishing the third coalition government was signed in September 1973, but the government itself was not sworn in until 5 April 1974, following neutralization of the two cities. The PL (the 'Patriotic forces side') and the right (the 'Vientiane Government side') each had equal representation in both the government and on the NPCC. Souvanna remained Prime Minister, while Souphanouvong took over the Chairmanship of the NPCC which met in Luang Prabang. Under Souphanouvong's effective direction the NPCC unanimously adopted an 'Eighteen-point Programme for the Current Construction of the Fatherland' calling for continuation of the monarchy, economic development, and a neutral foreign policy. A second document outlining 'Ten Democratic Freedoms' espoused equally liberal principles. In the following twelve months both these documents gained widespread mass support among ethnic Lao in the 'Vientiane zone' who accepted them at face value as the PL-inspired blueprint for the future of the country. The extent of popular disillusionment was correspondingly great when they were later abandoned.

By the end of 1974, despite such heated disagreement over recognition of the Provisional Revolutionary Government of South Vietnam that Souvanna suffered a heart attack, the third coalition government was functioning remarkably smoothly. Pathet Lao ministers had been moderate in their statements and diligent in the administration of their offices. Prisoners of war had been exchanged, Luang Prabang and Vientiane had been effectively neutralized under joint control of equal RLG and PL military and police contingents, and the cease-fire was generally holding. At the same time, the

PL resolutely opposed every attempt to gain access to their administrative zone as they set about repairing the damage caused by American bombing. Whereas American and Thai forces had been withdrawn by 4 June, all indications were that though DRV troop levels had been reduced in northern Laos, substantial numbers remained in the south along the Ho Chi Minh trail where a military build-up was again taking place in preparation for the final DRV offensive of 1975.

Formation of the Lao People's Democratic Republic

There is reason to believe that when the PL initialled the Vientiane Agreements of 1973, they fully expected the coalition government to last for a number of years. During this time, the LPF hoped to increase its appeal among lowland Lao in the 'Vientiane zone' through stepped-up political education and mass mobilization in preparation for an eventual seizure of power when circumstances permitted. The unexpectedly rapid collapse of right-wing regimes in Cambodia and South Vietnam significantly altered the balance of political power in Laos and 'created conditions more favourable to the cause of the Revolution' (Documents of National Congress of the People's Representatives of Laos, n.d., p. 5).

Already in the latter part of 1974, the Vientiane side was subject to increasing political, military and social pressure from the PL. Political pressure took the form of agitation by students and workers in support of the reasonable and moderate 'Eighteen-point Programme', together with selective criticism of uncooperative and unpopular right-wing leaders, and of the American presence. On the military front the cease-fire generally held, despite numerous protests by the RLA alleging LPLA violations. The PL meanwhile actively sought to undermine RLA morale, especially in remote posts. This brought results in December 1974 and again in January 1985 when RLA troops garrisoned in what is now Bokeo province in the northwest and in Kammouane province in central Laos mutinied and went over to the LPLA. Social unrest, fuelled by the deteriorating economic situation, took the form of strike action and walkouts affecting an increasing number of organizations and industries. Students were particularly active in organizing protests against all forms of corruption and foreign interference.

In April 1975, military pressure was suddenly increased when PL forces wrested control of the strategic junction of Routes 7 and 13 from Hmong 'secret army' forces, and thrust south. This limited offensive coincided with the opening phase of the final assault in South Vietnam, perhaps fortuitously as PL forces halted their advance 130 kilometres north of Vientiane. Thereafter the Lao revolution was pursued by political, not military, means—though the threat of renewed fighting with the possible involvement of Vietnamese forces remained ever-present.

As events in Cambodia and South Vietnam reached their climax in April, political tensions mounted in Laos. Protests and walkouts from government departments and institutions occurred in Vientiane and Luang Prabang, while student demonstrations, particularly critical of the presence and activities of the massive United States Agency for International Development (USAID), were mounted in other centres as well. On May Day, and again a week later, large demonstrations in Vientiane organized by students and trade unionists vigorously denounced right-wing government ministers and leading rightist military and police officers. On 9 May, fearing for their personal safety, five right-wing ministers and deputy ministers resigned their portfolios and crossed to Thailand together with a number of leading rightist generals. This was the sign for hundreds more Lao civil servants and military officers and their families to leave, along with many Chinese and Vietnamese merchants and businessmen. Meanwhile an American airlift flew thousands of Hmong soldiers and their families out of bases in northern Laos to Thailand.

The tide of protest next focused on the American presence in Laos. On 21 May the USAID compound in Vientiane was occupied by students and workers after earlier seizures of USAID offices in Savannakhet and Luang Prabang. In negotiations which followed with student representatives and PL officials, the United States agreed to withdraw its USAID mission completely by 30 June 1975. Other facilities, such as the offices of the United States Information Service, were later also seized. By the middle of the year, the huge American presence in Laos had been reduced to an embassy staff of twenty-two people.

By the end of May, the PL had achieved their major political goals and were in a position to seize power. Nevertheless, what one authority has described as the 'quasi-legalism' of the PL road to power was even then not abandoned (Brown, in Stuart-Fox, 1982a). Even as the acting minister of defence 'patriotic neutralist' General Khammouane Boupha, moved to neutralize the RLA in the absence of its leading generals, and LPLA forces took control of the cities of southern Laos, the façade of the coalition Provisional Government of National Union was retained. New ministers, more acceptable to the PL, were appointed to take the place of those who had fled. Not until August, after dissolution of the joint military and police forces responsible for assuring the neutrality of Luang Prabang and Vientiane, were the two cities taken over by revolutionary committees. Even then there was no suggestion that the coalition government would be dissolved or the monarchy abolished. Elections for a new National Assembly were officially scheduled for 4 April 1976.

It has been suggested that the decision to cut short this process and install a communist government in Laos was taken following the decision to consolidate relations between the northern and southern zones of Vietnam (Brown & Zasloff, 1976). It seems more likely, however, that internal considerations were paramount. The major concern of PL leaders towards the end of 1975 was to consolidate political power. They feared that resistance to the government would begin to crystallize, with the backing of Thailand. However, though many civil servants and military officers crossed the Mekong, many more remained in the hope that they could contribute to building the new peaceful, neutral, democratic and united Laos proclaimed in the 'Eighteen-point Programme'. For the PL, these former enemies nevertheless posed a threat to the security of the new socialist regime. From July to November 1975, most remaining senior public servants and military officers above the rank of captain were sent for political re-education at camps set up near Viengsay in Houa Phan province. Officers up to and including the rank of captain were despatched to other camps north of Vientiane, and in Saravane and Attopeu provinces in the south. All were given to understand that re-education would last no more than a few months, and most went willingly. (Many of those sent to Viengsay and Attopeu were still there ten years later.)

Early in November elections were held at the village, sub-district (*tasseng*), and district (*muong*) levels for people's administrative committees. Voting was by secret ballot for candidates duly ratified by local LPF representatives. Elected members appointed standing committees whose chairmen replaced village and district chiefs. This was to have been the first stage of the electoral process, to be followed later by provincial and national elections. The sequence was cut short, however, when Thailand closed the border with Laos in mid-November after an exchange of fire across the Mekong. The resulting economic blockade produced severe hardships in Vientiane with consequent social unrest. Towards the end of November, the decision was taken to assemble the PGNU and the NPCC in joint emergency session in Vieng Say. Remaining senior military and civilian officials of the RLG were ordered off to seminars. Some went; others, including Souvanna Phouma's son, fled to Thailand. In Vientiane, orchestrated demonstrations on 26 and 28 November called for dissolution of the coalition government and the NPCC, and abolition of the monarchy. The next day, at the urging of Souvanna Phouma and Souphanouvong, King Savang Vatthana abdicated his throne and Souvanna stepped down as Prime Minister. On 1 and 2 December, a secret two-day National Congress of People's Representatives in Vientiane unanimously voted to abolish the six century old monarchy and form in its stead the Lao People's Democratic Republic with political institutions modelled closely on those of other communist states. The 'national democratic' phase of the Lao revolution was complete: the 'dictatorship of the proletariat' had begun, exercised by the newly revealed Lao People's Revolutionary Party, the name adopted at the Second Party Congresss.

The First Decade of Communist Government

The stated task facing the new regime was to pursue the second phase of the Lao revolution, to 'advance, step by step, to socialism without going through the stage of capitalist development' (FBIS, 24 March 1976). The guiding role in this transformation was to be played by the LPRP, on behalf of the multi-ethnic Lao 'worker-peasant alliance'. But the Party itself had first to consolidate its monopoly of political power. This it did with remarkable efficiency. From the first days of the new regime a high degree of internal security was maintained. The general fund of goodwill with which the Pathet Lao were welcomed in the RLG zone was not yet exhausted. Most Lao saw no alternative but to continue to cooperate with the victors. The great majority of RLA and police officers and senior civil servants was safely out of the way attending political re-education courses in the Pathet Lao zone. Opposition as a result remained inchoate and disorganized.

Opposition to the new regime when it did develop was organized in Thailand by Lao exiles with the tacit or overt support of local Thai officials. Although in retrospect the threat posed by the politically, ethnically and geographically divided Lao refugees in Thailand was slight, the Pathet Lao leadership took it seriously. In fact the exiles were politically discredited, lacked organization and could generate little popular support. A trial *in absentia* of thirty-one prominent rightists staged in Vientiane after the liberation of the city, at which six were given death sentences served notice that opponents of the new regime would be punished as criminals and traitors. The people were exhorted to increase their revolutionary vigilance, report anti-State activities and identify enemies. Publicity was given to the arrest of all 'spies', 'saboteurs' and 'rightists' accused of plotting to create disturbances or undermine the revolution.

Natural, but exaggerated, PL concern for security during the crucial transitional period had the effect of generating a climate of uncertainty and fear which notably increased the outflow of refugees. Constant emphasis on the need for vigilance against vaguely defined 'enemies' accused of equally vague 'crimes' led to the arrest of people guilty of no more than expressing an opinion critical of Pathet Lao actions. This increased the circle of 'enemies' of the revolution to include an unnecessarily large proportion of the Lao educated class in the former RLG zone who were otherwise sympathetic to the need for radical change in Lao society, and were prepared to work with the Pathet Lao. As it was, the Pathet Lao encountered no real threat to their political control or to the security of the new regime, but lost, as a result of heavy-handed policies, a substantial proportion of the few skilled managers and technicians the country possessed.

The social and economic problems faced by the new regime were far more daunting than were problems relating to security and the consolidation of political power. A first priority was to resettle as many as 700,000 internal refugees who in the previous decade had fled the expanding PL zone largely to escape American bombing. On the economic front the regime faced equally serious difficulties. The withdrawal of American economic assistance, including substantial subsidies for the Lao budget, the termination of the Foreign Exchange Operations Fund which underwrote the value of the Lao currency, and the Thai economic blockade all contributed to the virtual collapse of the artificial Lao urban economy. Inflation increased. Unemployment soared as the rightist army and police were disbanded and factories closed for lack of imported raw materials, or because managers and technicians had fled to Thailand. As Nayan Chanda noted:

The guerrilla leaders of the Pathet Lao, who had so long presided over a subsistence economy in a limited area (relying greatly on commodity assistance from China, the Soviet Union and North Vietnam) and condemned the economy of the Vientiane zone as 'neo-colonialist', suddenly found themselves called upon to manage that very system, but in a bankrupt state. [Chanda in Stuart-Fox, 1982a, p. 116.]

The government's response took the form of an ideologically orthodox political decision to solve the problem of economic shortages and rising prices through imposition of state controls. Industries were nationalized and the properties of the more prominent 'traitors' and 'reactionaries' confiscated. So too were the stocks of merchants accused of profiteering. Traders were forbidden to purchase rice or other food supplies in the countryside or trade between provinces. In place of private commerce the government introduced state trading. The principal market in Vientiane was closed and goods chanelled through state-run stores and marketing cooperatives. To deal with immediate shortages, people were encouraged to grow their own vegetables and raise livestock. Each ministry and government department set up its own farm. So too did each army unit.

The economic effects of these measures will be discussed below. Suffice it to note here that prices spiralled for the few goods available, and the value of the kip plummeted. Imposition of a new rice tax in kind to enable the government to stock state shops lost it support in the rural areas. Popular disillusionment and discontent over the deteriorating economic situation were reinforced by resentment over a series of new social controls, and the way these were enforced. Personal liberties were curtailed. Passes were required even to move from one village to the next. Permission was needed even to slaughter a pig. People were discouraged from attending religious festivals, and were forced to spend hours and even days at political seminars. Personal dress and lifestyle were rigidly controlled. Western clothing, music and dancing were condemned as 'decadent bourgeois culture'. Towards the end of April, 1976, some 1,200 of Vientiane's most incorrigible youth—drug addicts, prostitutes, 'hippies', gamblers, etc.—were rounded up and despatched to re-education camps on separate islands (for men and women) in the reservoir of the Nam Ngum dam, 80 kilometres north of the capital.

During 1976 popular support for the new regime dwindled rapidly as unrealistic hopes for a prosperous new order faded. The extent of disillusionment was all the greater due to widespread ignorance in the Vientiane zone of Pathet Lao methods and intentions, and the perceived failure of the new regime to honour its promises as set out in the 'Eighteenth-point Programme'. In summary, PL performance failed to meet the expectations of those initially sympathetic to the new regime (Stuart-Fox, 1977b).

Friction developed between PL cadres and the lowland Lao population in a number of ways. Most of the young soldiers who were brought down from the PL zone to police the Mekong river towns belonged to tribal minorities. Their training had stressed unquestioning obedience to the Party. Their experience had been limited to the mountains of their birth and the rigours of war. Their attitude to the lowland Lao was that of victors, suspicious and resentful of urban standards of living and ways of life. The response of ethnic Lao in the Vientiane zone was coloured by racial prejudice and cultural superiority. At the village level, mutual antagonism developed for a number of reasons. Young PL cadres treated village elders with arrogance and disdain. In response to criticism they simply repeated slogans or threatened re-education for reactionaries. Another cause for resentment was over PL interference in the choice of candidates and voting procedures for elections to village administrative committees which often led to inclusion of unpopular opportunists who had quickly learned to recite the new slogans.

By early 1977, the regime was facing something of a crisis. The deteriorating economy, harsh political controls, and constant fear of arbitrary arrest for an indefinite period of 're-education' sent a continuous stream of refugees across the Mekong to Thailand. In 1976, almost 20,000 lowland Lao fled the country: in 1977, another 18,000 joined the exodus (UNHCR Report, 1985). In these first two years, Laos lost most of its professionally and technically qualified middle class. While LPRP leaders seem to have been unconcerned at this flight of 'class enemies', its effect was seriously to undermine the administrative capabilities of the government and long-term development prospects for the country.

Concern over security remained high, especially after a third assassination attempt was made against Kaysone. Stringent precautions were taken to guard Party leaders. Severe drought resulting in a second year of poor harvests, together with resentment over collection of the new tax on agricultural production, created conditions which anti-government insurgents could readily exploit. In response to insurgent activity in northern Laos, both by former Hmong members of the 'secret army' and by Thai-based groups, the authorities ordered the preventative arrest of both the ex-King and Crown Prince and their indefinite imprisonment in Houa Phan province. As LPA troops proved incapable of suppressing the continuing insurgency, the government requested Vietnamese assistance. Even then it took combined Lao and Vietnamese forces the best part of a year to contain the Hmong resistance.

Throughout 1977 and 1978 the Party maintained policies aimed at consolidating political power and bringing about a rapid socialist transformation of Lao society. Early in 1978, a three-year development plan was announced designed to prepare the way for the first five-year plan in 1981 in coordination with other communist states. In May 1978 a political decision was taken to press ahead with the rapid cooperativization of agriculture. Low-level cooperative production in the form of mutual aid teams had been introduced in some areas, mainly in the former PL zone, as early as 1976. The success of these teams, really no more than an extension of traditional modes of peasant labour exchange, was given as the principal reason for the decision to cooperativize agriculture. The real reasons, however, were ideological. From the perspective of Marxist ideology only the cooperativization of rural production could bring about the revolution in relations of production that constituted the necessary next step in the socialist transformation of Lao society. Concurrently, the government hoped both to increase production and to improve security through strengthening economic and social controls in the countryside (Stuart-Fox, 1980b).

The economic effects of this decision were disastrous. In Laos cooperativization was not preceded by land reform. A few larger land holdings belonging to exiled 'feudalists' were confiscated, but no attempt was made to equalize peasant holdings through a programme of land redistribution (Khan & Lee, 1980). As a result, though there were few, if any, landlords as such, land holdings varied quite considerably and peasants were by no means equally motivated to pool their resources. Opposition to the formation of cooperatives was widespread. Lack of effective preparation, the shortage of qualified cadres and counter-productive use of coercion all contributed to peasant resentment. Reaction took the form of passive resistance and non-cooperation, destruction of property and crops destined for cooperative use or even migration either to towns in Laos or more often to Thailand. In 1978, almost 50,000 lowland Lao fled to Thailand, well over double the number that left in 1977. A substantial number were peasant farmers mainly from southern Laos.

Severe flooding following upon the drought of the previous year again seriously reduced the 1978 rice harvest. But it was also clear that peasant opposition to cooperativization had reduced production. The gains that had been expected from cooperativization did not materialize because reduced incentives were not compensated for by improved agricultural techniques and inputs. In addition, cooperativization was beginning to have an adverse effect on national security, as peasant fear and incomprehension were exploited by resistance groups to undermine government credibility and gain recruits. In mid-July 1979, after being 'strongly advised' by both Soviet Premier Alexei Kosygin and high-ranking Vietnamese leaders to terminate the cooperativization drive, the CC of the LPRP issued a directive calling for 'immediate and absolute suspension' of the programme. Any cooperative member who wished to withdraw was given permission to do so. Of the 2,800 cooperatives the government claimed had been set up incorporating twenty-five per cent of all peasant families, most collapsed. The count was in any case inflated, and many cooperatives existed only on paper. Henceforth, cooperativization while not abandoned was to proceed gradually as resources permitted (Stuart-Fox, 1980b; ADB Report, 1980).

The failure of the cooperativization programme, continuing poor economic performance, and new regional tensions resulting from Vietnam's invasion of Kampuchea and subsequent border war with China together forced a radical rethinking of policy on the part of the Lao leadership. It also led to a purge of LPRP members suspected of being pro-Chinese. At its seventh plenary session held in November 1979, the CC of the Party decided to implement a new and softer political line. This was endorsed by the Supreme People's Assembly in December in a document known as the Seventh Resolution, the economic impact of which will be discussed below. Suffice it to say that the changes introduced affected every aspect of the Lao economy and society. A whole range of economic controls was loosened. Private production was encouraged by reducing agricultural taxes and increasing procurement prices. Government subsidies were cut and salaries increased. Productivity and profit were recognized as necessary criteria for the efficiency of state enterprises. Henceforth, economic results were to take priority over ideological orthodoxy. This tactical change of economic policy in the direction of 'market socialism' was justified by reference to Lenin's New Economic Policy.

By the end of 1980 when the regime celebrated its fifth anniversary in power, it was already evident that the reforms were having the desired effect. Food and consumer goods were freely available in Vientiane's markets. Rice production reached one million tonnes of paddy. The security threat was being contained. In 1981, the reforms of the Seventh Resolution were adopted as the basis for Laos' first five-year plan to run to the end of 1985. Ambitious targets were set for agricultural and industrial production, in infrastructure development and transportation, and in education and public health.

In April 1982, the LPRP held its Third Party Congress. This endorsed the general line contained in the Seventh Resolution, but addressed itself more specifically to one of the priority areas listed in the first five-year plan— namely to consolidate and restructure those 'organizations responsible for managing the economy and the state'. The government was reorganized on three levels (see below). The new governmental structure preserved the dominance of the established Party leadership while introducing at the vice-ministerial level a number of younger technocrats, some of whom were Western trained and had even served the former RLG regime. It was hoped that the appointment of about eighty vice-ministers would decentralize administrative decision-making processes.

It appears, however, that some opposition was voiced to the restructuring of government, liberalization of the economy and the overall pragmatic approach to the socialist transformation of Lao society confirmed as Party policy at the Third Congress. Opponents of these changes were critical of the resurgence of 'bourgeois' and 'petty capitalist' tendencies, and alarmed at the relaxation of state controls in the economic sector. Much of this criticism was effectively contained within the Party, but an indication of the intensity of 'the struggle to resolve the problem of who is winning over whom between the two lines—socialism and capitalism', as Kaysone put it (FBIS, 29 January 1985), was provided by the series of arrests and in some cases subsequent release and rehabilitation of vice-ministers which occurred between 1983 and 1985.

In March 1983, two vice-ministers, both of whom had previously worked for the RLG, together with a number of lesser officials were arrested on charges of corruption and anti-state activities. Thirty-two persons in all were later convicted and given prison sentences. Then early in 1984 two more vice-ministers were arrested. Charges were never made public, but one vice-minister had been instrumental in denouncing officials already convicted, while the other had been openly critical of government economic policies. In mid-1984, after a month-long investigation by a 'special appeals tribunal' into allegations that evidence against the first group arrested had been manufactured, most of these, including both vice-ministers, were released and restored to their former positions. In November 1984 two more vice-ministers were arrested, one of whom was later released and the other charged with corruption (for a detailed discussion of these arrests, see Stuart-Fox, 1986b).

There are multiple dimensions to these events which throw some interesting light on how Lao politics were by then being conducted. It would seem that the 1983 arrests reflected dissatisfaction on the part of some PL veterans over the elevation to vice-ministerial status of technocrats associated with the former regime. Personal jealousy and antagonism evidently played a part in these arrests, but power conflicts seem to have been just as important. Evidence appears to have been deliberately fabricated in order to dispose of certain opponents. Ideological criticism was another important means of attack. Criticism of policies by those who are not Party members carries with it the threat of denunciation as a secret enemy of the regime.

These events also throw light on two further aspects of modern Lao society—the prevalence of corruption and the workings of the system of justice. By 1985 corruption had become widespread, though not at a level to compare with that of the former regime. This increase in corruption occurred partly because salaries of government servants remained absurdly low and partly because new opportunities for corrupt practices became available. Liberalization of foreign trade and the possibility of private investment and joint private-state enterprise had come to provide such opportunities on a relatively lavish scale.

Revolutionary justice in the LPRP operated at first on an *ad hoc* basis, mainly because of the lack of any constitution or legal guarantees. In the early days of the regime, accused were tried by 'people's courts' without benefit of legal advice or any right of appeal. The re-examination of evidence in the case of the first two vice-ministers arrested was the first known occasion when the authorities were forced to admit that anyone had been wrongly arrested and convicted. This might reflect well on the appeal system were it not that the 're-trial' was ordered not as a result of legal process, but because families and friends of the accused brought personal pressure to bear on senior Party leaders.

The arrests of 1983 and 1984 illustrate above all how power is exercised in the LPDR: not primarily via institutionalized procedures or through rational debate on the merits of particular lines of action, but via personal relationships, family influence and clan affiliation. Position and preferment depend to a large extent on family relationships by blood or marriage, and on the patronage provided by powerful figures in the Party. Civil servants and Party cadres are frequently identified as belonging to the clan of one personality or another, reference to which provides an explanation of their fortunes. Perhaps these developments should not cause surprise. After all, politics in Laos have traditionally been conducted by manipulating power relations between clans and families. In the LPDR, much of the old Laos remains.

In January 1985, Kaysone told the annual sitting of the Supreme People's Assembly that the struggle between the 'two lines'—socialism and capitalism—'developed to a new phase in a fiercer and uncompromising manner in the past year'. Clearly this reflected ongoing debate over the direction the Lao revolution was taking; for clearly too the 'enemy' was inside the Party, as well as outside it. In the future there would exist 'possibilities for a complicated, fierce, and furious change in the struggle', Kaysone said. The struggle extended 'to all respects and . . . all domains', but the primary 'battlefront' was that of 'circulation and distribution and economic relations with foreign countries'—handled by just those ministries from which most arrests had occurred (FBIS, 29 January 1985). Where Kaysone himself stood in relation to this 'two-line struggle' remained unclear, though he did confirm that the government was determined to implement more flexible management procedures.

Despite these warnings of increased political tension, the year passed quietly with celebrations marking the 'two great, historical days of the nation'—the thirtieth anniversary of the founding of the LPRP, and the tenth anniversary of the establishment of the LPDR. As 1985 also marked the completion of the country's first five-year plan, it provided an occasion for sober examination of the fruits of a decade of socialism in Laos. However, whether measured in terms of economic development, socialist transformation of Lao society, or creation of new Lao socialist men and women imbued with the ideals of Marxism–Leninism, achievements were less than anticipated. Laos remained a desperately poor country with limited human resources, low productivity, and low life expectancy, still chronically dependent on foreign aid for any slight improvement in the standard of living. Regrettably, no matter what political or economic decisions are made in the future, it is likely to be many years before this picture alters appreciably.

2　Social Structure

Ethnic Divisions

The outstanding characteristic of the social structure of the LPDR is that its primary divisions are determined not on the bases of social class or economic role, but on ethnogeographic criteria. The boundaries of the Lao state as these have existed this century have never marked off the living space of a single integrated Lao society. Indeed the term 'Lao society' has usually referred to the social community formed by one ethnic group—admittedly the group which has historically been, and still remains, politically and culturally dominant, but one which comprises only about 50 per cent of the total population of the country. The creation of an integrated Lao society drawing together as Lao all those who live within the frontiers of the Lao state constitutes perhaps the major challenge facing the present regime. On how this challenge is met depends the future of Laos as a political entity.

Since the founding of the LPDR, the Lao population has been said officially to be made of sixty-eight different nationalities. However, no list of these sixty-eight nationalities has ever been published and it has proved impossible to obtain any such list from any Lao official. Interviews with the Chairman of the Nationalities Committee and researchers in the ethnographic section of the Ministry of Culture revealed, however, that the list did not include urban-dwelling ethnic Chinese, Vietnamese, Thai, or Indians resident in Laos, even though many possess Lao citizenship. Nor does it include the most primitive ethnic group in the country, jungle nomads known as the Phi Tong Luang, 'spirits of the yellow leaves' for their habit of constructing makeshift shelters of banana fronds which they abandon once the leaves turn yellow. It does, however, include the Ho (or Haw), ethnic Chinese originally from Yunnan who have settled in northern Laos, mainly in Phong Saly province. It appears that the main reason why the list of sixty-eight 'nationalities' remains secret is that the count may not be accurate. Agreement has evidently not been reached on a definitive basis of classification: whether the primary criterion should be cultural or linguistic. Ultimately for the present regime, the decision as to what is to count as a distinct ethnic group is a political one—which the Lao authorities have been reluctant to make. How many different ethnic groups actually exist in Laos therefore remains a mystery.

Based on a combination of cultural, linguistic and geographical criteria, however, it is usual to divide the population of Laos into three broad groups. These have been designated as the Lao Theung, or 'Lao of the mountain slopes', speaking Mon-Khmer languages; the Lao Soung, or 'Lao of the mountain summits', speaking Tibeto-Burman languages; and the Lao Loum, or 'Lao of the mountains and plains', speaking T'ai languages. The ethnic, or lowland, Lao of the Mekong valley constitute but one of the groups making up the Lao Loum.

Lao Theung tribes were the earliest inhabitants of what is now Laos. They appear to have been driven from the more productive alluvial plains by the gradual migration of T'ai-speaking peoples during the first millennium AD. Prior ownership of the land by the Lao Theung was symbolically acknowledged in the ceremonies and accompanying myths performed until 1975 at the court of Luang Prabang. Various Lao Theung tribes in both northern and southern Laos were forced into dependent relations with the dominant ethnic Lao amounting to slavery, an institution which was only abolished by the French. The pejorative term used by ethnic Lao to refer to the Lao Theung is *kha*, meaning 'slave'. A few tribes, such as the Phu Noi, the So and the Sek have adopted Lao language and culture and become assimilated into Lao society. Such assimilation has also occurred in the case of a few individual families of other tribes, particularly the Khmu (Kunstadter, 1967). By contrast, most Lao Theung tribes have fiercely guarded their cultural autonomy and independence.

Lao Theung tribes are scattered through most of the mountainous regions of Laos, but are concentrated in parts of the north, and in the region of the Bolovens Plateau in southern Laos. Most tribes practise a similar economy of partially nomadic slash-and-burn agriculture (upland rice, maize, legumes, vegetables), raise chickens, pigs and cattle, and produce whatever other commodities they need in the way of clothing, tools and weapons. This virtually self-sufficient economy is supplemented by trade with lowland Lao, Vietnamese, or Chinese merchants for a few consumer goods, medicines, salt and metal in exchange for skins and forest products such as benzoin and sticklac. Most tribes practise their own forms of animism, in rites demanding the sacrifice of buffalo and consumption of quantities of rice wine. Authority lies in the hands of hereditary chiefs, the old and the wealthy, and of sorcerers revered for their ability to placate or expel malevolent spirits (*phi*).

Lao Theung villages are usually constructed around a men's house at the centre. Houses built of timber and woven bamboo are often large enough to shelter an entire extended family. The social structure is patriarchal and patrilinear. Some Lao Theung tribes recognize an hereditary chieftain, but most have never developed any political organization above the village level. In cases when a supratribal organization was temporarily developed, as during the revolt against French authority by Lao Theung tribes on the Bolovens Plateau from 1910 to 1918, this centred on a respected traditional chieftain whose position was reinforced in the eyes of other tribes by his claims to magic powers. Within the village, social stratification is minimal. Even where an hereditary village headman exists, he is no more than first among equals. In cases where there is no village headman as such, the leading figure in the village is usually whoever is responsible for officiating at essential religious festivals and ceremonies. Among some tribes—for example, the Lamet of northern Laos—this position of religious leadership is hereditary (Halpern, 1964).

By contrast with the Lao Theung, the Tibeto–Burman speaking Lao Soung tribes, notably the Hmong (also pejoratively known as *Meo*, meaning 'savage'), and the Yao or Man, were latecomers in Laos. The first small groups to arrive migrated from southern China less than two centuries ago. Most are concentrated in the provinces of Houa Phan and Xieng Khouang, but others have moved west to Sayaboury and northern Thailand, or south into the northern parts of Vientiane province. A few families have even penetrated as far as Khammouane province in central Laos. In general, the Lao Soung have occupied the higher altitudes left vacant by the Lao Loum and Lao Theung. Traditionally they have built their villages on well defensible mountain ridges and maintained a vigorous independence. Like the Lao Theung, the Lao Soung practise slash–and–burn agriculture, growing in addition to food crops their principal commercial item—opium. This they trade for salt, iron, textiles and simple consumer goods. They raise small, sturdy, mountain pack horses essential for the transportation of goods in areas where roads are unknown. Like the Lao Theung, the Lao Soung are animists, but practise in addition, under Chinese influence, both divination and ancestor worship. They accept the authority of hereditary chiefs of major clans.

The Hmong in Laos are grouped into a number of patriarchal and patrilinear clans, the most prominent of which traditionally elected their own clan leaders (*kiatong*) (Lee, in Stuart-Fox, 1982a). With the extension of French control over northern Laos, the Hmong were brought within the French system of local administration. Resentment over imposition of taxes and demands for corvée labour led to the revolt of 1918–22, after which the Hmong were granted a greater degree of control over their own affairs (Larteguy & Dao, 1979). This semi-autonomous status was preserved under the Royal Lao government, and reinforced by formation of the CIA-funded

Hmong 'secret army' in northern Laos, when General Vang Pao became a virtually independent Hmong warlord.

Hmong social structure is based above all upon respect for age symbolized in the cult of ancestor worship. The family head is the oldest male member, while the village chief was traditionally the oldest family head, though this was not always the case. The chief of a Hmong village is a powerful figure whose word is usually sufficient to regulate village affairs and solve disputes. In consultation with other heads of families he decides on the need to open up new fields or to move the whole village. Another powerful figure is the village shaman. Although Hmong society has a close-knit hierarchical structure at the village level, no permanent institutionalized structure exists above the village level. What unites the Hmong from time to time is the messianic belief that a Hmong king will some day rise up to unite the clans and create an independent Hmong kingdom. This collective dream (or folk memory of an earlier Hmong state in southern China) gives rise to millennarial movements of revolt, which the Hmong call *oa phoa thay* ('to make a king') (Halpern, 1964, p. 73). The Hmong have in the past been prepared to follow any charismatic or powerful leader who claims to possess divine powers and promises to carve out a Hmong state. Even as recently as 1976 the Chao Fa ('God's Disciples') resistance movement against the new Lao regime was animated by similar notions (Lee, in Stuart-Fox, 1982a).

The largest of the three broad ethnic groups in Laos is the Lao Loum. This comprises in addition to the ethnic Lao of the Mekong valley, the culturally closely related Lao Phuan of Xieng Khouang, the Lao Yuan of Sayaboury, the Lu of northern Laos, as well as the Tai Neua of Houa Phan, and the mountain Tai peoples. The Lao Phuan, Lao Yuan and the Lu are Buddhists, though they have retained a number of animist beliefs and practices. All are thoroughly assimilated and integrated into the dominant ethnic Lao society and culture. The mountain Tai are divided into a number of distinct groups, including the Tai Dam (the Black Tai), Tai Deng (Red Tai) and Tai Khao (White Tai) named for the predominant colour in the traditional costumes of their womenfolk. Of these, the Tai Dam may be taken as typical.

Like all Lao Loum, the Tai Dam practise the cultivation of wet rice, often using complex systems of irrigation and terracing in their narrow upland valleys. Much of the rice grown is of the glutinous variety characteristic of Lao Loum cuisine. Like all Lao Loum, but unlike either the Lao Theung or Lao Soung, the Tai Dam use buffalo and oxen for ploughing or as draught animals, not to sacrifice. They raise poultry and pigs, cultivate vegetables and gather forest products. Like the Lao Soung, the Tai Dam and other mountain Tai also breed pack horses. Like all Lao Loum, the Tai Dam build wooden houses raised on piles above the ground, under which the women weave or men make fishing nets or tools. Unlike the ethnic Lao and other Lao Loum groups, however, the mountain Tai are animists who revere a variety of spirits associated with the sky, the earth and the subterranean world. A substantial spirit house is constructed near each village for their worship.

The Tai Dam are patriarchal and patrilinear. In Laos they are organized into small principalities, or *muong*, each presided over by a *chao muong*, or prince, who is always a member of a single royal clan or one of its collateral branches. Traditionally, the mountain Tai principalities were organized into a loose federation known as the Sip Song Chau Tai (the Twelve Tai Principalities, sometimes the Sip Hok, or Sixteen, Chau Tai), most of whose territory now forms the mountainous northwestern region of Vietnam. The Tai *muong* in Laos, however, rarely extend beyond a single mountain valley and form part of no wider political grouping of Tai peoples. Instead the *muong* are integrated into the provincial administrative structure of the Lao state.

The Tai Dam traditional social structure comprises three classes. At the apex stands the princely clan of the Cam (or Lo Cam). Below these in prestige and social standing rank two clans, the Luong and the Ka, making up the priestly class. Below these again rank all remaining Tai Dam families forming a broad commoner class of peasant farmers and village artisans. The Cam owe their prestige to the belief that four of their thirty-two souls were created by the supreme celestial deity, in whose worship they perform an essential role. Priests are of three ranks depending on the nature of the ceremonies they are competent to perform. Since all irrigated land nominally belongs to the *chao muong* it is regularly redistributed among the families of the village according to need, for which a tax is demanded in corvée to work the land reserved for the *chao muong* and his family.

Because of the geographical remoteness of many of the mountain villages, and the poor means of communication over much of northern and western Laos, the traditional social structures of the peoples of these regions, whether Lao Theung, Lao Soung or mountain Tai, still significantly influences the politics and society of present-day Laos. Attempts to transform traditional beliefs and practices have encountered concerted opposition from tribal minorities. Social relations at the village level still reflect traditional values, and are likely to continue to do so until such time as minority groups can be drawn more closely into the economic and political life of the country.

Lowland Lao Social Structure

The changes brought about in lowland Lao society through installation of a communist government in Vientiane have been most apparent in urban areas. In part these changes have been due to population movements which will be discussed below; in part they have resulted from a deliberate policy of socialist transformation. Ten years, however, is too short a period in which to create entirely new social structures. Traditional social relationships which played an important role in structuring lowland Lao society during the period from 1949 to 1975 have proved remarkably resistant to change during the early period of socialist government. A discussion of the traditional structure of Lao society is essential, therefore, to an appreciation of those changes which have occurred since 1975.

At the apex of traditional Lao society stood the king together with the royal family of Luang Prabang and members of its collateral branches. Below them ranked an aristocratic elite numbering probably no more than 200 families (Halpern, 1964, p. 5), who traced their ancestry back either to the other royal families of Champassak or Xieng Khouang or to high officials who served the courts of Luang Prabang, Vientiane, Xieng Khouang or Champassak. (There are no direct descendants of the former royal family of Vientiane.) All other ethnic Lao formed a population of peasant farmers dispersed over those areas where the cultivation of wet rice was possible.

Under the French, and during the period of the Royal Lao government, a small degree of upward social mobility existed for those with a French education, though this was limited by the fact that French educational facilities in Laos were monopolized by the children of the elite themselves. During the same period, a Lao middle class began to develop composed of lower ranking civil servants, primary school teachers, police and army officers, small merchants and businessmen. Some sought to improve their social standing by entering politics as candidates for election to the National Assembly. Even if elected, however, they very seldom gained positions in the ministry, for these were reserved for members of the elite. Even representatives of the Pathet Lao who participated in the three coalition governments prior to 1975 were like Souphanouvong or Souk Vongsak related to the royal family of Luang Prabang, or like Phoumi Vongvichit were high ranking or well-educated former French-trained administrators or government officials.

If political power in the areas under Royal Lao government control remained firmly in the hands of the ethnic Lao elite, the same cannot be said for the Pathet Lao. Power in the Lao communist movement was shared between former members of the Lao elite and those leaders of more humble social origins who had gained positions of authority within the Lao Patriotic Front or the clandestine Lao People's Party (as it was called until 1972). Throughout the various negotiations which led to the formation of the three coalition governments, the former group was most in evidence; the latter remained in the background. Even after the formation of the LPDR, the distinction remained important as a basis for differing tendencies within the LPRP (Stuart-Fox, 1977a).

The Lao elite was not rigidly exclusive. Entry was possible for those with educational and professional qualifications or with the right family ties through marriage. Kinship constituted the primary structural basis of elite Lao society. Important families, together with collateral branches and those to whom they were related by marriage, formed clans which competed for political power, wealth and social prestige. Clan interests and clan loyalties all too often were placed ahead of national loyalties and interests (Deuve, 1984). Clan divisions were exacerbated by regionalism. The elite families of Luang Prabang and southern Laos jealously guarded their prerogatives against the families of Vientiane, such as the Souvannavongs, the Sananikones and the Voravongs. The influence of the major clans penetrated all aspects of Lao national life. Clans would have representatives not only in politics and in government service, but also in business and in the army or police. Members of powerful families entered into partnership with Vietnamese or particularly Chinese businessmen in such areas as banking, hotels, airlines, construction companies, timber milling and road transport. Many invested also in land and in construction of villas to rent to diplomatic and foreign aid personnel (cf. Halpern, 1964).

Prior to 1975, much of the urban economy of Laos was in the hands of Chinese and a few French merchants and businessmen, who profited from the massive inflow of American aid by catering to the demand for imported consumer goods. Together with the Lao elite, these constituted the Lao bourgeoisie. Below them in the social hierarchy stood a petty bourgeoisie of shopkeepers, small merchants, teachers and lower ranking civil servants. Below these again came a small working class concentrated in Vientiane employed in construction and industry. A few small factories in Vientiane making cigarettes, soft drinks, beer, soap and detergent, cheap plastic items, textiles, furniture, and agricultural implements, plus rice mills, saw mills and brickworks, together employed perhaps 15,000 workers. Industry outside the Vientiane area was minimal. Apart from the tin mines at Phou Tiou in Savannakhet province, employment was mainly in government service, transportation, construction and in small machine shops or garages. More than 90 per cent of the population outside the Vientiane area were peasant farmers.

The ethnic Lao peasantry was and remains numerically by far the largest class in the country. In fact, in view of the minute size of the urban proletariat, it can be said to constitute the dominant class in the Lao socialist state. Lao villages are essentially self-sufficient, semi-isolated units producing most of what is necessary for daily existence. Inter-village commerce is minimal, unless villages are situated along a main road. Only around Vientiane and some smaller towns are villages fully integrated into a market economy. Work is seasonal and divided according to sex and age. In most areas, still only one rice crop is produced a year after the rainy season, usually necessitating no more than 100 days of labour. For the rest of the time, men make simple implements, repair whatever needs repairing, go fishing or sit and talk. Women grow vegetables, weave, cook and look after the home. Children care for the livestock. Life is lived at a leisurely pace, for nature is abundant.

The basic social unit is the nuclear family. Younger sons usually build their own houses after they marry, but relations within the extended family remain close. Lao society has often been described as 'loosely structured', but this is a misleading concept. It is true that the Lao village lacks the close-knit social structure characteristic of Chinese or Vietnamese villages—social obligations are less exacting, and social relations less constricting. But Lao society does not lack structure; it is simply structured with reference to different criteria based not predominantly on relationships within patrilocal extended families and ancestral clans, but on relationships of relative superiority and inferiority calculated according to a variety of considerations including kinship, age, sex, occupation, wealth and religious standing (cf. Barber, 1979).

The centre of village life remains the Buddhist *wat*, or pagoda, where much of the social life of the village is still concentrated. *Bouns*, or festivals, are frequent and the occasion of expenditure of wealth, both in gifts to the monks and in consumption. Surplus wealth is therefore neither accumulated nor invested. It goes, rather, to ensure merit and a comfortable rebirth—much to the despair of those who are attempting to drag Laos along the path of socialist development.

Population Movements and Social Structure

The events of 1975 set in train a series of population movements which have permanently altered the demographic and class structure of Lao society. From May 1975 to June 1985, a total of 309,694 people left Laos to cross as refugees into Thailand. Of these 194,220 were described as 'lowland Lao', a designation which included ethnic Chinese and Vietnamese resident in Laos, and 115,474 were from various hill tribes, the great majority of whom were Hmong. As many as 60,000 more, predominantly lowland Lao, are estimated to have avoided registration and been absorbed into Thai society. In May 1975, the exodus was led by those Lao most closely identified with the discredited political right, but included a group of more than 2,000 Tai Dam who had come as refugees to Laos in 1954 from North Vietnam. Later in the year thousands of Hmong families whose menfolk had fought for the CIA-funded 'secret army' in northern Laos against the Pathet Lao were either airlifted out, or trekked across Sayaboury province to the Thai border. In all, more than 10,000 lowland Lao and almost 45,000 hill-tribe people left before the LPDR was officially established. The number of lowland Lao leaving almost doubled in 1976, held steady in 1977 and more than doubled again in 1978 to over 48,000. Over the same period, the number of hill-tribe departures declined dramatically. In 1979, the number of lowland Lao refugees dropped by more than half, to just above the level in 1976 and 1977, though hill-tribe departures tripled to just on 24,000 with the final crushing of Hmong resistance by Vietnamese and LPA forces. The refugee outflow eased considerably in 1981, and declined further the following year to a mere 3,200 lowland Lao and 1,800 hill-tribe people, as more lenient policies in Laos coincided with tighter Thai controls. In 1984, however, the number of Lao leaving again increased to just on 15,000, and remained high through the first half of 1985. A new Thai policy of sending back 'illegal immigrants' cut the outflow again in July 1985. (All figures are from UNHCR Report, 1985.)

These figures are of interest for a number of reasons for they reflect both the expectations of those leaving and the policies of the new regime. Reasons for the two major waves of Hmong departures in 1975 and 1978 have already been noted. Lao departures in 1976 and 1977 comprised those who feared their political involvement with the former regime would be held against them (leading to indefinite detention in re-education camps); the families of many of the 10,000 former officials already undergoing re-education who had given up hope of their release; and the remaining Vietnamese and Chinese merchants progressively forced out of business by new economic policies and controls. The spectacular increase in 1978 was in large part composed of former middle- and lower-level civil servants, former police and army personnel, and members of the urban middle class who had been prepared to stay and help build a new, prosperous and peaceful Laos under the leadership of the Pathet Lao, but who over a period of three years had used up all their savings and saw no prospects of economic improvement or political liberalization. Their numbers were swelled for the first time by peasants, especially from southern Laos, reacting against the cooperativization of their land. Termination of the cooperativization drive in mid-1979 brought this peasant exodus to an end, but overall numbers of refugees remained high in 1979 and 1980 as more and more families, especially from the Vientiane area, made the essentially economic decision to leave and seek new opportunities elsewhere. Already in 1981, however, economic policy changes ushered in by the Seventh Resolution were beginning to have an effect. Food was more readily available and other conditions of life had improved. Why then the sudden increase in 1984? According to officials of the UN High Commission for Refugees, the reason had mainly to do with the 'pull-effect' exercised by relations already settled abroad and their glowing reports of life in America, or Australia or France; and with the 'snowball effect' accompanying a rumour that no one who left after the end of 1984 would be accepted for resettlement overseas. Many people left because they saw others leaving, and so thought the rumour must be true. Because very few of those who left in 1984 and the first half of 1985 could conceivably be called political refugees, however, Thailand began in July 1985 to treat most Lao as illegal emigrants subject to forced repatriation—a policy which promised eventually to put an end to the haemorrhage of population from Laos.

The net effect of the outflow of refugees from the LPDR over the first ten years of the new regime has been to reduce the population by about 10 per cent. This in itself is serious enough for a country already underpopulated. The policy of the LPDR is in fact to increase population by all available means, which is why birth control measures are unavailable. Without this loss, the population of Laos would have been about 3.9 million at the time of the 1985 census instead of less than 3.6 million. More significant, however, is that the outflow not only included most of the former Lao elite, but also represented a substantial proportion of the educated middle class. Laos lost not only almost all its professionally qualified doctors, engineers, managers and administrators, but also a large proportion of its mechanics, tradesmen and artisans. Such a loss of so many trained civil servants, teachers and technicians from a country as underdeveloped as Laos could not help but set the country back several years in its programme of development. The

Table 2.1 Population of Laos (Census taken 1–6 March 1985)

Area	Total population	Male	Female
Vientiane Municipality	377,409	193,136	184,273
Luang Namtha Province	97,028	46,435	50,593
Phong Saly Province	122,984	59,925	63,059
Oudomsai Province	187,115	90,570	96,545
Bokeo Province	54,925	26,360	28,565
Luang Prabang Province	295,475	146,202	149,273
Houa Phan Province	209,921	104,740	105,181
Sayaboury Province	223,611	109,763	113,848
Xieng Khouang Province	161,589	80,611	80,978
Vientiane Province	264,277	132,572	131,705
Bolikhamsai Province	122,300	59,931	62,369
Khammouane Province	213,462	102,040	111,422
Savannakhet Province	543,611	263,856	279,755
Saravane Province	187,515	88,240	99,275
Sekong Province	50,909	24,657	26,252
Champassak Province	403,041	195,240	207,801
Attopeu Province	69,631	32,837	36,704

number of hill-tribe people, especially Hmong, who left altered the ethnic balance slightly, but it was the loss of a substantial proportion of the urban population that was most significant.

In terms of social classes, the outflow of refugees virtually eliminated the Lao bourgeoisie, together with the petty bourgeois class of small urban merchants and shopkeepers, mostly Chinese and Vietnamese. By 1978, the commercial centres of the Mekong towns were but dead shells of barred and shuttered shops, only a few of which had been taken over by the state. All but a minute fraction of the 30,000 strong Chinese community in Laos had left by the end of 1978, during the period when Vietnamese pressures against the Chinese community in Vietnam were at their height. Many Vietnamese left too, but these were partially replaced by Vietnamese who moved to Laos from northeastern Thailand. These population movements altered the population profiles and class composition of the Mekong river towns in Laos since those who left were replaced by peasant guerrillas of the Pathet Lao and their supporters from outlying villages and provinces. Lao Loum from Houa Phan and Xieng Khouang provinces and from villages in Vientiane province moved into Vientiane city to take the place of those who left, while in Luang

Prabang and in southern Laos a number of Lao Theung families have taken up residence in administrative centres. The new townsfolk form a small urban population composed of workers in state industrial enterprises, construction and transportation, plus civil servants, soldiers and a few remaining shopkeepers and merchants—altogether far fewer in number than in 1975.

Two other groups are significant in Lao society, not in terms of numbers, but in terms of the political and economic power they wield. The first is, of course, the new communist leadership; the second is composed of those few members of former elite families who chose to remain in Laos. Some of this latter group were poorer relatives of those who had fled, most of whom have taken possession of family residences. (Rather surprisingly very few homes of those who have fled the country have been confiscated by the state.) From 1975 to 1980 members of the former elite kept a low profile. Most survived on remittances from abroad. With the economic liberalization of 1980, those who had stayed were in a position to take advantage of the new policy of stimulating the capitalist and joint state–capitalist sectors of the economy, for they alone had the knowledge and skills, the contacts abroad, and the necessary finance (usually also from abroad). By 1985, a new class had begun to emerge, at least in Vientiane, comprising those families which through the perquisites of power (high Party and state officials) or accumulation of wealth (former members of the bourgeois elite) enjoyed patterns of consumption and a standard of living well above that of the mass of the urban population.

The outward signs of membership of the new Lao elite were possession of television sets and video recorders, use of cars (official or private) without shortage of petrol, attendance at private parties, and so on. Just as significant, however, was the presence of their children at one of the two former lycées in Vientiane where some attempt has been made to maintain educational standards, and their assurance of scholarships to study abroad. Once again, by 1985, family relationships were important, and the former phenomenon of 'clans' centred upon a politically powerful or wealthy 'patron' was again evident. Members of the 'national bourgeoisie' were beginning to play a more influential political role through their membership not of the LPRP, but of the Lao Front for National Construction. Their children also exercised increasing influence on the People's Revolutionary Youth organization. If trends towards a *de facto* social alliance between Party leaders and remnants of the national bourgeoisie, reinforced by marriage and political influence, were to continue, it would clearly represent a phenomenon of considerable significance in the evolution of Lao social structure, with implications for the socialist transformation of Lao society.

Socialist Transformation and the Structure of Lao Society

Changes in the structure of Lao society which have taken place during the first decade in power of the new regime have been significant as far as the urban population is concerned, but have left rural society almost untouched. If, however, Thai policy of sending back to Laos all who cannot prove their status as political refugees is adhered to, the exodus of refugees seems likely to come to an end. Change in social structure as a result of population loss will not, therefore, continue. Yet if Laos is to develop in the direction desired by the leaders of the LPRP, such development must needs be accompanied by substantial changes in social structure, particularly in rural areas and in the proportional relationship between the urban proletariat and the peasantry. How likely is this to occur?

In terms of a Marxist analysis, there exists in Laos a 'difference between the politically advanced regime and the insufficiently developed economic base' that will have to be bridged (Mikheév, 1985, pp. 69–70). The chosen method is to pursue simultaneously three revolutions: in relations of production, in science and technology and in culture and ideology. It was in pursuit of the first of these goals that the regime attempted to socialize the means of production and distribution of goods between 1976 and 1979. To this end controls were exercised over commerce and trade, industry was nationalized, and the programme of cooperativization of agriculture was initiated. The failure of these measures, and especially peasant opposition to cooperativization, forced the change of policy embodied in the Seventh Resolution. Many cooperatives were disbanded: others did little more than formalize traditional mutual assistance at times of planting and harvest. Clearly in the Lao context where 85 per cent of the population are peasant farmers hardly producing above the subsistence level, a revolution in the means of production will not be easy to achieve.

The scientific and technical revolution has proved equally difficult to promote in Laos. Most technically competent Lao have left the country. Levels of education and expertise among those who remain are depressingly low. Also the state has very limited resources either for promotion of mechanized, input intensive agriculture, or for modern industry. Fertilizers and pesticides are not readily available, even for state farms. Wet rice production does not lend itself to mechanization; and maintenance of equipment leaves much to be desired. What factories there are function well below capacity. Thus the burden of the socialist transformation of Lao society has perforce had to be borne by the third revolution, in culture and ideology, which is supposed to stay a step ahead of the other two.

Essentially the third revolution consists in trying to get people to think of themselves as socialists and to act accordingly. In particular, it entails convincing them that they are 'the true masters of their own country' and so able, through force of will and hard work, to transform it into a modern socialist state. Propaganda to this end, however, comes up against a number of deep-seated Lao beliefs and character traits. The Lao are individualistic; their primary loyalties are to their own families. Traditionally they have preferred to devote excess production to the accumulation of religious merit and the pleasure that accompanies this rather than invest it, for there has been little need in Laos to be concerned for the future. Such attitudes continue. For most Lao what matters far more than 'national construction' are convivial pleasures with family and friends won with a minimum of unnecessary effort.

Not surprisingly, therefore, in the light of these difficulties, the transformation of Lao society has been and in all likelihood will continue to be slow. The necessary prerequisites for social change are the production of an agricultural surplus through intensive farming, investment in processing and import-substitution industries along with the mechanization of agriculture, all of which should bring about a net movement of population from the countryside to urban areas. The rapid conversion of an impoverished peasantry into an industrial proletariat that occurred in the Soviet Union is likely to take far longer in Laos, however. For the foreseeable future, therefore, Lao social structure seems set to retain its present features—peasant farmers making up the mass of the population; a small urban proletariat of industrial workers and civil servants; a petty bourgeoisie composed of shopkeepers, merchants, private tradesmen and the like; and an elite comprising both top Party leaders (the political component) and what remains of the national bourgeoisie (the economic component).

3 The Political System

The Lao People's Revolutionary Party

The Lao People's Revolutionary Party, as the communist party of Laos is known, traces its origins back to the Indochinese Communist Party founded by Ho Chi Minh on 3 February 1930. This is a proudly proclaimed heritage. In the words of LPRP Secretary-General Kaysone Phomvihane in an interview for Radio Hanoi on the occasion of the thirtieth anniversary of the Party, the LPRP has inherited 'the glorious historic mission of the Indochinese Communist Party founded and trained by great President Ho Chi Minh' (FBIS, 21 March 1985). It was not until 1936, however, that a Committee for Laos, or 'Lao section' was set up within the ICP (Mikhéev, 1985, p. 9). This date apparently marks the formation of a branch of the ICP in southern Laos which probably included the first Lao communist, a civil servant by the name of Kham Sen, who may have been recruited by Ho Chi Minh himself when Ho was working in northeastern Thailand. Almost all members of the ICP in Laos at this time, however, were Vietnamese (Brown & Zasloff, 1986).

It was not until the mid 1940s that recruitment of Lao into the ICP was actively stepped up. Nouhak Phoumsavanh, then driving a truck between Laos and Vietnam, was recruited at about this time. So too was Kaysone Phomvihane, a young law student in Hanoi known by his Vietnamese name Quoc. (His father, Luan, was a former secretary in the office of the French *résident* in Savannakhet; his mother was Lao. The name Kaysone Phomvihane was taken to emphasize the Lao side of his ancestry.) Communist activists in Laos have been variously described as forming 'a party organization of the Indochinese Communist Party', or a 'Party Committee for Laos'. What is clear, however, is that at this time all Party directives were issued from Vietnam. It was under the auspices of the ICP that Vietminh support was organized for the Lao nationalist movement. The ICP policy of 'Viet–Lao Cooperation' led initially to the signing on 30 October 1945 of a military convention between the Lao Issara government and Ho Chi Minh's fledgling Democratic Republic of Vietnam, and later to formation of a Lao–Viet Allied Armies General Staff to co-ordinate anti-French resistance. Following the defeat of the Lao Issara forces by the returning French in April 1946, ICP agents organized the Committee for Lao Resistance in the East. As noted above, this organization constituted the nucleus around which radical anti-French resistance centred from 1946 until 1949 when the Lao Issara government in exile in Bangkok was formally dissolved.

The period from 1946 to 1949 was one of organization and consolidation for the Lao branch of the ICP. Not until 20 January 1949 was the first Lao combat unit officially established in what was to become the Lao People's Liberation Army. On 13 August 1950, this organizational phase came to fruition when the first Resistance Congress was held, grouping members of the Committee for Lao Resistance in the East with former members of the Lao Issara who refused to compromise with the French and followed Souphanouvong to Vietnam. The congress established the Free Laos Front (Neo Lao Issara), and formed a Lao government of resistance, key figures in which were members of the ICP.

In February 1951, the Second Congress of the ICP resolved to disband the party and form instead three separate parties representing the three states of Indochina. In immediate response to this resolution, the Vietnamese declared the formation of a Vietnamese Worker's Party (Dang Lao Dong). It is not entirely clear, however, what organizational form the Lao response took. Some authorities believe a Lao Worker's Party (Phak Khon Ngan) was formed in direct imitation of the Vietnamese (Deuve, 1984, p. 33). Other writers make no mention of such an organization (Langer & Zasloff, 1970; Zasloff, 1973). Nor has any official publication of the LPDR ever made reference to such a party. Kaysone Phomvihane, writing in the March 1985 issue of the Vietnamese journal *Tap Chi Cong San*, says only that after 1951 'the Lao Communists in the Free Laos Front and the resistance government continued to lead the Lao people in their resistance war and at the same time prepared conditions for the founding of their own party' (FBIS, 27 March 1985). It seems at least possible, therefore, that no formal Lao communist organization existed before 1955, and that individual Lao communists either formally or informally transferred their membership to the Vietnam Worker's Party (cf. Brown & Zasloff, 1986, pp. 58-9; see also my discussion above, p. 20).

The decision to establish a 'leading party' in Laos may not have been taken until 1954, after the signing of the Geneva Agreements on Indochina (cf. Langer & Zasloff, 1970, p. 93). In any case, the official founding of what was then called the Lao People's Party (LPP) has since been taken as 22 March 1955. It is this date, not the founding of the ICP, nor its dissolution in 1951, which has consistently been commemorated in subsequent anniversary celebrations. Some 25 delegates representing 300 to 400 members are said to have attended the founding congress of the party, since described as 'an authentic Marxist–Leninist party, a party of the Lao working class, organized in order to direct the Lao revolution' (*Pages historiques*, 1980, p. 6). Kaysone Phomvihane was elected Secretary-General. In January 1956, the LPP organized a new front organization to replace the Neo Lao Issara. Thus was founded the Lao Patriotic Front (Neo Lao Hak Sat) which was to serve as the mass political organization of the communist movement in Laos, directed and controlled at all times by the clandestine LPP.

The LPP directed the negotiations which led to the formation of the first and second coalition governments in 1957 and 1962. Members of the Party represented the Pathet Lao in both governments. In February 1972, at a time when negotiations between Washington and Hanoi over conditions for an American withdrawal from Vietnam were well advanced, the Second Congress of the Lao People's Party was held to review the events of the previous seventeen years, and to determine a course of action in Laos to take advantage of the changed international situation. At this congress, the name of the Party, then claiming a membership of 21,000, was changed to the Lao People's Revolutionary Party (Phak Pasason Pativat Lao). Kaysone Phomvihane was re-elected Secretary-General, a seven-member Politburo was nominated, and the party continued to function clandestinely.

Subsequent negotiations leading to the formation of the third coalition government in 1974 were directed at all stages by the LPRP. The agreements signed in Vientiane on the 21 February 1973 and the protocol of 14 September 1973 effectively opened the way, through neutralization of the cities of Vientiane and Luang Prabang and formation of a Provisional Government of National Union, to increased activity by the Party in those areas of the country previously under Royal Lao government control. It would appear from a subsequent comment by Souphanouvong in 1975 to the effect that the Pathet Lao had gained power five years too soon (cf. Stuart-Fox, 1981b) that the Party had envisaged a period of at least five years of propaganda and organization among the ethnic Lao of the Mekong valley before seizing power. The opportunity created in 1975 by the collapse of rightist governments in Phnom Penh and Saigon cut short this programme of political education and mobilization, and enabled the Party to establish a people's democratic republic by the end of the year. Only then did the LPRP officially reveal its existence as the guiding force behind the Lao revolution: only subsequently was the membership of the Politburo and the Party Central Committee made public.

The structure of the Party which revealed itself at the end of 1975 is similar to that of other communist parties. Nominally the supreme decision making body is the Party Congress which meets every three or four years.

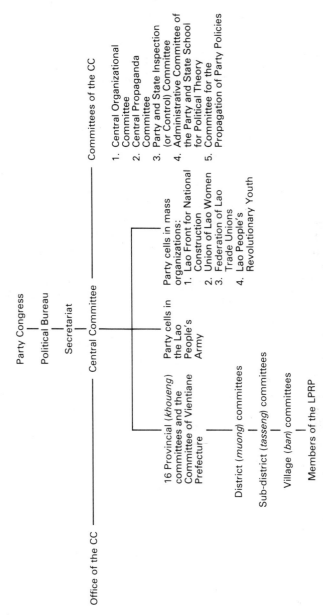

Figure 3.1 Structure of the Lao People's Revolutionary Party

(The Third Party Congress was not held until April 1982, ten years after the Second; but the Fourth Congress was planned for 1986.) At each congress, Party members theoretically elect the Political Bureau, the Central Committee, the Secretariat of the Central Committee and the members of its various committees. In reality, however, the Congress meets to ratify decisions already taken by Party leaders as to who should fill these positions.

As in most other communist parties, the Political Bureau (Politburo) is the real centre of power in the LPRP. Since the Party was founded in 1955, it has been presided over by LPRP Secretary-General Kaysone Phomvihane. Other members of the Politburo have also served since the Party was founded. They are, in the order published after the Third Party Congress, Nouhak Phoumsavanh, Souphanouvong, Phoumi Vongvichit, Khamtay Siphandone, Phoune Sipaseuth, and Sisomphone Lovansay. All are full members: the Lao Politburo has never had alternate members. How often the Politburo meets and how it comes to decisions are unknown. Nor is it known whether anyone but actual members is ever invited to attend meetings—as is rumoured to have occurred in the case of certain Vietnamese advisers. Reports that a sort of inner Politburo consisting of Kaysone and Nouhak in consultation with senior Vietnamese representatives meets regularly are also unconfirmed.

Five of the seven members of the Politburo are also members of the nine-man Central Committee Secretariat. They include Kaysone, Nouhak, Khamtay, Phoune and Sisomphone. Other members following in order of listing are: Saly Vongkhamsao, Sisavath Keobounphanh, Saman Vignaket and Maychantane Sengmany. Of these Khamtay, Saman and Maychantane were added to the earlier six-member secretariat after the Third Party Congress. The Secretariat acts on behalf of the Central Committee whenever the CC is not meeting. It is responsible for issuing all Party decisions and directives. Since the CC meets normally only once or twice a year, the Secretariat effectively controls the day-to-day affairs of the Party. As such it constitutes a focus of power second only to the Politburo. From its members is almost certain to be chosen any eventual successor to Kaysone as Secretary-General of the Party.

The Central Committee of the Party is elected by the Party congress for the period until the next congress meets, when theoretically all positions on the CC become vacant and any member can be replaced. The CC has the task of leading the Party until the sitting of the next Party congress. From its members are drawn both the members of the Politburo and of the Secretariat. The CC has no fixed size. When the Party's role in guiding the Lao revolution was revealed in 1975, the CC consisted of twenty-one full and six alternate (non-voting) members. (One member died in 1978.) After the Third Congress of the LPRP, this was more than doubled to forty-nine full and six alternate members. No member of the former CC was dropped, and all former alternate members became full members. Two members died soon after the congress, and were not replaced.

Membership of the 1982 CC was made up of veteran communists who fought throughout all or most of the Thirty-Year Struggle. The first eleven members in order of listing were members of the Politburo and Secretariat. These were followed by the seven surviving full members of the 1975 CC. Then came the powerful secretary of the Champassak Provincial Party Committee, Sounthon Thepasa. Next in order were the six former alternate members, followed by seven new members representing the Party, government and mass organizations, including Thongvin Phomvihane, Kaysone's wife. Next were listed two groups significant for their increased representation on the CC—six more secretaries of provincial committees (bringing the total to seven), followed by six military officers, two of whom concurrently held government positions as vice-ministers of defence. The six alternate members included two more army officers appointed as government ministers and another provincial representative from Vientiane province. Thus of the twenty-nine additional full and alternate members promoted to the CC at the Third Party Congress, eight were provincial representatives and eight were military officers. Of the remaining thirteen appointees, seven held ministerial or vice-ministerial portfolios, while the remainder held positions in the Party or in mass organizations.

Membership of the Central Committee appears to have been carefully balanced. Most government ministries and state committees, with some exceptions, such as Education, Public Health, the National Bank, and Justice, were represented by their minister or chairman. Interior and Foreign Affairs were represented by the minister and two vice-ministers, while the Ministry of Defence alone was represented by the minister and all four vice-ministers—thus confirming the increased political influence of the LPA. (The minister and one vice-minister of the Ministry of the Interior were also army officers.) The presidents of all major mass organizations were also represented, as were the chairmen of all important Party committees. Provincial Party representatives were drawn from four northern and three southern provinces, together with Vientiane province. Only in the matter of ethnic affiliation was the balance not maintained. No more than eight members of the CC were Lao Theung and only two were Lao Soung (both Hmong). The remaining forty-three surviving members in 1985 were Lao Loum, though a few of these were Tai Dam, Tai Phuan or Tai Lu and rather than ethnic Lao.

Nevertheless, ethnic Lao representation on the CC far outnumbered that of all other ethnic groups combined.

In the Party structure six organizations are described as serving the CC. The first of these serves a dual function as both the office of the Party CC and the office of the Council of Ministers—an overlap of duties which dramatically emphasizes the overlap of personnel between Party and government. The director of the office until 1985, Thongsavath Khaykhamphithoune, was both a member of the CC and had ministerial rank in the government. He was assisted by five deputy directors (with vice-ministerial rank) and two other committee members, none of whom in 1985 were on the CC. The other five organizations are special committees of the Central Committee. They are the Central Organizational Committee, the Central Propaganda Committee (also known as the Propaganda and Training Board), the powerful Party and State Inspection (or Control) Committee, the Administrative Committee of the Party and State School for Political Theory (middle and upper levels) and the Committee for the Propagation of Party Policies. Each of these committees has been chaired by a CC member and has included from two to four vice-chairmen and up to five additional members, almost none of whom were on the CC. Only two committee chairmen, Maychantane Sengmany of the Party and State Inspection Committee, and Chanmy Douangboudy in charge of the State School for Political Theory, were known to hold the concurrent rank of minister in the government.

Party committees direct local affairs in each of the sixteen provinces (*khoueng*). Each is presided over by a provincial Party secretary who wields considerable political power, both within the province and on the national level. Below the provinces stand the Party committees of the 112 districts (*muong*), 950 sub-districts (*tasseng*) and an increasing number of the 11,424 villages (*ban*) into which, by official count, the country is divided. Many villages, however, do not yet boast a branch of the Party, or have one or two members only—insufficient to constitute a branch. As a result, branches at the sub-district level tend to function as branches for those larger villages which serve as sub-district administrative centres, rather than as the next stage in a hierarchy of branches. Only at the district level are branches properly representative. Branches at this level (though not for all districts) met during 1985 in preparation for the calling of the Fourth Party Congress.

Party cells are also constituted in government ministries, units of the armed forces, mass organizations and economic enterprises. Party members are expected to take a leading role in the affairs of each institution, to ensure compliance with Party policies, and to provide information on their fellow workers to the central organs of the Party. Party members are instructed not

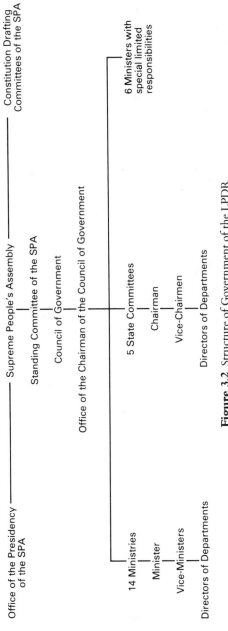

Figure 3.2 Structure of Government of the LPDR

to reveal the fact, though most can be identified. Even senior Party members are most reluctant to reveal the least sensitive information about the Party to visiting researchers, even when that information is already available in published sources.

Membership of the LPRP has grown steadily since 400 members came together at the founding congress in 1955. Ten years later, party membership was estimated to have reached 11,000, climbing to between 12 and 14,000 by 1969 (Norindr, in Stuart-Fox, 1982a, p. 41). According to Kaysone, the LPRP counted 21,000 members at the time of the Second Party Congress in 1972 (FBIS, 27 March 1985). Membership was probably close to 25,000, therefore, when the Pathet Lao seized power in 1975, and more than 30,000 by 1980. A Soviet source states that Party membership at the time of the Third Party Congress in 1982 stood at 35,000 but that as a result of an appeal to increase recruitment, membership had risen to 43,000 by mid-1985 (Mikéev, 1985, p. 58).

Most of those responsible for founding the LPRP were ethnic Lao, even though during the first twenty years of its existence, the Party drew its strength primarily from ethnic minorities in the north and east of the country (Langer & Zasloff, 1970). These included notably Lao Theung tribes in the southeast and in the north, Hmong loyal to Faydang Lobliayao, and Lu, Tai Neua and Lao Yuan in north and northeastern Laos. By the time the Second Party Congress met, more than half the rank-and-file membership may have been Lao Theung (cf. Norindr, in Stuart-Fox, 1982a, p. 41), though this was not reflected in the central organs of power. One of the aims of the Party in entering into the third coalition government in 1974 was certainly to increase its membership and extend its organization among the ethnic Lao of the Mekong valley. Recruitment among the small Lao working class in Vientiane and other towns was stepped up after 1975, and much of the subsequent increase in membership appears to have been among ethnic Lao. Thus the ethnic imbalance in terms of the proportional population of the major ethnic groups which resulted from the historical and geographical accidents of the liberation struggle is gradually being corrected. In the meantime, more minority cadres have been promoted in the Party hierarchy, and some wield considerable power in traditional ethnic Lao centres, such as Luang Prabang.

Despite recent recruitment, the LPRP remains overwhelmingly a peasant party. All minority cadres come from peasant backgrounds. Only the ethnic Lao come from a variety of social backgrounds: from the small industrial working class, from the army and the civil service, from the former Lao elite and from the peasantry. In the upper echelons of the Party, members of the former elite such as Souphanouvong and Phoumi Vongvichit remain influential, but power rests primarily in the hands of those of more humble 'proletarian' background, such as Nouhak Phoumsavanh and Khamtay Siphandone who, like Kaysone, enjoy the support and trust of the Vietnamese.

Despite the publicity surrounding the Third Party Congress and the emulation campaign launched to celebrate the thirtieth anniversary of the Party, the LPRP still functions essentially as a semi-secret organization. Members of the Party are instructed not to flaunt the fact. Party meetings at any level are not a matter of public knowledge. Times and locations of meetings may be changed at the last minute as a security measure. Entry into the Party is not by application, but by a process of co-option. A prospective member must first be nominated as a candidate for membership by two existing members. Only after a year's probation during which the candidate's suitability is systematically investigated can he or she become a full member. The final decision to join the Party must be taken by the candidate alone in full appreciation of what his or her action entails. Only then is a written application submitted and accepted.

The quality of new members has not been high, as is indicated by frequent references to the need to educate cadres and improve their ideological understanding. Cadres are expected to have as revolutionary qualifications, loyalty to the Party and determination to carry out its instructions. They should be disciplined and organized, maintain a close relationship with the masses, and diligently study Marxism–Leninism (FBIS, 15 January 1985). To this end Party members meet for regular 'criticism, self-criticism' sessions at which Party policies and instructions are discussed. The Party also organizes longer ideological and organizational training courses (seminars) for members at various levels, lasting from one week at the local level to four months for higher cadres at the Central Committee's School for Political Theory at which Marxist–Leninist theory is taught by Soviet and Vietnamese instructors. As of March 1985, more than 260 senior Party cadres are reported to have graduated from such courses (FBIS, 20 March 1985). More advanced theoretical studies are pursued at the Nguyen Ai Quoc school for Senior Party cadres in Hanoi. In March 1985, the Party launched a new theoretical journal, *Alum May* (New Dawn), to supplement its daily newspaper *Pasason* (The People) and raise the theoretical understanding of Party cadres.

The LPRP is hailed in a Vietnamese publication as 'an avant-garde party of the worker and peasant class, attached to the communist ideal and faithful to the interests of the proletariat' (quoted in Norindr, in Stuart-Fox, 1982a, p. 46). To this the Lao add that it represents also the interests of 'the Lao people of various tribes' (Tass interview with Phoune Sipaseuth, FBIS, 19 March 1985). Since its founding the Party is said to have 'always held aloft the banner of national independence, closely associated with socialism, creatively applied Marxism–Leninism to the true situation in the country, set forth a correct and clear-sighted policy and methods for the revolution, and led the entire Lao people to win one great victory after another' (*Pasason* editorial, FBIS, 28 March 1985). The Party is said to have achieved the national democratic revolution in Laos, and to be leading the country in the revolution of socialist transformation, bypassing the stage of capitalism. But as Kaysone ruefully admitted:

It is an extremely difficult and complex task to advance the country directly to socialism without passing through the stage of capitalist development at a time when our economy is poor, backward, and heavily dependent on agriculture, and when we have to struggle against the enemy's obstinate and insidious schemes and acts of sabotage. [Interview broadcast over Radio Hanoi, FBIS, 21 March 1985.]

In theory the LPRP applies such Marxist–Leninist principles as the dictatorship of the proletariat, class struggle, democratic centralism and proletarian internationalism. In practice, however, these are tailored to take account of Lao conditions. At this stage in its development, Laos is a 'worker and peasant state' in which even the national bourgeoisie have a role to play in the Lao Front for National Construction. Proletarian internationalism is invoked principally to justify provision of aid by fraternal socialist states. Democratic centralism is accepted as the principle underlying the system of government of the LPDR, but power is concentrated firmly in the hands of fewer than a dozen men making up the Politburo and Permanent Secretariat of the Party. The degree of concentration of power in Laos will become more evident after analysis of the structure of government, and of the implications of the failure of the regime to promulgate a constitution during its first decade in power.

The Constitutional Situation

Despite a number of references to work in progress and to the imminent appearance of the final document, the LPDR was still without a constitution when it celebrated its first ten years of existence. Given that a new constitution was promulgated for the People's Republic of Kampuchea within weeks of the Vietnamese invasion, it is even more surprising that the LPDR should be so long without a constitution, especially since East German legal advisers have reportedly been working on the project since 1983. In light of the failure of the Lao authorities to provide any explanation for this extraordinary delay, any reasons advanced can only be speculative. It seems safe to assume that the leaders of the LPRP were not prepared to accept a ready-made constitution of the Kampuchean variety. One possible reason for the delay, therefore, may be that there exist profound differences between the Lao leadership and their Vietnamese counterparts and advisers over what form the Lao constitution should take, or perhaps over whether, and if so how, reference should be made in the Lao constitution to the 'special relationship' between the two countries. Another possibility is that difficulties have been encountered over how to resolve the nationalities problem. A most difficult question for the regime to determine is what constitutional guarantees should be provided to define and protect the rights of those minority groups making up half the national population.

A Constitution Drafting Commission, presided over by Souphanouvong, was set up as a special committee of the Supreme People's Assembly (SPA) immediately after its inception. It included as members the three other vice-presidents and eight SPA members. Three additional members, not members of the SPA, were also co-opted on to serve on the Commission. The five-member standing committee of this commission consisted of Souphanou-vong, Faydang Lobliayao, Khamsouk Keola (concurrently secretary-general of the SPA), Thit Mouane Saochanthala, and Leuam Insisiengmay. No sign of progress, no announcement even that the commission or its standing committee was meeting, occurred for a number of years, except in response to the occasional questions of visiting journalists, who were assured that a constitution would be forthcoming in due time. Then in 1984, it was announced that two additional Constitution Drafting Sub-Committees had been appointed. The first of these was given the task of collecting, compiling and studying the work that had been done; the second was charged with 'studying and grasping the social situation'. The first committee consisted of two SPA members of the Constitution Drafting Commission, two of the additional members co-opted on to that Commission, and three new co-opted members. The second committee, whose task was far from clear, consisted of two full Commission members, plus another group of three co-opted members. A constitution was promised 'without delay', but hints that it would be ready in time for the tenth anniversary celebrations were unrealistic given the tasks of the sub-committees. It was not until early in 1986 that the SPA approved a report on progress made in drawing up a 'fundamental draft' of the constitution and electoral law (FBIS, 4 February 1986).

Not only does the LPDR lack, at the time of writing, any constitution, but it also lacks any duly elected body to serve as the supreme organ of state power. Elections were due to be held in July 1975 to elect a National Assembly in conformity with the agreements signed in 1973 setting up the third coalition government. These elections were postponed in June 1975. In November, under the careful supervision of the LPRP, 264 delegates were chosen to represent the districts, towns and provinces of the country, together with member organizations of the Lao Patriotic Front, and the Front itself. No elections took place to choose these representatives: the choice was made by the LPF, directed by the LPRP. One of the actions of this National Congress of People's Representatives meeting on 2 December 1975, was to appoint a forty-six member Supreme People's Assembly comprising, in addition to a majority of LPRP members, a number of 'patriotic neutralists', and even a few former RLG officials prepared to work with the new regime. It is this appointed body which acts in the absence of a constitutionally elected parliament as the supreme organ of state power in the LPDR.

Because of the lack of any constitution, the function and powers of the SPA remain unclear. The resolution of the National Congress establishing the SPA made mention of 'the necessity of establishing the legislative power to study the new Constitution and to proclaim the laws of the People's Democratic Republic'. The SPA was thereby charged both with drawing up the constitution and with acting as the supreme legislative body. If similar institutions in other communist states are anything to go by, it is also responsible for appointing the government and for nominating members of the People's Supreme Court. According to the Ministry of Justice, the SPA does have the latter power, but appointments to all government positions in Laos are decided by the Party Secretariat and merely ratified by the SPA, and it seems very likely that members of the Supreme People's Court are similarly appointed.

The National Congress named Souphanouvong as President of the SPA with four vice-presidents representing four ethnic groupings: Sisomphone Lovansay (hill Tai), Faydang Lobliayao (Lao Soung), Khamsouk Keola (lowland Lao) and Sithon Kommadan (since deceased) for the Lao Theung. A small standing committee, consisting of Khamsouk Keola as Secretary-General with Say Phetrasy and Souvannarath Sayavong as deputy secretaries, and five other members, acts as the secretariat of the SPA. Apart from the Constitution Drafting Commission, the SPA has three other commissions dealing with Presidential Decrees, Economy and Finance, and the State Budget. There is no indication that any of these meets regularly or enjoys any power at all. The three commissions are chaired by Somphavan Inthavong, Thit Mouane Saochanthala and Leuam Insisiengmay respectively.

During the first ten years of its existence the SPA lost a number of members through death or because they left the country as refugees. Crown Prince Vong Savang, originally a member of the SPA, was placed under house arrest in Houa Phan province in March 1977 where he reportedly later died of complications following an attack of malaria. Former King Savang Vatthana, originally named as supreme adviser to the President of the Republic, was arrested at the same time. He is understood to have subsequently died of old age. None of the missing members of the SPA was replaced. By 1985 the Assembly had been reduced to about three-quarters of its original membership.

Since its formation in 1975, the SPA has met once or twice a year including a combined session with the Council of Ministers to hear and adopt the annual political report prepared by LPRP Secretary-General Kaysone Phomvihane. Only in the sense of adopting the political report as a resolution of the SPA does the Assembly have any role to play in directing the affairs of the country. The SPA also ratifies, without revision, those laws which it is asked to approve. Many 'laws', however, are issued in the form of government ordinances or decrees which are not presented to the SPA even for routine ratification. Nevertheless, the fiction that the SPA is the supreme legislative body continues to be maintained even though its insignificance is apparent to all. For example, decisions taken at the Third Party Congress to increase the size of the government were duly passed by the SPA as law 1/82/SPA dated 20 July 1982. However, nominations of particular members of the government were not even put before the SPA, let alone ratified. Positions were decided by the Secretariat of the Central Committee meeting a week after the SPA in accordance with 'the regulations of the Party which were passed at the Third Party Congress'. Appointments were made at the same time to 'the various organizations which serve the Party Central Committee, the various ministries and government committees, and the various mass organizations'. All were direct Party appointees. The decisions were communicated in an internal Party document signed by Kaysone as Secretary-General and dated 5 August 1982.

In Laos, therefore, it is evident that the Supreme People's Assembly, perhaps because it is not a popularly elected body (as are, for example, the USSR Supreme Soviet or the Vietnamese National Assembly), is even more insignificant and wields even less power than is usual in communist systems.

The Structure of Government

The structure of government in the LPDR is similar to that in any modern state, capitalist or communist. The chief of state is the President of the Republic, a post held since 1975 by Souphanouvong. He is assisted by a small staff under the direction of a *chef de cabinet* with the rank of vice-minister. In Laos, the governing body is known as the Khana Rathaban, which strictly translates as the Council of Government rather than the Council of Ministers (which in Lao would be Khana Rathamontri). The term 'Council of Government' follows Vietnamese usage, but Soviet and Eastern European writers consistently refer to the LPDR Council of Ministers (Mikéev, 1985).

The government of the LPDR was constituted at the same time as the Supreme People's Assembly by the National Congress of People's Representatives. It consisted at first of the Office of the Prime Minister, twelve ministries and three state committees. Souvanna Phouma, former Prime Minister in the third coalition government, was appointed adviser to the government, a position he continued to hold until his death in January 1984. After the Third Party Congress, the size of the government was increased to fifteen ministries and five state committees. The Ministry of the Interior lost responsibility for veterans and social affairs, which became a separate state committee. Similarly the Ministry of Propaganda, Information, Culture and Tourism was divided into a Ministry of Culture and a State Committee for Propaganda, the Press, Radio and Television. Propaganda was given over to the Central Propaganda Committee of the Central Committee of the Party. The Ministry of Industry and Commerce was divided into two separate ministries, and the Ministry of Communications, Public Works and Transport was divided to form a Ministry of Transportation (incorporating the former Ministry of Posts and Telecommunications), a Ministry of Construction, and a new Ministry of Equipment and Technical Supply.

At the same time as the number of ministries and committees was expanded, the structure of government was reorganized to form three distinct levels. At the apex stands an 'inner cabinet' comprising the Chairman and five Vice-Chairmen of the Council of Government. These six men, five of them concurrently members of the Politburo, are responsibile for taking major decisions of government policy and for overall direction of the principal sectors of government activity. Below them come the nineteen ministers and chairmen of state committees who are responsible for managing their individual portfolios. At a lower level still comes a group of some eighty vice-ministers and vice-chairmen, many of them with technical

Chairman: Kaysone Phomvihane

Vice Chairmen:

Nouhak Phoumsavanh	Saly Vongkhamsao	Phoumi Vongvichit	Khamtaiy Siphandon	Phoune Sipaseuth
Economy	*Planning*	*Information and Culture*	*Defence and Security*	*Foreign Affairs*
with broad responsibility for ministries or state; committees of Finance; National Bank; Industry, Handicrafts and Forestry; Equipment and Technical Supply; Construction; Commerce; Agriculture, Irrigation and Cooperatives; Transportation; Posts and Communications.		with broad responsibility for ministries or state, committees of Education; Culture; Nationalities; Public Health; Social Affairs and Combat Veterans; Information, Press, Radio and Television.	with broad responsibility for ministries of Defence, Interior, Justice.	

Figure 3.3 Responsibilities of the 'Inner Cabinet' of the Council of Government

qualifications and specific functions and responsibilities. Each of these levels requires analysis.

The Chairman of the Council of Government is Kaysone Phomvihane whose dual position as Secretary-General of the Party and head of government makes him incomparably the most powerful figure in Laos. He is assisted by the Office of the Council of Government comprising the same staff making up the Office of the Party Central Committee, presided over by a director (*chef de cabinet*), who has full ministerial rank. With the appointment of Thongsavath Khaikhamphithoune as Ambassador to Moscow in 1985, this position fell vacant. The director is assisted by five deputies, each of whom has vice-ministerial rank. These were, in 1985, Khamsai Souphanouvong, Somsavath Lengsavath, Khampong Soulinphoumi, Khambon Keokinnaly and Phao Phimphachanh. The office has responsibility for drawing up the agenda for Council meetings, for correlating essential information for decision making and for verifying implementation of decisions taken.

Each of the four powerful special ministers previously attached to the office of the Chairman of the Council of Government in the 1975–82 government has since been assigned specific functions, either in government (Saly Vongkhamsao became chairman of the State Planning Committee; Sisavath Keobounphanh retained the Ministry of the Interior) or in the Party (Chanmy Douangboudy is Chairman of the Committee of the Party and State School for Political Theory; Maychantane Sengmany is Chairman of the Party and State Inspection Committee). Both of the latter, however, retained the rank of minister in the government, and are still officially attached to the Office of the Chairman of the Council of Government. What role they perform remains unclear, but it seems likely that they act, together with Saly and Sisavath, as personal advisers to Kaysone.

Five vice-chairmen of the Council of Government were named in 1982. Of these, four had been vice-chairmen in the previous government. The First Vice-Chairman, Nouhak Phoumsavanh, had been Minister of Finance in the previous government, a position he relinquished to take over responsibility for supervision of the economy as a whole and thus of the overall functioning of all economic ministries. Nouhak serves as acting chairman in Kaysone's absence. Second-ranking Vice-Chairman, Phoumi Vongvichit relinquished his Ministry of Education in order to take over broad responsibility for social and cultural affairs. The third and fourth vice-chairmen, Khamtay Siphandone and Phoune Sipaseuth retained their ministries of Defence and Foreign Affairs, but with extended responsibilities for internal security and relations with fraternal parties respectively. The fifth vice-chairman named was Saly Vongkhamsao, who moved from being senior minister in the Office of the

Chairman of the Council of Government to become Chairman of the State Planning Committee. Not only did this constitute a promotion for Saly himself, it also marked the increased importance of the Planning Committee in determining economic priorities and directions.

An interesting distinction is made in appointments to positions at the next level of government, that of ministers and chairmen of state committees. Appointees are either full ministers or acting-ministers, depending on whether or not they are members (either full or alternate) of the Party Central Committee. Acting-ministers appear to be on probation until nominated to the Central Committee. There is, however, one exception to the general rule that full ministers must be CC members. This is the ageing Kou Souvannamethi, Minister of Justice since the founding of the LPRP, who may not be a member of the Party at all. Kou was one of the founders with Quinim Pholsena of the Santhiphap Pen Kang (Peace and Neutrality Party) and of the patriotic neutralist faction which sided with Pathet Lao after 1964. Judging by the size of his ministry, and by the lack of activity shown by it during the first ten years of the LPDR, Kou exercises little influence within the government.

The most influential ministries are undoubtedly Defence and the Interior. The Defence Ministry is presided over by Politburo member and Commander-in-Chief of the LPA, General Khamtay Siphandon, with the assistance of four vice-ministers, all of whom were in 1985 serving officers and all of whom were full members of the Party CC. They included the Director of the General Political Department of the LPA, Major-General Siphone Phalikhan, and his deputy, Brigadier-General Osakan Thammatheva, and the Acting Chief of the General Staff, Major-General Somsak Saysongkham. Army officers also hold important positions in the Ministry of the Interior. The Minister of the Interior, General Sisavath Keobounphanh, is still listed as Chief of the General Staff of the LPA, though his duties have been largely taken over by Major-General Somsak. In addition to being a member of the CC Secretariat, Sisavath is also Secretary of the Party Committee of Vientiane Prefecture. One of the three vice-ministers in the Interior Ministry was also an army officer.

Four other ministries were headed in 1985 by former army officers—Agriculture, Irrigation and Cooperatives by Brigadier-General Inkong Mahavong; Construction by General Khemphone Phouiphaseuth; Finance by General Yao Phonevantha; and Transportation, Posts and Communications by Colonel Phao Bounnaphone. All were full ministers with the exception of General Khemphone. Other ministries with full ministers were Industry, Handicrafts and Forestry (Maisouk Saisompheng), Commerce

(Vanthong Sengmuang), Culture (originally Sisana Sisane until he was relieved of his portfolio in March 1983, then given to Thongsing Thammavong), Justice (Kou Souvannamethi) and Foreign Affairs (Phoune Sipaseuth). Ministries with acting-ministers were, in addition to Construction, Public Health (Khamlieng Pholsena), Education, Sport, Physical Education and Fine Arts (Bountiem Phitsamay), and Equipment and Technical Supply (Thongsouk Saisankhi). The five state committees were Planning (Saly Vongkhamsao), Social Affairs and Combat Veterans (Mune Somvichit), Nationalities (Nhiavu Lobliayao), Propaganda, the Press, Radio and Television (originally Thongsing Thammavong, then Sone Khamvanvongsa when Thongsing went to the Ministry of Culture), and the National Bank (Boutsabong Souvannavong). Of the five chairmen of these state committees, the first three held full ministerial status as members of the Party CC; the last two did not.

As part of the government changes which followed the Third Party Congress a miscellaneous group of ministries was created especially for those ageing former ministers relieved of their duties. Thus Ma Khaikhamphithoun, previously Chairman of the State Planning Committee, became 'Minister with Special Responsibilities'; former Minister of Agriculture, Khamsouk Sayaseng, became 'Minister Responsible for the Expansion of Coffee Production', and Thongchanh Ouplavan, former Chairman of the State Committee for the National Bank, became 'Minister Responsible for Pricing Problems'. Soth Phetlasy was named as 'Minister Responsible for Mapping and Boundaries', but was never heard from throughout the protracted border dispute with Thailand during 1984 and 1985. One vice-minister with 'special duties' was also named. In addition, Professor Souly Nanthavong was named President of a government Scientific and Technical Committee, with the rank of minister and responsibility for scientific and technical inspection and control of government projects.

Of the vice-ministers or vice-chairmen of state committees appointed in 1982, most had proven technical or managerial skills. A number had received their higher education in the West and some had worked for the previous regime. The number of vice-ministers attached to different ministries and state committees varied from six on the Planning Committee and five in Foreign Affairs, in Industry, Handicrafts and Forestry, and in Transportation, Posts and Communications, to none in Justice (although Ounneua Phimmasone, President of the Supreme People's Court, apparently concurrently held the rank of vice-minister in the Ministry of Justice) and two each in the Ministries of Culture and Education. Most ministries and state committees have three or four vice-ministers in charge of specific tasks. Thus in the

Ministry of Public Health the three vice-ministers are in charge of preventive medicine, pharmacy and administration; and in the State Committee for Propaganda, the Press, Radio, and Television, the three vice-chairmen are in charge of the official news agency (Khaosan Pathet Lao), radio and television broadcasting, and administration. All vice-ministers apparently have equal standing within the government, except in the case of Foreign Affairs, where Khamphay Boupha was named senior vice-minister to serve as acting minister during the not infrequent absences of the ailing Phoune Sipaseuth.

A certain fluidity exists, however, at this third level of government. Vice-ministers may be seconded for other duties, to serve on *ad hoc* committees, or to organize specific projects. Thus Bounkeut Khamphaphongphane, one of the vice-ministers of Industry, Handicrafts and Forestry, was appointed vice-chairman of one of the Constitution Drafting sub-committees; Ouloth Chounlamountry was seconded from Agriculture to assist in the organization of the Vientiane Prefecture; and Soulivong Daravong was moved from Equipment and Technical Supply to Industry. Such changes are never publicly announced in Laos. Nor are arrests or investigations of members of government accused of corruption or some less specific 'crime'. Nor is it announced when vice-ministers are sent on ideological training courses in Vietnam. One of the games played by Western embassies in Vientiane, therefore, is to discover from airport welcoming lists, aid receiving ceremonies, or discreet inquiries, whether the absence of some vice-minister means he is in Hanoi, under arrest or just working hard elsewhere.

The three levels of government in Laos correspond roughly to levels of decision making and areas of competence. The 'inner cabinet' of vice-chairmen makes policy decisions in the broadest sense. These are then creatively applied by ministers in their respective areas of responsibility, an activity which requires making decisions about interpreting policy, assigning priorities and so on. At the third level, vice-ministers are responsible only for technical decisions that arise in implementing policy. They have next to no influence on the formulation of policy—though they may, at some risk, as the arrests of 1983 and 1984 showed, criticize policy directives or their implications. Vice-ministers, and those acting ministers who are not members of the LPRP Central Committee, play next to no political role therefore. The government exists to apply the decisions of the Party, not to take those decisions. Policy decisions are taken by members of the government only in their capacity as influential members of the Party. Criticism of the government thus becomes criticism of the Party and the Party line is always correct. Thus despite the broadening of the structure of government by inclusion of the third level after the Third Party Congress, very little decentralization of decision making occurred. In fact the broadening of government was accompanied by a reinforcement of the principle of democratic centralism which found expression in the new three-level hierarchy of government, and by a reinforcement of the pre-eminence of the Party which found expression in the distinction drawn between full and acting ministers on the basis of their position in the Party hierarchy rather than their competence in government.

Local government in Laos is concentrated at the province (*khoueng*) level, both because the provinces enjoy a remarkable degree of administrative autonomy, and because below the province level, district and village administrators seldom have the authority, the expertise or the resources to decide upon and implement important decisions materially altering local conditions. Development projects at the district or village level require the concurrence and support of provincial authorities. The administration of the sixteen provinces and the Prefecture of Vientiane is in the hands of people's administrative committees. These are responsible for implementation of Party policy as this is interpreted by, or in the case of provincial matters, formulated by the provincial Party committee. Membership of the two committees is overlapping, but not identical, though the majority, if not all, of the members of provincial administrative committees are normally Party cadres. Provincial administrative committees are presided over by a chairman and two vice-chairmen, and comprise from ten to thirteen members responsible for implementation of policy in specific areas corresponding to central government ministries.

The policy of encouraging provincial responsibility for regional economic development and planning has led to the setting up of provincial departments (*phuek*) paralleling the structure of central government ministries. There are provincial departments of agriculture, industry and handicrafts, commerce and construction; of education, public health, nationalities, and social affairs. Each is responsible for its appropriate area of interest. There even exist provincial departments of 'foreign affairs' whose staff arrange for the accommodation and transportation of foreign diplomats, technical advisers and other visitors to the provinces, and for exchange visits of delegations between Lao and Vietnamese sister provinces. Important provincial departments deal with finance, planning and security. Finance and planning depend in large part on the activities of provincial commerce departments responsible both for supplying state shops and for trading with Vietnam and Thailand, or in the case of appropriately situated provinces, with Kampuchea or China. Provincial security departments work closely with local army commands and village militia.

Since provincial Party committees effectively have the power to interpret central Party decisions and instructions at the province level, some provinces take a much 'harder line' than others. Champassak province is one such. The cooperativization programme was put into effect there more enthusiastically than in most other provinces, and the majority of peasant refugees crossing into Thailand were from this area. Champassak is frequently singled out for special praise, however. In Kaysone's political report of January 1985 Champassak was specifically mentioned for having 'basically' eliminated malaria among children, having increased trade, for being 'the leading area in carrying out extensive agriculture', and for scoring a 'fundamental success' in increasing the number of agricultural cooperatives to include 82 per cent of farming families and 77 per cent of total farmed land (FBIS, 29 January 1985). It is worth noting that Champassak Party Secretary, Sounthon Thepasa, at number nineteen in the Party CC ranks significantly higher than any other provincial Party representative.

The degree of provincial autonomy in Laos is surprising for a centralized socialist state. There are a number of reasons for this. One has to do with the nature of the war fought by the Pathet Lao. Because of the difficult terrain and poor communications, regional commanders were left with a high degree of freedom of action where local situations were concerned. By all accounts, these powers and prerogatives have been jealously guarded since 1975. Local freedom of action was reinforced by the policy of provincial self-sufficiency in food supplies. In the lean years from 1976 to 1978 this was a matter of necessity. The government possessed no means of transporting rice from surplus to deficit areas—roads were poor or non-existent, means of transport lacking, and guerrillas active. From self-sufficiency in food supplies it was a short step to making provinces responsible in large part for their own development programmes, to be financed by whatever agricultural surplus they could produce. This both provided an incentive for provincial officials to encourage production, and shifted much of the burden of economic responsibility from the central to provincial administrations. Provinces were given the right either to exchange their surplus agricultural and forestry production in barter agreements with designated sister provinces in Vietnam, or to sell directly to Thailand without passing through the Ministry of Commerce. A variable percentage of income in convertible currency had to be remitted to the central government, but the remainder could be used by the province to finance its own economic and social programmes.

By 1985, some ill effects of the policy of provincial autonomy were becoming evident. One effect was to bring inter-province trade virtually to a standstill. Provincial officials much preferred to use surplus production to obtain consumer goods from Vietnam or Thailand than to meet the needs of other provinces. Some provinces even began to levy a tax on products crossing province boundaries, thus erecting what amounted to internal customs barriers against inter-provincial trade. A second effect has been to direct trade away from Vientiane. Thus provinces such as Luang Prabang or Xieng Khouang whose natural trade routes pass through Vientiane prefer to seek alternative means of trading directly with Thailand (Luang Prabang province sends forest products up the Mekong to Ban Houei Sai, rather than downstream to Vientiane) or with Vietnam (in the case of Xieng Khouang). One result of this has been to deprive factories situated in or near Vientiane of essential raw materials. In 1985, Vientiane's two furniture factories had to resort to using unseasoned timber because supplies available from other provinces had been insufficient to permit stockpiling for seasoning.

The most significant political effect of the policy of provincial autonomy has been to increase the power of provincial Party and administrative committees—as is apparent from the increased representation of provincial Party secretaries on the LPRP Central Committee. No studies have yet been made of provincial administration in the LPDR, but it is clear that even though provincial departments may count no more than two or three cadres, prerogatives are jealously guarded. Provincial 'foreign affairs' departments, for example, insist on authorizing all visits to a province. Thus, foreign diplomats, UN officials and aid workers all have to obtain, in addition to travel papers supplied by the appropriate central government ministry, written permission from provincial authorities. Clearance for a visit may be given by central government authorities and the visit held up for weeks by the refusal of provincial authorities to provide authorization. Those arriving in a provincial capital without such authorization risk waiting around for days until travel papers are issued or may even have to return to Vientiane.

The next level of local government in Laos is the *muong* or district, previously the lowest level at which central government appointments were made. Below the *muong* is the *tasseng* (sub-district), a somewhat artificial entity introduced by the French consisting of five to ten villages; and below the *tasseng* is the *ban*, or village, numbering usually between 200 and 300 people. In traditional Laos, the essential entities in Lao society were the village and the *muong*, meaning not an administrative district, but any larger political entity in which village and villagers were situated. The *chao muong* (local princeling) owed allegiance to the king, or to some foreign power, but these lay beyond the village horizons. The *muong* and *tasseng* as administrative entities continue to exist in the LPDR, but it is interesting to note that the political predominance of the province in effect reconstitutes the ancient *muong* as the larger political entity grouping the villages of a region.

People's administrative committees exist at both the district and sub-district levels. At the village level, the administrative committee usually consists of the village chief, the local Party secretary and other Party members (where a branch exists in the village), local representatives of the Lao Front for National Construction, the union of Lao Women, and the Lao People's Revolutionary Youth and also co-opted influential villagers. The committee concerns itself with village affairs, including the regulation of disputes and dispensation of justice. In addition, it acts as the intermediary between the village and higher authority, at the district or province level. The village committee is responsible for communicating government decrees, for example on rates of taxation, and for implementing policies, such as the formation of cooperatives. The committee is also responsible for organizing village political meetings or seminars to discuss the Party line, and for explaining the importance of political events. How government directives are received depends greatly on the enthusiasm, or inertia, of the village committee, and on the dedication and influence of members of the LPRP serving on it. Members of the committee have the power to act as petty tyrants, placing constraints on personal activities, movement, and even consumption (as occurred particularly during the period 1976-8). Often, however, village authorities are more lenient, and the relationship between villagers and the committee more nearly approaches the traditional pattern.

Party-State Relations

It is really a misnomer to talk about Party-state relations in Laos, as if two separate sets of institutions exist which relate in certain definable ways to each other. The extreme overlap in membership between the top echelons of the LPRP and the Council of Government makes it impossible to draw any clear line of demarcation of function which would permit an analysis of the relationship to be carried out. In addition, the fact that the LPDR had no constitution during the first decade of its existence meant that even the pretence of elections for a Supreme People's Assembly charged with appointing the government was dispensed with. In Laos in 1985 the SPA was still an *appointed* body, nominally by the 1975 National Congress of People's Representatives, in fact by the leaders of the LPRP. As already noted, members of the government formed in 1982 after the Third Party Congress were appointed not by the SPA, but by the Secretariat of the LPRP. There is no question, therefore, of there being a separate focus of administrative power which interprets and applies Party policies. In Laos, not only does the Party appoint the government as executor of its decisions, but most key members of the government as members of the Party CC carry out their own agreed policies (see Table 3:1).

Because of the relatively small number of educated senior cadres in the LPRP, both during the 'Thirty-Year Struggle' and after formation of the LPDR, the concentration of power in Laos has been more obvious than in larger communist states. Five of seven members of the Politburo hold five of the six positions in the 'inner cabinet' composed of the chairman and vice-chairmen of the Council of Government. Six out of nine members of the CC Secretariat are senior ministers, five of them also members of the 'inner cabinet'. Twenty-six out of fifty-three, or half the members of the Party CC, hold government positions. Or to put it another way, only seven members of the Council of Government (six until Sisana Sisane was relieved of his portfolio) out of twenty-four are not members of the Party CC. The overlap is much less striking at the third, or vice-ministerial, level of government—but this is the level of technical implementation of policy, not of its formulation. Decisions are made at the top level only, and there by ministers acting in their capacity as senior members of the Party, not the government.

A similar overlap is evident at the provincial level. In six out of the sixteen provinces the secretary of the provincial Party committee was in 1985 concurrently chairman of the provincial administrative committee. In the remaining ten provinces, as a general rule, the chairman of the administrative committee is the deputy-secretary of the Party for the province. In addition, Party members hold a majority of positions on administrative committees at and below the province level. Even in a village where the Party is poorly represented and Party members are outnumbered, they still frequently monopolize political power by virtue of their Party affiliations with district and provincial authorities. Even though detailed studies are lacking, therefore, it is true to say that at all levels of government above, and often including, the village level the Party is in command and makes not only all political but also all administrative decisions.

The precedence the Party takes over the government does not, however, mean that all Party decisions are uniformly applied, or that all Party exhortations bear similar fruit in all areas or at all governmental levels. Even though at times the central government issues remarkably detailed instructions (for example on the spacing to observe when transplanting rice seedlings (cited in Brown & Zasloff, 1985)), many policies are couched in terms so broad as to permit a wide range of interpretation as to how they

Table 3.1 Overlap between membership of the LPRP Politburo and Secretariat, and State organs of the LPDR

Name	Party		State			
	Politburo	Secretariat	Committee of the CC (Chairman)	Supreme People's Assembly	Council of Government	
					Inner Cabinet	Minister or Chairman of State Committee
Kaysone Phomvihane	*	*			*	
Nouhak Phoumsavanh	*	*			*	
Souphanouvong	*			*		
Phoumi Vongvichit	*	*			*	
Khamtay Siphandone	*	*			*	
Phoune Sipaseuth	*	*			*	
Sisomphone Lovansay	*	*		*		
Saly Vongkhamsao		*				*
Sisavath Keopbounphanh		*				*
Saman Vignaket		*	*			*
Maychantane Sengmany		*	*			*

should be implemented. At the provincial, and even at the local level, Party cadres reserve the right to promote Party policies in the light of local conditions which may vary enormously from region to region. Although the Party dominates government, policies are not uniformly applied, nor does the writ of the Politburo extend throughout the country: where power is exercised, it is channelled through the Party and through the Party alone. Local government does not constitute a basis of power independent of the Party. Administrative committees are simply the principle means by which the Party exercises political power at the local level.

Mass Organizations

There are five popular or mass organizations in the LPDR. The first and most important is the Lao Front for National Construction (LFNC), successor to the Lao Patriotic Front which served as the front organization for the LPRP during most of the 'Thirty-Year Struggle'. The other four are the Federation of Lao Trade Unions, the Lao People's Revolutionary Youth, the Union of Lao Women and the Lao Committee to Defend World Peace. Of these the first three have some importance, but the last is devoid of political significance. The first national congress of the LFNC was held in 1979, three years before the Third Party Congress. National congresses of the other mass organizations were held after the Third Party Congress, as part of the process of strengthening the Party's political foundations and administrative effectiveness. Organizing and mobilizing committees were appointed for each mass organization by the Secretariat of the Party CC. These were responsible for organizing the respective national congresses, which then elected their own office bearers, in many, but not all, cases confirming previous Party appointees.

The Lao Front for National Construction

As the latest manifestation of a united national front in Laos, the Lao Front for National Construction traces its origins back to the first congress of the Lao Resistance Front held in 1950. That congress drew up a twelve-point programme, and adopted the name Free Laos Front. In 1956, this was changed to the Lao Patriotic Front, and in February 1979, at the first national congress since the founding of the LPDR, the name was changed again to the Lao Front for National Construction (Neo Lao Sang Sat). The reason for the change in name, Souphanouvong told assembled delegates, was that the LPF had 'gloriously fulfilled its historic mission' in assisting to bring about the national democratic phase of the Lao revolution. In the new socialist phase of the revolution a new front was required, one which would 'enlarge the bloc of national union, organize and mobilize all the patriotic forces which approve of socialism . . . and employ all its forces to victoriously accomplish the work of socialist construction and fully assure the defence of our socialist fatherland (*Les Principaux Documents Importants du Congrès du Front*, 1980, p. 5). The action programme of the new Front committed it to bring together all popular organizations, all ethnic groups, and all social classes on the basis of the worker-peasant alliance following the leadership of the LPRP in order better to develop the role of collective mastery of the people, stimulate socialist transformation, contribute to national defence, form new socialist men and women, bring about equality between all ethnic groups and between the sexes, develop culture and education, improve conditions of living and intensify international solidarity. The leading role of the Party in the Front was clearly defined by Kaysone in his speech to the Congress:

Committees of the Party at all levels must appoint cadres and members capable of participating in leading the Front at the local level, to effectively assist the Front in its activities. Those cadres and members of the Party appointed must actively take the initiative in the activities of the Front. . . . [Ibid., p. 66.]

According to the statutes of the LFNC, membership is open to all patriotic organizations and individual citizens who accept its action programme and constitution. Members have the right to put forward their own proposals at Front meetings, but must respect the decision of the majority once it is taken. Front committees exist at the central, provincial, district and village levels, each composed of representatives of the Party, administration and mass organizations at the same level, an LFNC representative from the next lower level, notables, intellectuals, class and ethnic representatives, and individuals with particular skills and a capacity for hard work.

The congress of the LFNC meets every five years and is the supreme body. It elects the LFNC Central Committee, which in turn appoints a standing committee to handle the everyday affairs of the Front. Provincial Front committees also elect a standing committee. The Central Standing Committee, and provincial committees meet at least once every six months. Committees at different levels have three main tasks: to bring about the union of all Lao of all ethnic groups and social classes; to raise the political consciousness of people through political instruction; and to mobilize the prople to exercise their right of collective mastery (Statutes of the LFNC, ibid., pp. 91-7).

The congress elected Souphanouvong as President, with Faydang Lobli-ayao (representing the Lao Soung), Bolang Boulapha (representing the Lao Theung) and Khamsouk Keola (Lao Loum) as vice-presidents. These, together with Thit Mouane Saochanthala, Madame Khampheng Boupha and Nhiavu Lobliayao, comprised the Central Standing Committee. Sixty-nine more representatives, among whom were only four women, made up the large and unwieldy Central Committee of seventy-six members. Representa-tives were listed by province, even though representation at the congress was by organization, ethnic group or social class, as well as by province. Represen-tatives of the Lao United of Buddhists Association, mass organizations, intellectuals, artists, 'patriotic and progressive personalities' and 'businessmen and industrialists' all addressed the first congress, and are represented at its regional meetings.

The LFNC is the only organization in the LPDR which provides a political forum for such groups as businessmen, Western-trained intellectuals and others associated with the former regime. It also includes as representatives a number of conservative tribal leaders. Overall, therefore, the Front has tended to exert a countervailing influence against those arguing for the rapid socialist transformation of Lao society. In Vientiane, the Front has been a vehicle for the increasing influence of formerly powerful families intent on taking advantage of the government's policy of encouraging capitalist investment, and joint state–private enterprises. Despite the overriding political influence of the Party, the Front has thus become an important channel for the expression of a variety of popular opinion in Laos. How far this democratic process of representation of popular opinion is permitted to go, however, remains to be seen. Preparations for the Second National Congress of the Front were authorized in 1985, and the Congress itself was expected to take place early in 1986, probably before the Fourth Party Congress.

The Lao People's Revolutionary Youth

The Lao People's Revolutionary Youth (LPRY) is the direct descendant of the Association of Patriotic Lao Youth, one of the mass organizations forming part of the Lao Patriotic Front. It was not until April 1983, however, that the LPRY held its first national congress in Vientiane, more than seven years after the founding of the LPDR. During this period youth groups were established in major centres throughout the former Royal Lao government zone of control, and a nationwide organizational hierarchy built up. Like the Associa-tion of Patriotic Lao Youth before it, the LPRY has two sections. The first, grouping children aged six or seven to fifteen years, is modelled on similar organizations in other communist states and called the Lao Young Pioneers. Children are taught revolutionary songs and slogans, learn the importance of collective labour in the construction of socialism and take part in official ceremonies welcoming foreign visitors and anniversary celebrations. The organization for older youths, the LPRY proper, covers the age group sixteen to twenty-four. It forms the training ground for young Lao communists, the avant-garde responsible for continuing the socialist transformation of the country.

The first national congress of the LPRY brought together 245 delegates representing a membership of 115,000 (said to be double the number in 1978). The congress heard Kaysone Phomvihane stress the need to build up the country-wide organization of the LPRY in order to train the next generation of Lao youth to carry on the revolutionary ideals of the LPDR with commitment and dedication. Through study combined with practice, Lao youth were urged to forge themselves into the new socialist men and women of the future, in a spirit of self-reliance and by renouncing the 'old ways' of selfish living, idleness, sexual pleasure and luxury that characterized the former regime. The nation's youth were to become 'shock troops' in carrying forward the three revolutions in relations of production, the application of science and technology, and in culture and ideology. They were to take the lead in building socialism, and in countering the destructive schemes and sabotage resulting from the collusion between American imperialism and Chinese expansionism, Kaysone told his audience (FBIS, 3 May 1983). Revolutionary Lao youth are expected to practise the 'three solidarities', and embark upon the 'four offensives'. The three solidarities are between one youth and another, between youth and the masses, and between Lao youth and their international counterparts. The four offensives are in improving one's own work performance, defending the country, building political awareness and technical competence, and increasing economic production.

The 1983 congress was also addressed by Kaysone's wife, Thongvin Phomvihane, who delivered a report on the revised statutes of the organization, and was elected first vice-president of the LPRY. This followed her earlier election as full member of the LPRP Central Committee, and confirmed her rising status in the Party hierarchy. Interior Minister General Sisavath Keobounphan, previous LPRY President, was replaced by Thongsavath Khaykhamphithoune, member of the Party CC and Director of the Office of the Council of Government. In 1985 Thongsavath was appointed Lao ambassador in Moscow. After some hesitation, during which she was referred to in the official media as acting-President, Thongvin was promoted to President of the LPRY. The LPRY congress also elected a seven-member Secretariat, or standing committee, and a twenty-nine member Central Committee. Secretary of the standing committee was Phandouang-chith Vongsa. Other members included a representative of the LPA and an ethnic Hmong representing minority groups.

The LPRY is most active in the larger urban centres, especially Vientiane. Its membership in November 1985 was put at 161,892 (NL no.5, November 1985). It has its own resources such as meeting rooms, transport, electronic equipment and musical instruments. It also has its own printing facilities where it produces a youth magazine and publishes occasional novels and poetry. Since 1983, the LPRY in Vientiane has been active in pressing for more latitude for youth in such areas as dress, music, dancing and access to foreign publications. Thongvin has reportedly argued in a similar vein within the Party with some success. Not only did Lao youths in Vientiane in 1985 play and listen to Western music, but it was not unusual to see girls wearing jeans, something unheard of during the early years of the regime.

For the privileged few, sons and daughters of high Party officials or of wealthier families, cassettes of the latest Thai or American music, Thai television and video films are available. In one Vientiane restaurant, young people gather on Saturday nights to dance and drink and listen to bands beating out the latest rock and pop from the West. A group may spend in a night on imported beer and snacks as much as a senior government official makes in cash (as opposed to coupons for use in government shops) in six months. The continuing attractiveness of the Western lifestyle, the ready proximity of Thailand and the presence overseas of relatives who have already left, constitute a permanent temptation for Lao youth to cross the Mekong. Temptation is avoided for sons and daughters of the Party hierarchy by sending them to study in socialist countries. Two sons of Souphanouvong who seemed to be developing too much liking for decadent Western amusements in Vientiane were sent to pursue further studies in Hanoi in part because it was feared they might cross to Thailand. Ten years after the founding of the LPDR, therefore, there were few signs that the next generation were conforming to the ideal of new Lao socialist youth.

The Federation of Lao Trade Unions

The next mass organization to hold its first national congress was the Federation of Lao Trade Unions, in December 1983. According to a Soviet publication, delegates represented half of all workers and 'employees' in the country (Mikéev, 1985, p. 57). It is difficult, however, to be sure who counts as a worker in Laos. It has been estimated that only 0.8 per cent of the workforce is engaged in manufacturing, half of them in handicraft industries. A further 0.2 per cent at most is engaged in mining, while 0.6 per cent work in each of the three sectors of construction, public utilities, and transport (Khan & Lee, 1980, p. 58). This would give a total of 2.8 per cent, which is somewhat greater than the estimate that the Lao working class accounts for only 3 per cent of the total population (Cahour, 1979, p. 138)—a figure which does not include those employed in trade or commerce or as civil servants in public administration. Not all the above sectors are covered by organized unions, however, and some of the unions which are said to exist are poorly organized and have limited membership. The national congress therefore probably represented no more than 20,000 workers.

Speakers at the congress urged workers to increase industrial production and improve the quality of transportation, communications and other services. The ageing Sanan Southichak was elected President of the newly formed Federation but died a little over a year later. His deputy, and fellow member of the Party Central Committee, Thitsoi Sombatdouang, was subsequently appointed president. The five-member secretariat comprises two vice-presidents and two additional members drawn from the twenty-one member Central Committee. Two women serve on the Central Committee.

The Union of Lao Women

The last of the mass organizations to hold a national congress was the Association of Patriotic Lao Women, like the Youth organization previously a member body of the Lao Patriotic Front. The name was changed to the Union of Lao Women at the congress held in Vientiane in March 1984. A seven-member organizing committee had been appointed by the Party Secretariat in August 1982, five of whose members, including the president and three vice-presidents, were confirmed as members of the standing secretariat by the congress. Both the president of the ULW, Madame Khampeng Boupha (wife of the First Vice-Minister of Foreign Affairs, Khamphay Boupha), and the First Vice-President, Madame Phetsamone Lasasima, are members of the Party CC. The Congress also elected a twenty-seven member Central Committee.

In his speech to the congress, Kaysone Phomvihane called upon delegates to raise the political consciousness of women, to motivate them to take the socialist path, and to improve their organizational capacities. Women should be mobilized to take an active role in building the socialist revolution because 'if the socialist revolution is not carried out, women cannot be completely emancipated'. Kaysone also admonished women to move into the work-force, for 'it is a law of socialist construction to promote the ever-increasing role of women in productive labour'. Women were also urged to take a more active role within the Party. 'All Party organs and . . . branches must be fully aware of the extremely important position, role, and functions of women as well as the position and role of the contingent of women cadres in the revolu-tionary course of the Party in general and in the emancipation of women in particular', Kaysone said. Party and state officials 'in many areas' were castigated for having 'failed to concentrate on organizing, rallying, educating, training and creating favourable conditions for women to carry out their activities'. Officials at all levels were instructed to draw women more into the 'daily political life' of the nation (BN 45, 23 April 1984; cf. also JPRS 1315).

Kaysone admitted, however, that 'there are comrades in Party and administrative committees at different levels who do not clearly conceive the problem of women's emancipation; they disregard women and do not pay enough attention to fostering and developing the great abilities of women'. On the other hand, women themselves did not have a thorough under-standing of their role. They too often exhibited an 'inferiority complex, with the tendency to depend on others' (BN 45, 23 April 1984). Yet Kaysone also stressed the family role of women in creating a 'new-type socialist family', and in 'moulding our children into a new socialist generation'. The two tasks set for women were to achieve their own emancipation, and to safeguard and build the country; but the 'three goods' to which women were to aspire were to be a good citizen, a good mother and a good wife to her husband—hardly a programme for women's liberation. In fact, after ten years of communist government in Laos the position of women in Lao society had hardly changed at all. There were four women out of fifty-three members of the Party Central Committee and not one in any of the three levels of government. The ULW however, does not see its role as urging greater representation—that is a decision to be left to the male-dominated Party. In November 1985, the ULW claimed a membership of 426,000 and published its own women's magazine, though with a limited print run.

Other Popular Organizations

The only other official organizations in Laos are the Lao Committee for the Defence of World Peace, the Lao United Buddhists Association (LUBA), and various friendship associations with other countries. The LUBA will be discussed below. The nine-member committee for the Defence of World

Peace (reduced to eight by the death of Dr Udom Souvannavong) was appointed by the Party Secretariat in August 1982. The President is Singkapo Sikhotchounlamany, a retired Pathet Lao general. One of the three vice-presidents is Madame Khamsouk Vongvichit, wife of Politburo member Phoumi Vongvichit. The committee exists as a welcoming delegation for visiting peace delegations and as Lao delegates to international peace meetings. It also assists in the organization of rallies in Vientiane to mark appropriate occasions.

A similar role is played by the various friendship associations. Presidents of committees are appointed by the Party Secretariat, often to reward stalwarts of the Party. Thus Khamsouk Sayaseng (former Minister of Agriculture, who was shunted aside as Minister for Coffee Production) was named President of the Lao–Soviet Friendship Association. Souk Vongsak, until his death, was President of the Lao–Vietnamese Friendship Association. In other cases presidents of friendship associations have greater political standing. The president of the Lao–Kampuchean Friendship Association is Chanmy Douangboudy, Director of the Party and State School for Political Theory. The mayor of Vientiane, Khambou Sounisai, is President of the Lao–Cuban Friendship Association. Membership of committees entails only the need to welcome occasional visiting delegations, and carries with it the reward of occasional overseas travel for the Party faithful, a reward much sought after in the LPDR.

Political Dissent

Dissent in the LPDR takes two forms: political opposition to the policies of the regime and armed insurgency aimed at overthrowing it. The two are interconnected, both by the fact that both draw upon external sources of inspiration and support, and because both feed upon popular dissatisfaction with present policies and their implementation. They are also interconnected by the fact that the principal form of expression of political dissent during the first decade of the LPDR has been the decision to leave the country. The insurgents are drawn from these refugees.

Forms of internal political dissent

Most Lao who are dissatisfied with the present regime for one reason or another merely grumble and get on with the problem of living. Only after dissatisfaction increases above a critical level does dissent find expression in action. Such action may be divided into dissent as attempts to modify the policies of the regime in some way, and dissent as reaction to those policies for one reason or another. Neither of these forms of dissent has any formal organization in Laos. While the former seeks informal means of bringing influence to bear on Party leaders, the latter provides occasional support for insurgents.

The limits of permissible dissent within the LPDR are strictly circumscribed, above all by the established policy of Indochinese solidarity and the 'special relationship' with Vietnam. Vietnamese influence within the Party, the Vietnamese civilian and military presence in Laos, and above all the effectiveness of the Vietnamese intelligence network, all make it inadvisable for anyone to voice opinions which could be interpreted as anti-Vietnamese—or, just as serious, as pro-Chinese. Even criticism within the Party or government based on Lao national interest runs the risk of being branded as the sin of 'narrow nationalism', as failing to take account of the principle of 'proletarian internationalism' and the 'law' of Indochinese solidarity. Those who persist in their errors risk being sent for 're-education' or expelled from the Party. The only alternative is to flee the country, as Sisanan Sayanouvong, former editor of the Party journal *Sieng Pasason*, and as a number of others did in July 1979 during the purge of 'pro-Chinese' elements.

Those who are concerned over the extent of Vietnamese influence in Laos are therefore forced to seek alternative means of countering that influence. Since neither China nor Thailand can be used as a counter-balance, they are forced to fall back on characteristically Lao values and resources, to emphasize what is characteristically Lao in terms of culture and lifestyle. One form of dissent is thus to emphasize what differentiates Lao from Vietnamese—not in any obvious or provocative way, but as a stubborn insistence upon what is Lao. A principal focus of this form of dissent is the popular and official support given to traditional Lao culture and to Buddhism. As a Lao official in Vientiane told the author in 1985: 'We must preserve Buddhism in Laos because so much of what is Lao is Buddhist'.

Ideological opposition to Buddhism in Laos has been greatly relaxed since 1978. Even members of the Politburo attend major Buddhist festivals. Pagodas in 1985 were well kept and well attended, and the number of monks and novices had increased—at least in Vientiane. Some pagodas which had fallen into disuse in the former 'liberated zone' under Pathet Lao control before 1975 were reportedly being renovated and monks invited to take up residence. The author photographed monks sculpting new Buddhas in a pagoda in Luang Prabang. The Party has even relaxed its prohibitions against members entering the *Sangha* (the order of monks) for the brief period necessary to perform traditional mourning and burial rites for close relatives.

Lao traditional culture is also being encouraged in a number of ways. Visiting Vietnamese delegations are almost invariably entertained with traditional Lao songs and dances. Party leaders frequently refer to the historical origins of the Lao state in the fourteenth century Kingdom of Lan Xang. Even the national war memorial to those who died during the Thirty-Year Struggle is in the form of a traditional Lao *that* or stupa. Taken separately, these points may not seem significant: taken together, however, they form a pattern of cultural nationalism that is reasserting itself particularly at the popular level, and which Party leaders are not only well aware of but seem prepared to accommodate.

Political dissent, or perhaps rather political dissatisfaction, has also been expressed by that group of young, often Western-trained, technicians and intellectuals who played no part in the Thirty-Year Struggle, but who stayed on in 1975, or returned subsequently, to serve the new regime. The source of their dissatisfaction is the monopolization of political power in the hands of the Party leadership, a monopolization which all but excludes the possibility for those often better qualified to influence decision-making. With the change of economic policy in 1980, lines of communication began to open up between the Party and this group. These were further reinforced by the decision taken after the Third Party Congress to appoint a number of officials who had served the former regime as vice-ministers in the new government. The dangers involved in acting too freely in their new capacities were amply demonstrated, however, in the series of arrests which took place in 1983 and 1984.

Outside the confines of Vientiane, popular opposition and dissent is even more inchoate. The primary means of expressing opposition to government policies has simply been to cross the Mekong to Thailand. This occurred particularly during the agricultural cooperativization drive of 1978-9. Dissatisfaction over government policies or the presence of Vietnamese forces also takes the form of willingness to listen to and provide a certain minimal level of assistance to anti-government guerrillas operating in the west and south of the country from Thailand, or tribal agit-prop agents operating in the north from China. The dominant theme of both groups, one which strikes a chord in many Lao, is that the leaders in Vientiane have sold the country to the Vietnamese.

Externally-supported insurgency

The origins of the anti-government insurgency in Laos go back even before the founding of the LPDR when rightist refugees who fled to Thailand in 1975 were reported to be organizing resistance forces to oppose the Pathet Lao-dominated coalition. In the event, these amounted to no more than a few rather amateur sabotage teams which, as agents of discredited politicians, could count on no popular support. The principal opposition to the regime during 1976 and 1977 came instead from Hmong remnants of the CIA-funded secret army who feared Pathet Lao reprisals. The Hmong resistance was largely contained, with Vietnamese assistance, by early 1978, though scattered incidents continued for some years. The Lao government consistently denied American charges that chemical weapons—the mycotoxins known as 'yellow rain'—were ever used in controlling the Hmong insurgency (Evans, 1983).

In April 1977, Thai newspapers reported the formation of a 'Free Lao National Liberation Movement' led by the brothers Iang and Sisouk na Champassak (FBIS, 26 April 1977), but this organization, if it existed in anything but name, proved incapable of co-ordinating the disparate Lao resistance groups which were then operating. In October 1978 a Lao government-in-exile was proclaimed in France, but gained no international recognition and was quickly denounced by the French government.

By mid-1978, however, Lao insurgents operating from bases in Thailand had become more active. The signing of the Lao-Vietnamese twenty-five year Treaty of Friendship and Cooperation in July 1977 lent substance to their claims that Laos had fallen under Vietnamese domination. Also relations between Vietnam and China were becoming increasingly strained over Kampuchea. In Laos, rumours began circulating of Chinese support for Hmong insurgents, and relations between the two states began to cool. The 1979 Vietnamese invasion of Kampuchea and subsequent Chinese border war with Vietnam had serious repercussions for Lao internal security, for it led to overt Chinese support for Lao resistance groups. As Chinese-Lao relations deteriorated further, Beijing warned darkly that 'mounting discontent and opposition . . . to Soviet-Vietnam control' of Laos would lead to a new insurgency (*Beijing Review*, 16 March and 6 April 1979). The shadowy existence of a Lao Socialist Party dedicated to expelling the Vietnamese from Laos was obliquely revealed, but turned out to be based in France. By early 1980 the Chinese had established facilities for Lao insurgents in Yunnan province where more than 1,000 recruits were reported to be undergoing basic political and military training. Lao accusations that the Chinese were recruiting a 'division' of between 6,000 and 7,000 men (the so-called 'Lanna' division) were, however, certainly exaggerated. Such reports may in fact have originated as part of a Chinese campaign of psychological warfare aimed at undermining Lao relations with Vietnam.

In addition to training and infiltrating anti-government agents into northern Laos, China was believed in Vientiane to be the guiding force behind attempts to co-ordinate, train and arm Thai-based insurgents. In May 1980, at Vieng Keo ('somewhere in southern Laos') a National United Front for the Liberation of the Lao People was formed with the stated aim of freeing Laos from *North* Vietnamese domination. President of the new Front was former RLG Cabinet Minister Impeng Suryadhay, while Commander-in-Chief of the Front's military arm, the Armed Forces for the Liberation of the Lao People, was former PL colonel Boualien Vannasay. The new organization was hailed by Beijing and condemned by the SRV. Initially the Front seems to have had some success in stimulating guerrilla activity in the Lao–Thai–Kampuchean border area of southern Laos (where up to 1,500 Lao recruits were reported to be receiving arms and training from the Khmer Rouge), and in co-ordinating resistance forces as far north as Savannakhet (Gunn, 1983). Several vehicles were ambushed and installations such as bridges and camps attacked. One foreign adviser was killed and a number of others wounded. Over the next two years, however, Lao government forces, with Vietnamese and Kampuchean assistance, seem to have effectively contained this threat. By 1983, fewer than a thousand insurgents were operating in all of southern Laos, and rebel activity along the Lao–Kampuchean border had virtually ceased. Small groups were still active in Sayaboury province and in Oudomsay and Bokeo. Former neutralist general Kong Le was reported to have 1,000 men under his command based in southern China, but his return to France at the end of 1983 left it unclear as to who was commanding these forces, and to what purpose, for military as opposed to propaganda activity in northern Laos had virtually ceased by the end of 1984.

By mid-1985, Lao anti-government insurgency was at a low level. By all reports, the Lao-Chinese frontier region was relatively peaceful with both Chinese traders and tribal peoples moving freely across the border. The Lao authorities continued to accuse the Chinese of attempting to subvert the Lao regime, but privately admitted that this was no longer by armed subversion. Rather than fighting, insurgents preferred to disarm local militia, disseminate anti-Vietnamese propaganda, return the weapons they had taken and move on (*Le Monde*, 5 November 1985). Insurgency in western and southern Laos continued with clandestine Thai support, but armed clashes were few. In the face of exaggerated claims from insurgent organizations, it is virtually impossible to place a figure on the total number of insurgents involved. American estimates of 9,000 insurgents country-wide are almost certainly too high (Brown & Zasloff, 1985; cf. Gunn, 1983). The authorities in Vientiane were taking no chances, however, as the tenth anniversary celebrations approached. The Lao people were continually exhorted to be on their guard against the schemes of the enemy, vehicles were regularly checked during night curfews, and security for the celebrations themselves was tight.

4   The Economic System

Economic Policy and Planning

Once the 'national democratic' phase of the Lao revolution had been achieved through victory in the Thirty-Year Struggle, the LPRP was faced with the task of bringing about the socialist phase of the revolution; that is, the socialist transformation of Lao society. At the same time, revolutionary gains needed to be protected. For this reason, the two 'strategic tasks' of this second phase of the revolution are defined as socialist construction (economic development according to socialist principles) and national security. The combination is significant: each task is expected to promote the other (cf. Stuart-Fox, 1981a). The clearest statement of this connection was contained in Kaysone's speech to the SPA in February 1977, where he stated:

Because our country is a socialist outpost, and because of the thoroughness of our country's revolution, we must always closely link the duties of national defense . . . with the duties of economic construction . . . both in the immediate and long-range future. We must regard the duty of fostering and consolidating security and national defense as an integral and interrelated part of the entire socialist revolutionary struggle.

For the Lao leadership the problem of economic development cannot be divorced from the requirements of national security.

Within this context, socialist construction is to be pursued through application of the 'three revolutions' and promotion of 'collective mastery' on the part of the multi-ethnic Lao people. Together these two borrowed Vietnamese concepts (cf. Doré, in Stuart-Fox, 1982a) form the ideological basis for economic development policy in the LPDR. The three revolutions are to be carried out simultaneously. Even though the first listed, the revolution in production relations, is in orthodox Marxist terms the most basic, the second, the scientific and technical revolution, is described as the 'keystone' of the whole programme, while the third, the ideological and cultural revolution, is to be 'a step ahead' of the others.

The above description leaves the exact relationship of the three revolutions unclear, though the broad lines of the economic strategy they entail are evident. The revolution in production relations is to be achieved through socialization of the means of production, in the financial, industrial and agricultural sectors. Accordingly banking and all larger industrial plants were nationalized in the first year of the new regime. Attempts were also made to cooperativize agriculture, though opposition from a substantial proportion of peasant farmers forced the government temporarily to curtail the programme and to proceed more carefully thereafter. As for the scientific and cultural revolution, this depends crucially on both levels of education and the level of transfer of technology. Weaknesses in the Lao education system affecting this programme will be examined below. Foreign aid programmes provide the principal means of transferring technology, which thus depends on the willingness of donors to furnish what is needed and on the capacity of Lao to absorb what is offered. The ideological and cultural revolution is to remain a step ahead of the others in the sense that all those who participate in the construction of socialism must already be convinced that this is a worthwhile task to which to devote their lives (Phomvihane, 1980).

'Collective mastery' is described as a 'right' belonging to the masses under socialism. The concept as used by the Lao was developed by the Vietnamese from the Chinese theory of the 'mass line'. For the Lao, the relationship between Party, government and people is summed up in the slogan: the Party must lead, the state must manage, the people are masters (quoted in Zasloff, 1981b). Although exact relationships expressed in the slogan are again unclear, the theory of collective mastery can be understood in the light of the notion of democratic centralism and the dictatorship of the proletariat (as exercised by the Party). In the socialist phase of the revolution, the people are responsible for their own future: the Party takes its direction from the popular will, while at the same time shaping and guiding that will. Or so it is in theory. In practice, economic development in Laos more often takes the form of 'a determined band of mentors handing down instructions via an unsophisticated vanguard to an uninspired nation' (Brown & Zasloff, 1985).

If collective mastery is still a distant vision, the ideology of Lao communism nevertheless provides the theoretical explanation for, and justification of, changes in economic policy which occurred during the first decade of the LPDR. Political consolidation of the new regime required socialization of the means of production in order to bring the previously *laissez-faire* economy under the control of the state. The problem was that in Laos measures to enforce state control through nationalization of the small industrial sector and regulation of the urban market economy left untouched the major proportion of the agricultural sector. Hence the need to collectivize agriculture, and to tax it to finance planned economic development.

Early economic policy decisions were not taken on an entirely *ad hoc* basis: they were, however, inappropriate as a response to the situation that faced the new regime. By the end of 1975 the artificial urban economy built on massive American aid had all but collapsed. The service sector was particularly hard hit. So too was the industrial sector as managers and technicians fled to Thailand. The Thai blockade resulted in shortages of food, fuel, spare parts and industrial raw materials, which only added to spiralling inflation and unemployment. Inflation was exacerbated by the collapse, consequent upon termination of American aid, of the IMF directed Foreign Exchange Operations Fund set up to support the Lao currency. By early 1976 the free market value of the kip had dropped to 4,000 to the US dollar. By the middle of the year, when the government was forced to replace and devalue the currency, the rate was 14,000 kip to the dollar (Chanda, in Stuart-Fox, 1982a).

Government policies did nothing to reduce inflation. Wages were increased to keep pace with rising costs of living (then increasing at 400 per cent per annum). Large subsidies were advanced to nationalized state industries and trading companies and to finance new state-run shops and marketing cooperatives. The massive resulting budget deficit was covered by printing more money, which further fuelled the inflationary spiral. In September 1976, the government turned to the only source of additional revenue available to it, apart from increased foreign aid—the agricultural sector. A system of progressive taxation was introduced, and immediately applied, without prior discussion or explanation, to the current harvest. Its effect on peasants who never previously had been taxed and were already wary of the new regime was disastrous. Evasion of tax was widespread and subsequent production was curtailed by wealthier farmers to avoid higher tax levels.

By 1977, the economy was in deep crisis. The 1976 rice harvest had been reduced by drought, necessitating costly imports to make up the deficit. Food supplies to towns had dwindled to virtually nothing due to controls on the movement and marketing of goods. Production of industrial crops was down. The trade deficit had increased. The only positive achievement was the resettlement with help from UNHCR of as many as 500,000 remaining internal refugees, together with many former rightist soldiers and police on abandoned or unused agricultural land, thereby reducing urban unemployment and augmenting the rural labour force. However a lack of draught animals and implements kept the productive capacity of these cooperative resettlement villages at a bare subsistence level.

During 1977, the government introduced a number of economic measures aimed at increasing productivity and at reducing expenditure and increasing revenue in order to reduce the budget deficit and lay the foundations for an interim three-year plan to run from 1978 to 1980.

Government controls were eased slightly; procurement prices were increased for some agricultural products; salaries were frozen; taxation was increased for the non-agricultural sector; subsidies were cut; and the prices of food and services provided by the state were increased. By the end of 1977, these policies were having some effect, though returns from the agricultural tax still remained disappointingly low.

At the beginning of 1978, the government launched its interim three-year plan, a principal goal of which was to make the country self-sufficient in food grains. This goal was not met. Poor harvests due to flooding in 1978 meant that 150,000 tons of rice had to be imported; and even after improvements in the two following years, the deficit still stood at an estimated 11 per cent of production (Stuart-Fox, 1983). The decision to collectivize agriculture was taken both for ideological reasons and in order to increase both production and government control over what was produced. Much was expected to flow from this move; the collective relations of production would soon demonstrate their superiority over private relations; collective mastery and socialist consciousness would be heightened; and the solidarity engendered would lend powerful support to the defensive capability of the state.

None of these anticipated benefits materialized. Soon after the cooperativization programme was launched in May 1978, it ran into concerted peasant opposition. Farmers objected to pooling their land and means of production (draught animals, ploughs, etc). Coercion by enthusiastic but ill-trained cadres only added to peasant distrust. By early 1979 it was clear not only that production was being adversely affected, but that internal security was suffering as anti-government resistance groups exploited growing peasant dissatisfaction. The decision to abandon the cooperativization programme half-way through the interim three-year plan was a victory for economic pragmatism over ideology. It was taken as part of a radical reconsideration of economic policy then underway in part provoked by a confidential World Bank report submitted to the Lao government in November 1978 (No 2282-LA). The outcome of this reconsideration was the announcement of sweeping economic reforms in December 1979 in the form of the Seventh Resolution of the LPRP Central Committee.

By any account this was a remarkable document. While candidly recognizing some of the regime's shortcomings, it announced a series of sweeping reforms touching on virtually every aspect of the economy. In particular, the document recognized the need to take account, in the current stage of the nation's economic development, of capitalist as well as socialist economic laws in order to promote economic growth. This was because the Lao economy actually incorporated five distinct sectors. These were: the state sector (consisting of nationalized banks and industries, state farms, and state transport and trading companies); the collective sector (mainly consisting of agricultural cooperatives); the individual sector (comprising individual farmers, traders, repairmen and other self-employed people); the capitalist sector (remaining small-scale industrial and commercial enterprises functioning in accordance with government regulations); and the joint state-capitalist sector (composed of those joint ventures utilizing investment from both private enterprise and the state) (cf. Luther, 1982).

Recognition of the need to stimulate all five sectors of the economy led to the liberalization of restrictions on private participation in manufacturing, transportation and commerce. Individuals were positively encouraged to become involved in everything from light industry to trucking. At the same time the government introduced more realistic pricing policies in line with free market rates, and made profit the primary criterion of economic performance of state enterprises. Two further measures consolidated the Seventh Resolution reforms. The first was a currency conversion and devaluation of 60 per cent against the US dollar. This move, which was supported by an IMF loan, replaced the so-called 'Liberation kip' with notes issued by the National Bank valued initially at 16 kip to one US dollar. The second measure was a new system of agricultural taxation based on average land fertility rather than actual output. Farmers were taxed a fixed amount of paddy according to the area farmed, leaving all increased production to be freely disposed of on the open market. Together with higher procurement prices, this provided an incentive to increase yields and to plant a second crop where possible.

The very extent of these reforms was indicative of the parlous state of the Lao economy after four years of communist rule. The loss of foreign aid, Chinese as well as American, and the massive flight (or imprisonment) of almost the entire educated, technically proficient middle class were clearly two factors much to blame; but government ineptitude was also responsible. Restrictions had all but eliminated petty trading; taxation policy and procurement prices that failed to keep pace with inflation had stifled rice production; and government enterprises had been hopelessly mismanaged by men more often appointed for their political reliability than their economic expertise.

By the time the new regime celebrated the fifth anniversary of its accession to power, the new policies were beginning to take effect. Rice production topped the one million tonne mark for the first time; livestock numbers and forestry production were up; and urban markets again had something to sell. Only industrial production, for which no figures were announced, remained disappointing. The economic picture as the country prepared to embark on its first five-year plan was therefore not entirely bleak. In addition to increases in agricultural and forestry production, hydroelectricity exports had tripled and mining showed promise. Serious attempts were being made to increase the efficiency of manufacturing industry. On the financial side, government revenues were up while expenditure, though still more than double internal revenue, was being kept within bounds. The domestic money supply was also being kept under control. Exports had increased, though imports had also risen, leaving a current account deficit of around double total exports—an amount which could only be made up by foreign aid. Still foreign debt servicing stood at a manageable 7 per cent of total exports, thanks to the non-refundable nature of most financial aid, and gross international reserves were around 28 per cent of annual imports (IMF Report, 1980).

On this basis the Lao government launched its first five-year plan, the outlines of which were revealed in the Eighth Resolution of the Party CC ratified by the SPA in January 1981. This document drew three lessons from the experience of the preceding five years during which the economy had 'failed to make progress': that there was clearly a need to understand and apply the Party line, improve economic management and promote international socialist solidarity (that is, to cooperate fully with and take the advice of the Soviet Union, Vietnam, and other Soviet bloc states). The 'two objectives' of the plan were to 'normalize the material and cultural life of the people', and to 'concentrate on building those enterprises which are strategically important to [the country's] economy and national defence'. The 'seven priorities' of the plan were listed as: to promote agricultural production; build strategically important enterprises; consolidate the economic bases of state enterprises; train economic managers and technicians; complete the literacy compaign; consolidate and restructure 'organizations which manage the economy and state'; and acquire and efficiently utilize foreign economic assistance (FBIS, 26 January, and 2 and 13 February 1981).

Actual targets for the five-year plan were announced in Decree 408 of the Council of Government of the LPDR, issued on 28 November 1980 (KPL/BQ, 28 November and 1 and 2 December, 1980; see also World Bank Report, 1983). Targets were given as percentage increases over unstated production figures for 1980, but did at least provide some measure against which actual performance over the years 1981–5 could be assessed—a task made difficult, however, by the inaccuracy of data provided by the Lao government and the variability of official statistics. To take an example, GDP at current prices for 1981 and 1982 were both revised upwards in the IMF report of January 1985 compared with the same organization's report of February 1984—not to mention changes in dozens of other officially provided figures included in the tables of basic data for these two years in the two reports.

The target of the five-year plan was for GDP to rise by between 65 and 68 per cent. In his speech marking the tenth anniversary of the LPDR, however, Kaysone noted only that GDP had more than doubled over the full ten year period, and that production per head of population had increased by 60 per cent. Presumably these figures were calculated on base figures for 1975 or 1976, both years of severe economic disruption and low production. No comparison was provided based on the year 1980, and no indication was given whether the plan target had been met (cf. Stuart-Fox, 1986b). It is possible, however, to assess economic development by reference to changes in GDP corrected for inflation over the course of the plan. A 6.6 per cent increase from 1980 to 1981 was followed by a rise of only 1.9 per cent in 1982 and a decline of 3.3 per cent in the depressed year of 1983. A recovery estimated at 8.1 per cent was registered in 1984 (IMF Report, 1985). Calculated on this basis, the plan target of a 65–68 per cent increase in GNP could not possibly have been met by the end of 1985—which may account for Kaysone's reluctance to provide relevant figures in his tenth anniversary speech.

An assessment of economic performance in relation to plan targets will be provided for various sectors to be discussed below. It is enough to note here that none of the major targets of the first five-year plan were actually achieved. In part this was due to problems of centralized planning and economic weaknesses that the LPDR shares with other underdeveloped socialist states (discussed in Stuart-Fox, 1982b); in part it was due to specific difficulties faced by the LPDR: including the debilitating loss of skilled workers the country has suffered; consequent low levels of technical expertise in the Lao workforce; the effects of an externally supported insurgency; and the regional balance of power which has forced Laos into close political dependency on Vietnam. All these factors adversely influenced Lao economic performance, either because they necessitated the uneconomic allocation and utilization of resources or because they closed off possible sources of economic assistance.

The disappointing economic results during the first decade of communist government have led to continuing political debate in Laos. That not all members of the Party were happy over the direction of economic policy was evident from statements released following the Party CC's 6th and 7th Plenary Sessions in August and December 1984. Some members clearly preferred a more rapid and orthodox transition to socialism. Renewed efforts to establish agricultural cooperatives and increased taxation and control of private businesses towards the end of 1985 both reflected this more conservative line. The majority view on the eve of the second five-year plan, however, seemed to favour more of the same. In particular, the 'new management mechanism' inaugurated in the course of the first five-year plan was reconfirmed as government policy: a resolution of the SPA called upon all authorities 'to completely transform the economic management and promptly lay out various detailed policies and measures with a view to totally switching from the centralized bureaucratic administration based on the state-financing system to the socialist economic and business calculation . . .' (FBIS, 7 February 1986). The wording may be tortuous, but the intent is clear. Basic economic objectives for the second plan appear to be virtually unchanged from those of the first. Agriculture will continue to have priority in order to maintain self-sufficiency in food and meet stockpile targets set but not achieved in the first plan. Increases in rice production are to be brought about primarily by extending dry-season irrigation and improving yields: no great increase in the area under cultivation is envisaged. Industrial crops and livestock production will continue to be encouraged. Improvement of agricultural support services is also high on the agenda. Now that the third stage of the Nam Ngum dam has been completed, no significant increase is expected in hydroelectricity production before 1990. Increase in export income is expected to come instead from exploitation of the LPDR's vast forestry reserves. By contrast, mineral production is not likely to increase significantly over the five years to 1990. Industrial strategy will not be overly ambitious. New industrial plants will be on a small scale, will not be capital intensive and will utilize local raw materials. One major project the government would like to see achieved is construction of the Vang Vieng cement works. Existing factories will be brought up to full capacity. Emphasis will be on improving management and efficiency in state enterprises and in encouraging the setting up of small private enterprises through a three-year tax exemption (FBIS, 2 August 1985). Transport and communications will continue to be upgraded. So too will levels of technical education.

As equally important goals for the second five-year plan, IMF experts have recommended adoption of policies aimed at better control of inflation, improved resources allocation and a strengthened balance of payments (IMF Report, 1985). To this end they suggest that the government should factor in consumer subsidies and forgone revenue from agricultural taxes when drawing up the budget. Public enterprises should be permitted to retain a large proportion of profits, with the effect on reduced government revenue offset by increased mobilization of domestic resources and the imposition of duties on aid financed imports and taxes on state enterprises. Exports must receive high priority if a favourable balance of payments is to be preserved. This will require improved marketing, devaluation of the kip, and increased domestic procurement prices. The government may or may not act on these recommendations, but they are not impossible demands. There seems no reason, therefore, why Laos should not improve its economic performance during the second five-year plan—providing sufficient international financial assistance is forthcoming.

Finance and Dependency

Since the early years of the French administration, successive governments in Laos have had continuing difficulty in balancing their budgets. The present regime is no exception. In 1983, the last year for which complete figures were available, the budget deficit stood at 3.199 billion kip, an increase of 17 per cent over that of the previous year but a reduction from 20 per cent to 16 per cent of GDP. Over the period from 1980 to 1984 government revenue increased six times to stand at just over 8 billion kip. Over the same period expenditure increased by a factor of four to reach 4.55 billion kip. This left the deficit in 1984 at just over three times the figure in 1980. (Statistics in this section are drawn from the *UNDP Draft Report of 1985*, and the *IMF Report*, 1985, unless otherwise stated.)

The deficit is entirely financed by foreign loans and grants. These pay for almost all the budget allocation for capital outlays, a figure consistently amounting to slightly more than half the total expenditure. In other words, Laos is entirely dependent on foreign aid for any economic development: the country's income from internal sources of revenue is just sufficient to meet current expenditure in the form of wages and salaries, subsidies on consumption, debt servicing, and materials and supplies. Military expenditures are never included in the budget, and in any case are met by Vietnam and the Soviet Union. Nor is the cost of the rice subsidy allowed for in budget estimates. Yet in 1984 this amounted to 1,884 million kip made up of 1,346 million kip in losses to the Food Corporation and 538 million kip in lost revenue to the government. The total figure represented 7.1 per cent of GNP, and 23.4 per cent of budget expenditure—an amount the government could ill afford. Revenues derive from transfers from state enterprises (accounting for just on 70 per cent of the total), taxes on the private sector (which by 1984 had risen to over a billion kip, or approaching 25 per cent of total revenue), and the remainder from the agricultural tax (5 per cent), import duties, and other sources (see Table 4.1).

Table 4.1 Estimates of National Income and GDP, * 1980–4 (kip, m.)

	1980	1981	1982	1983	1984
National income at 1982 prices	8,974	9,564	9,746	9,422	10,189
Agriculture and forestry	7,428	8,085	7,933	7,616	8,372
Industry	679	660	682	657	686
Construction	255	203	331	331	331
Transport and communication	191	156	166	166	166
Commerce	334	368	517	517	517
Other	87	92	117	117	117
Depreciation	538	574	585	565	611
Nonmaterial services	2,864	3,053	3,111	3,007	3,252
GDP at 1982 prices	12,376	13,191	13,442	12,994	14,052
(percentage change)	(10.0)	(6.6)	(1.9)	(−3.3)	(8.1)
GDP deflator	48.7	64.9	100.0	155.1	189.2
(percentage change)	(...)	(33.3)	(54.1)	(55.1)	(22.0)
GDP at current prices	6,022	8,654	13,442	20,152	26,580

Source: UNDP Draft Report, 1985, based on IMF estimates and data provided by the Lao authorities.

* Laos' national accounts are established acording to the Material Product System (MPS), which differs from the United Nation's System of National Accounts (SNA). The basic difference between the two systems is that the MPS does not include the value of depreciation and non-material services.

In addition to its budgetary problems, Laos runs a chronic trade deficit, with exports covering only around 30 per cent of import costs. In 1982, the current account balance showed a deficit of US$103.6 million. By 1984 this had dropped to US$71.4 million due to decreased turnover. For the period 1980 to 1984 the deficit averaged US$93.1 million or around 20 per cent of GDP. In 1984, private remittances from Lao living abroad amounted to around US$3 million, while private sector financing of imports was twice that sum. The level of international reserves fell to US$48.5 million by the end of 1982, or just over two months of imports from the convertible currency zone. By June 1984 reserves had climbed back to US$20 million, equivalent to eight months of imports (see Table 4.2).

By the end of 1983, Laos had a foreign debt of US$385.5 million, comprising debts of US$127.7 million to the convertible zone (of which US$50.2 million was owed to multinational lending institutions), and US$257.8 million to Soviet bloc states in the form of thirty-year loans at 2 per cent interest repayable after a ten-year grace period. Debt service payments to the convertible area present problems because apart from electricity, exports to the convertible area have steadily declined (from US$13.3 million in 1979 to US$3.3 million in 1984). If this pattern continues, Laos will find itself desperately short of convertible foreign currency during the course of the second five-year plan, which in turn would have serious repercussions for the country's continuing economic development. Debt servicing to the non-convertible zone was due to increase from US$2.5 million in 1985 to US$5.5 million by 1987. Overall, the cost of debt servicing quadrupled over the period of the first five-year plan (*IMF Report*, 1985).

What this means is that, given the financial difficulties faced by the regime, Laos cannot afford to accumulate further substantial international debts. Aid towards infrastructure developments with no immediate financial return or for development programmes in such fields as public health or education can only be accepted in the form of gifts. Even feasibility studies and technical assistance at the pre-investment stage cannot be financed through loans in case projects fail to reach fruition. Laos is now in a position where it can only contract loans, and then only on the most favourable conditions, for projects aimed at generating export income at a high rate of return on investment.

Aid to Laos has averaged in the vicinity of US$80 million per year over the course of the first five-year plan—an upper limit in terms of the country's ability to absorb and make proper use of it. No accurate figures are available for total aid to Laos because Communist donors refuse to provide estimates of the value of their aid. Programmes whether in the form of capital investment or technical assistance are listed, but not costed. Amounts of military assistance from Vietnam and the Soviet Union are never revealed, but recent estimates place the figure at US$100 million for 1982 (*The Military Balance*, 1985). Overall, the Soviet Union provides more than half the total value of aid to the LPDR, involving the services of more than a thousand experts. In return, the Soviet Union has signed certain contracts for small quantities of Lao raw materials, the details of which have never been made public. More importantly, the Soviet Union also assumes the right to influence the direction of Lao economic planning and development through experts permanently attached to the State Planning Committee.

The second largest donor, despite its own poverty, is Vietnam, which has as many as 5,000 civilian advisers and technicians in Laos, not to mention an estimated 50,000 troops. Aid takes the form primarily of joint exploitation of mineral and forestry resources, the terms of which remain undisclosed, assistance in equipping and running state farms and provision of small industrial plants. (Details of Vietnamese economic and military assistance to

Table 4.2 Basic financial data

	1981	1982	1983	1984
GDP per capita (US$)	97	97	143	184
Output (percentage change)				
Real merchant GDP	6.6	1.9	−3.3	8.1
Production of rice	9.6	−5.4	−8.3	14.8
Gross industrial production	−1.7	0.4	1.9	1.6
of which: electricity	−4.5	7.6	−5.1	2.0
Prices (percentage change)				
Consumer price index (end of period)	22.5	43.4	66.1	19.2*
Official prices	−	38.4	25.4	−2.2*
Free market prices	31.9	45.0	78.4	23.6*
GDP deflator	40.9	46.0	61.0	21.4
Budget (percentage change)				
Revenue	32.2	178.6	26.9	30.1
Expenditures	10.1	179.9	22.3	20.0
Current	−	119.7	30.4	33.6
Capital	23.9	246.5	16.6	9.3
Monetary survey (percentage change)				
Domestic credit	25.1	23.4	20.3	31.1[†]
of which: credit to public enterprises	(29.9)	(24.4)	(20.8)	(31.3)[†]
Total liquidity	2.3	51.8	38.7	14.2[†]
Cash in circulation	7.6	39.6	35.6	40.0[†]
Balance of payments (US$ m.)				
Exports	19.4	39.8	42.8	36.2
Convertible area	14.0	26.9	29.8	28.2
of which: electricity	(7.9)	(23.9)	(23.5)	(24.0)
Nonconvertible area	5.4	12.9	13.0	8.0
Imports	−109.5	−132.2	−135.1	−98.4
Convertible area	−36.2	−44.0	−52.1	−31.4
Nonconvertible area	−13.8	−30.2	−40.0	−25.0
Under aid programmes	−59.5	−58.0	−43.0	−42.0
Trade balance	−90.1	−92.4	−92.3	−62.2
Current account	−96.4	−103.6	−101.1	−71.1
Capital account	95.9	93.5	107.5	73.1
Overall balance	−4.6	5.0	10.3	1.0
International reserves (US$ m.)				
Gross international reserves	13.53	8.54	18.85	20.01[‡]
(in months of merchandise imports)	(1.5)	(0.8)	(1.7)	(2.4)[‡]

	1981	1982	1983	1984
(in months of Nonaid imports from the convertible area)	(4.5)	(2.3)	(4.3)	(7.6)[‡]
Net international reserves	−1.49	−5.55	4.76	7.34[‡]
External debt operations (US$ m.)				
External debt outstanding (disbursed)	312.4	342.5	385.5	414.3[§]
of which: convertible area	(110.0)	(120.0)	(127.5)	(138.3)[§]
External debt servicing	7.2	7.4	6.6	16.8
of which: convertible area	(7.1)	(5.8)	(6.0)	(14.9)

*September 1984 over September 1983; [†] June 1984 over June 1983;
[‡] Outstanding in June 1984; [§] Outstanding in September 1984
Source: IMF Report, 1985

Laos are given below in the section on Lao-Vietnamese relations.) As in the case of the Soviet Union, the scale of Vietnamese aid is such as to give the SRV a major say in the planning and development of the Lao economy.

Other members of the Soviet bloc with aid programmes in Laos include the German Democratic Republic, Hungary, Czechoslovakia, Bulgaria, Cuba and Mongolia, but not Poland or Romania. Among Western donor countries, Sweden and Australia have substantial technical assistance programmes, while Sweden, Japan and the Netherlands have capital investment or commodity supply programmes (valued in total at just under US$11 million in 1983) (UNDP summary of aid to Laos, 1985).

The United Nations Development Programme and other UN agencies funded fifty-five projects in Laos over the period 1982-6 to the value of US$27 million. Of this sum half went to agriculture and livestock programmes, 8 per cent to forestry, 9 per cent to industry, 9 per cent was for communications, 13 per cent for education and 6 per cent for public health. Other UN projects were mounted by UNICEF (in health care, training, immunization, nutrition, sanitation and education, including teacher training and educational materials), by WHO (in control of diseases—malaria, leprosy and tuberculosis—health education and services, rehabilitation of the handicapped and war wounded, etc.) and by FAO (in agriculture, forestry and fisheries training and development). The Asian Development Bank (ADB) and the International Development Association provided loans of US$62 million and US$140 million respectively over the course of the first five-year plan for projects including rural electrification and road improvement in the Vientiane area, forestry development, manufacture of agricultural implements, dry season irrigation and extension of agricultural support services.

The thrust of Lao foreign policy during the course of the first five-year plan was towards establishing friendly relations with a variety of states with a view to ensuring a continuing flow of international aid, the need for which is clearly recognized by the Lao authorities. Given the weakness of the Lao economy, the requirement of the LPDR for foreign financial assistance is certain to continue for the foreseeable future. The very extent of such aid, however, inevitably places Laos in a position of extreme dependency, especially where an overwhelming proportion is provided by one or two states, as is currently the case for the Soviet Union and Vietnam. Diversification of aid donors might lessen this dependency marginally, but it seems unlikely that any other country would be prepared to shoulder a major share of necessary aid for Laos. The change of political system in Laos in no way has altered the fact that the LPDR is a desperately poor developing Third World country, acutely dependent on the international community to fund programmes of economic development.

Agriculture, Livestock and Fisheries

Agriculture accounts for 65 per cent of GDP, but occupies some 85 per cent of the Lao population. Cultivated land covers less than a million hectares out of a total land area of 23.68 million hectares, or just on 4 per cent. Of this area, rice in either its upland or paddy varieties, accounts for more than 75 per cent of the area planted. Upland rice grows on approximately 40 per cent of the total area under rice, while wet rice, mainly of the glutinous variety preferred in Laos, is grown on the remaining 60 per cent. The total area presently cultivated only amounts to about 20 per cent of the five million hectares of potentially cultivable land. Of this total, two million hectares constitute alluvial plains suitable for wet rice production, while a further three million hectares of prairie land could be given over to the cultivation of industrial crops such as coffee, pepper or rubber, or improved as pasturage for intensive livestock production. (Figures in this section are drawn from the government's *LDC Report*, 1983, the *UNDP Draft Report*, 1985, and IMF reports of 1984 and 1985, unless otherwise stated.)

When the present regime came to power in 1975, Laos imported around 150,000 tonnes of rice per annum. A major goal of the interim three-year plan was to become self-sufficient in rice. This was not achieved, mainly because of adverse weather conditions, lack of incentive due to low procurement prices and lost production resulting from popular opposition to cooperativization of agriculture. With the temporary curtailment of co-operativization, improved climatic conditions, and higher procurement

Table 4.3 Production of Major Agricultural Crops 1978–1983 (in '000 tonnes)

	1977	1978	1979	1980	1981	1982	1983 estimate
Paddy	693.0	724.0	867.0	1,053.0	1,154.0	1,092.0	1,112.0
Rainfed lowland area	(473.0)	(501.0)	(574.0)	(705.0)	(782.2)	(730.5)	n.a.
Irrigated area	(3.7)	(8.8)	(15.0)	(11.1)	(12.3)	(12.4)	n.a.
Upland area	(216.0)	(274.0)	(278.0)	(377.0)	(360.2)	(349.5)	n.a.
Vegetables	30.8	35.4	42.7	42.6	43.6	45.1	45.0
Maize	31.4	27.0	21.3	28.3	32.8	33.5	33.0
Cotton	2.4	3.7	4.8	4.9	5.0	5.3	5.4
Coffee	2.8	3.0	3.5	4.4	5.0	5.2	5.7
Tobacco	0.7	1.8	2.1	2.4	2.7	3.1	2.2
Root crops	48.7	50.6	68.6	80.3	97.1	105.0	99.2
Soybeans	1.9	2.9	3.3	3.3	3.9	4.2	4.8
Tea (tonnes)	–	27.0	30.3	29.0	46.0	48.0	48.0
Peanuts	3.5	7.1	7.6	7.9	8.6	n.a.	n.a.

Source: IMF Report, 1984 and data provided by the Lao authorities.

prices, paddy production improved in 1979 and again in 1980 and 1981—only to fall in 1982 and 1983 before increasing again to 1.3 million tonnes in 1984.

Rice is still cultivated predominantly by traditional means. Few farmers use fertilizers and little or no organic manure is applied to the fields. As a result yields remain among the lowest in the world at 1.7 tonnes per hectare for wet rice; between 1.9 and 2.2 for irrigated dry season crops and a miserably low 1.1 tonnes per hectare for upland rice grown by the slash-and-burn method. Increased total production has been largely due to increases in the area under cultivation, mainly through renewed use of abandoned paddies, rather than to improved yields through use of improved seed varieties, improved agricultural methods or increased agricultural inputs.

Agriculture was designated the priority area for development during the country's first five-year plan. The goal set of 1.4 million tonnes of rice per annum by 1985 was supposed not only to meet consumption requirements but also to enable the government to establish a strategic stockpile of rice equal to six months of commercial sales for emergency use in case of poor harvests. At the end of 1985, the government claimed that production had doubled over the decade since 1975, effectively wiping out the average annual deficit of 150,000 tonnes per annum under the former regime, and permitting individual consumption to rise from an average of 280 to 350 kilograms of paddy per year (equal to 210 kilograms of husked rice). This is a considerable achievement, though as noted above, progress was by no means steady during the first five-year plan. The harvest for 1985 of just over 1.3 million tonnes was about 100,000 tonnes below the target. Despite some improvement (except for upland rice), yields still remained extremely low.

Increase in rice production remains one of the principal goals of the second five-year plan (1986–90). This is to be achieved by four means: increase in double cropping; increase in yields; increase in incentives through improved price support for producers; and promotion of agricultural cooperatives (LDC Report, 1983). Increase in double cropping will depend on suitable incentives. In 1985 the area actually planted was only about half the area available for dry season irrigation. Increases in yield will be equally difficult to obtain, given constraints on the importation of chemical fertilizers and pesticides. Improved agricultural methods, better care of crops, and greater use of organic manure would raise yields particularly of upland rice, as would settled production through terracing, though the labour involved would be enormous. The steady increase in government acquisition prices for paddy rice, allied to reduction of taxation and increased provision of consumer goods in rural areas, have all provided some incentive for increased production. Whether continued cooperativization will also increase production is rather more questionable, however. Much will depend on the effectiveness of government support for cooperatives through provision of agricultural inputs and extension services, neither of which has been forthcoming to the extent necessary in the past. The government places much store on the mechanization of agriculture which is said to have increased five times over pre-1975 levels during the first decade of the regime (Kaysone's tenth anniversary speech, KPL/NB 3 December 1985). But mechanization has been almost entirely limited to resettlement cooperatives and to the thirty-one state farms which together occupy only 1,400 hectares, or 0.2 per cent of the total cultivated area, and for the foreseeable future most agricultural crops in Laos will continue to be planted and harvested by hand.

Even if production of rice does substantially increase, opportunities for export will be limited. Not only would the cost of transportation for sale to any but a neighbouring country be exorbitant, but the world demand for glutinous rice is small. Rice grown for export would have to be of the normal variety. As it is, the 6 per cent to 18 per cent (8.75 per cent average) of rice harvested which goes to pay government taxes in kind and meet procurement quotas is barely enough to feed government employees and the army. None is available for export. There would seem, therefore, to be only limited opportunities for rice to become a major source of export revenue that could be used for investment in development projects.

The principal secondary cereal crop in Laos is maize which is grown on about 31,000 hectares and gives yields of around one tonne/hectare. Another 11,000–12,000 hectares are devoted to root crops, mainly manioc and sweet potatoes, with yields of 8.5 tonnes/hectare while various vegetables are grown in another 5,000–6,000 hectares. All these crops are grown almost entirely for home consumption, as are about 4,000 hectares of fruit trees. Most are grown on small private plots and around houses. Sugar cane (1,000 hectares planted with low yields of around 27 tonnes/hectare), and leguminous crops such as peanuts, soya beans and mung beans (together grown on some 19,000 hectares for a total production of somewhere around 15,000 tonnes) are also for local consumption and offer limited prospects for export.

The principal industrial crops grown in Laos are coffee, cotton, tobacco and tea. Coffee is grown on more than 8,000 hectares mostly in small plantations on the Bolovens plateau. A further 4,000 hectares of former plantations abandoned during the war are gradually being rehabilitated. Yields are low at 400 kgms/hectare, and total production is only about 5,000 tonnes. The quality of the coffee produced is poor, due to inadequate processing and storage facilities, but despite the fact that an unknown percentage of production finds its way illegally to Thailand, coffee is the LPDR's principal cash crop and the government is working to upgrade treatment and handling. Cotton is grown on about 7,000 hectares with a yield of 0.6 tonnes/hectare. It is used almost entirely in cottage industries. Tobacco is grown commercially in the Vientiane area to supply the country's only cigarette factory. Much of it is grown along the banks of the Mekong river, erosion of which was held to be responsible for the decline in area under cultivation in 1983 from 4,900 to 3,600 hectares and associated decline in production from 3,100 to 2,200 tonnes. Tea is grown on 160 hectares producing 48 tonnes per annum. (Figures for increased production between 1980 and 1981 reflect improvement in the gathering and correlation of statistics, rather than increases in area cultivated or yields achieved.)

The extension of dry-season irrigation is a major agricultural priority for the government during the second five-year plan. At present only 13,000 hectares are irrigated for dry-season production contributing a mere 1.25 per cent of the total rice harvest. The potential for increased production through irrigation is considerable, though the expense involved in mounting large-scale irrigation projects will be a constraining factor. UNDP has estimated that 75,000 hectares of existing paddies could be irrigated. The goal for the second five-year plan is to increase the area under irrigation by 10,000 to 12,000 hectares. In line with these relatively modest targets, it is planned to scale down the target for storage of paddy to 10 per cent of production, or around 150,000 tonnes. Sixty per cent of this is to be stockpiled by individual families and cooperatives, and 40 per cent in state silos (constituting 50 per cent of commercial rice sales). Since installed storage capacity amounts to only 15,000 tonnes, silos to contain an additional 45,000 tonnes will have to be constructed, at an estimated cost of US$6.5 million (*UNDP Draft Report*, 1985).

The government also intends to improve agricultural support services, which have been woefully inadequate. A rural road programme is a major priority in order to draw villages into an integrated national economy. So too are the training of extension personnel and application of agricultural research, especially in the areas of improved seed production and improvement of agricultural techniques. In 1984, the extension service numbered only about 200 cadres. Some 200 students were studying agriculture, forestry and irrigation in Soviet bloc countries; while another 400 students were training as agricultural technicians at the Na Bong Agricultural College. These numbers will be increased. The two agricultural research stations at Salakham and Hat Dak Keo will be upgraded, and the Na Phok seed farm further developed. Incentives to increase production will take the form of realistic procurement prices and increased availability of consumer goods. In addition, the government intends to press ahead with the cooperativization of agriculture as a means of raising production. It argues that

the gradual restructuring of the existing individual property ownership to a system of collective property under agricultural cooperatives is the indispensable way to permit a rapid diffusion and application of techniques permitting, thereby, an increase in unitary yields and a diversification of crops. [*LDC Report*, 1983, p. 16.]

The government estimated in 1982 that of the country's 500,000 farming families, 90 per cent still used traditional methods to cultivate average private holdings of 1.5 hectares per family. Some 70,000 families were said to be (in some cases nominal) members of 1,800 cooperatives (LDC Report, 1983). This was down from the 2,800 cooperatives supposed to be functioning at the end of 1979 comprising 25 per cent of all peasant families (FBIS, 18 January 1980). By the end of 1985, Kaysone claimed that more than 3,000 cooperatives had been established comprising half of all peasant families farming half the total area under cultivation (KPL/NB, 3 December 1985). Another set of official figures placed the number of cooperatives at 3,184 comprising 61.5 per cent of all peasant families farming 58 per cent of all cultivated land (NL, December 1985). Such discrepancies in statistics have marked the cooperativization programme since its inception (Stuart-Fox, 1980b).

Part of the problem is due to difficulties in deciding what constitutes a cooperative. The first stage in the cooperativization of agriculture comprises little more than the traditional form of mutual assistance between villagers during planting and harvest. The second stage merely formalizes labour exchange between designated groups. Even in the third stage land may continue to be privately owned, as are farm implements and draught animals. Only in the final stage are the means of production owned in common. Very few cooperatives in Laos meet the criterion of common ownership. In most a small rental is paid for use of land. At any time land can be withdrawn from stage-three cooperatives. In some cases land is farmed cooperatively during the wet season, and privately during the dry season. Many such stage-three cooperatives have only an informal institutional base, and may only include a few families in a village. All such 'cooperatives' are nevertheless included in government statistics, and the suspicion remains that in order to reach the planned target of 60 to 70 per cent cooperativization by the end of 1985, even stage-two labour exchange arrangements have been counted as 'cooperatives'. As is so often the case in Laos, the gap between government rhetoric and reality over the extent of cooperativization of agriculture appears to be both wide and deep.

Livestock production in the LPDR is essential both as a source of animal protein and in order to maintain a supply of draught animals. After 1975, the policy of the government was to build up the number of draught animals to replace those lost during years of war. Controls were placed on the slaughter of cattle and buffaloes, particularly during religious festivals among highland minorities. These controls have since been relaxed, though it remains government policy to encourage bovine breeding and their use as draught animals before they are slaughtered. Breeding productivity remains low, however, with high incidences of disease in all species. The LPDR boasts fewer than twenty qualified veterinarians, together with perhaps 250 veterinary technicians trained to administer vaccines and provide rudimentary animal health care. Not more than a third of the total herd of cattle and buffaloes has been vaccinated.

According to official figures livestock breeding in all species nevertheless exceeded targets set in the first five-year plan. Buffaloes and cattle combined increased from 1.324 million to 1.550 million; sheep and goats increased from 54,000 to 66,000; pigs increased from 1.176 million to 1.433 million; while poultry increased from 5.568 to 7.834 million (NL, December, 1985). These figures need to be treated with caution, however, in a country where the gathering of statistical information is rudimentary. United Nations estimates are very much less 'exact'—nearly a million buffaloes, about half a million cattle, between half and one-and-a-half million pigs, around 50,000 sheep and goats and between five and ten million poultry of one kind or another (*UNDP Draft Report*, 1985). Laos also has probably fewer than a thousand working elephants, and an unknown number of horses.

Almost all livestock raised in the country is for private slaughter or for use as draught animals. There exist few commercial herds or flocks. Almost every household raises poultry and an estimated one in three fatten a pig or two. Buffaloes are mostly limited to the rice growing plains, while cattle thrive in the upland areas. In the vicinity of larger towns, particularly around Vientiane, livestock are raised for commercial slaughter but only to meet local demand. The Bolovens plateau offers the greatest potential for large-scale cattle raising, but even there state or cooperative cattle ranching will only become possible with much improved management and technical support from trained personnel. In fact, training of livestock and veterinary personnel is probably the most important priority in the field of animal production for the second five-year plan, together with improved selection techniques and nutrition.

Fish constitutes the second major source of animal protein in Laos, with average national consumption running at about seven kilograms per person per annum, though over twice this amount is consumed in the Vientiane area. Fishing is well developed from the Mekong and its many tributaries, from dams and reservoirs such as the 37,000 hectare Nam Ngum dam, and from streams and flooded rice paddies during and immediately after the rainy season. In addition, fish culture is extensively practised at the village level in ponds totalling some 5,000 hectares in area.

In view of the fact that river fishing has declined over the last decade, fish culture is being actively encouraged with support from FAO and the Mekong Committee. This takes the form of construction of major new ponds, training of management and technical personnel, and distribution of fingerlings of selected species. The goal for the second five-year plan is to increase national production from an estimated 27,000 tonnes in 1985 to 35,000 by 1990.

Forestry

More than 40 per cent of the total land area of the LPDR is covered by forests, including such valuable timbers as teak and rosewood. If inaccessible forests and those of marginal value are excluded, between 3 and 7 million hectares are available for economic exploitation. If the lower figure is taken, and the net average production is estimated at 2 cubic metres of timber per hectare per year, annual production could be in the order of 6 million cubic metres per year. This compares with a production level of not more than an average of 150,000 cubic metres per year during the course of the first five-year plan, far short of the goal of 400,000 cubic metres by 1985. The potential for increased production and exploitation of timber is thus considerable, and constitutes a major source of increased foreign earnings.

Lao forests also produce a number of other valuable products. These include sticklac, benzoin, cardamom, bamboo and rattan, and various resins. In 1981, the last year for which full statistics for forest products were available, production of sticklac was put at 718 tonnes and benzoin at 16 tonnes. Forty-two tonnes of cardamom were produced, but by 1983 this had decreased to 15 tonnes. The estimated 500 cubic metres of bamboo and rattan produced in 1981 also dropped the following year. These figures may well be inaccurate, however, and fail to reflect actual production. Forest products are gathered mostly by mountain dwelling tribes, and either smuggled to Thailand or marketed by provincial administrations (which have every reason to hide the amounts involved) or through the State Trading

Company. Even provinces such as Luang Prabang which do not share common borders with either Vietnam or Thailand go to some lengths to avoid sending their exports via Vientiane. (Luang Prabang exports to Thailand via Ban Houei Sai even though the border is not officially open at this point.) Increased procurement prices for forest products in 1983 and again in 1984 reportedly increased production channelled through the Trading Company, but figures were not available. (Production in 1984 is said to have increased by 29 per cent over the 1983 level, according to the *UNDP Draft Report*, 1985.)

Similar problems plague the timber industry itself. Forestry exploitation was decentralized in 1981 when provincial administrations were given the right to exploit local timber resources and nine regional state forestry enterprises were established—three in areas of Vientiane province, two in Khammouane and one each in Savannakhet, Sayaboury, Saravane and Champassak. These enterprises are virtually autonomous with only the most tenuous formal links with the Ministry of Industry, Handicrafts and Forestry. As of 1985, the Lao People's Army was also permitted to establish its own timber extraction and marketing organization, free of Ministry control.

There are, of course, ample resources in Laos for these various enterprises to exploit. The problem is not in the area of extraction, but in marketing. In 1982 the government set up a Lao Corporation for Wood Commercialization which was granted the monopoly of timber exports previously under the control of the State Trading Company. But provincial administrations, and now the Army, have the right to export timber directly to pay for commercial imports. In addition, as an IMF report notes, 'part of the exploitation and trade of logs has remained outside official channels' (*IMF Report*, 1984). Declining exports revealed by official figures which show a reduction in income earned from US$8.7 million in 1979 to US$5.1 million in 1981 may not therefore accurately reflect production (*LDC Report*, 1983).

One factor which does tend to reduce the value of timber exports and which also reflects tensions between the central government and provincial administrations is the serious under-utilization of capacity for processing timber, thus adding export value to the product. Laos boasts fifty-four sawmills with a capacity of 521,000 tonnes per annum; yet only about 20 per cent of this capacity has normally been utilized due to shortages of timber, spare parts and fuel. Just as serious, however, was the fact that only three of the larger sawmills in 1985 were able to produce sawn timber to international standards. A 1981 ban on the export of logs (in order to increase profits through processing) had by 1985 built up an inventory of at least 50,000 cubic metres of timber, valued at between US$15 and 20 million, which yet remained unavailable for Vientiane factories (*IMF Report*, 1985). Illegal export of logs has, however, continued.

Other forms of timber processing suffer from a shortage of timber. For example, the state company Lao Plywood in Vientiane has a capacity of 100,000 cubic metres per annum, but produces less than half that amount. State factories producing furniture and parquet flooring suffer from shortages of seasoned timber and bamboo. Such shortages occur because of difficulties of access and lack of means of transportation, both of which require extensive investment in roadbuilding and heavy equipment. Extraction becomes practically impossible during the rainy season from May to October. In addition there is a desperate shortage of trained personnel (only eleven forestry engineers and 120 technicians in the entire country in 1983). Finally, procurement prices paid by these enterprises frequently fail to meet inflationary costs of extraction: inadequate increases in 1983 again failed to stimulate production.

Marketing has been a major problem for the Lao timber industry, mainly because of inexperience and competition between provincial exporters. In the early 1980s unrealistic pricing reduced exports of sawn timber, while the permission granted to all provincial authorities to export logs permitted foreign buyers to play one off against another. The eagerness of provincial administrators to sell timber for convertible currency is all the greater for the fact that much of Laos' timber production is tied up in barter agreements, mainly with Vietnam and the Soviet Union.

In the long term, timber production in Laos will have to overcome a number of other problems. One is that at present between 200,000 and 300,000 hectares of exploitable forests are destroyed each year through slash-and-burn cultivation by highland minorities. At the very least such land, once it is abandoned, should be reafforested. No means yet exist to encourage this. In 1985 reafforestation programmes involved less than 2,000 hectares. Modern forestry management is a major priority for the future, in order to protect the most valuable areas and ensure regeneration of timber. So too is the training of personnel, both on the extraction and the marketing sides. Once these problems are overcome, timber could well surpass electric power as the LPDR's most valuable export commodity.

Industry and Mining

The entire industrial sector in the LPDR, including both electricity and mining, accounts for only around 7 per cent of GDP, and employs no more than 10,000 people, a level well below the average for even the least developed countries. Apart from electricity production, manufacturing industry registered disappointing results during the course of the first five-year plan. In retrospect the target of doubling production was quite unrealistic. After the economic stagnation of 1981-2, total manufacturing output rose by almost 5 per cent in 1982, and by a further 9 per cent in 1984 (*IMF Report*, 1984). However, these figures were calculated on extremely low base production rates running as low as 30 to 35 per cent of installed capacity. Poor results were due mainly to shortages of raw materials, a lack of trained technicians, and poor maintenance and management. Production did improve during 1985, but still remained well below installed capacity.

Eighteen larger factories run by the Ministry of Industry, Handicrafts and Forestry account for 80 per cent of Laos' industrial production. All are located within a 15 kilometre radius of Vientiane, manufacturing such products as corrugated iron, agricultural tools, industrial gases (oxygen), plastic items, detergents, insecticides, beer and softdrinks, matches, cigarettes and ceramics. Other factories, a number of them still in private hands, retread tyres, produce handicrafts, weave cloth and make furniture. Factories processing agricultural crops, including rice mills, fall under control of the Ministry of Agriculture. Productivity is low in all industrial areas, with the exception of electricity production, and distribution and marketing are inefficient. The industrial services sector is almost non-existent.

The remaining 20 per cent of industrial production is divided approximately evenly between smaller workshops in Vientiane (most still in private hands) and small-scale manufacturing and handicraft enterprises located in the provinces, mostly in Luang Prabang, Savannakhet and Pakse, catering for local demands. In 1985, according to government figures, no fewer than 4,670 private businesses were registered in Vientiane alone, though a high percentage of these were commercial rather than industrial enterprises. Licence fees and taxes brought the government 10 million kip in annual revenue (FEER Yearbook, 1986).

Increased industrial investment in the provinces was provided for under the first five-year plan, but finance for the largest enterprise outside Vientiane, the cement factory that was to have been built at Vang Vieng, was not forthcoming. Nor does the outlook for greatly increased industrial production during the second five-year plan appear much brighter. No systematic integration exists between the basic agricultural and the industrial sectors; nor are there adequate support services especially in the provinces. Poor internal communications result in fragmentation of the market and difficulties in distribution. In any case, demand remains low due to low levels of purchasing power possessed by most of the population. But probably the major constraints against increased production at present are the lack of trained personnel at all levels, both technical and managerial, and the cost and uncertainty of supply of raw materials.

Only electricity has been an area of industrial growth, with output tripling between 1977 and 1985. Installed capacity in 1985 amounted to 167.5 megawatts (MW), of which 150 MW were produced by five generators at the Nam Ngum dam site, 3.5 MW were produced by six small hydroelectric stations, and the remaining 14 MW were produced by diesel generators serving regional urban centres. Of this amount, only about 27 MW are consumed locally, the remaining 140 MW being exported to Thailand. (The Lao towns of Thakhek and Savannakhet are in turn supplied by the Thai network, since neither the southern nor the northern provinces are yet connected to the Nam Ngum power grid.) In 1984, electricity valued at US$24.9 million accounted for about 85 per cent of total exports to the convertible currency area. With the installation of the fifth generator at the Nam Ngum hydroelectric station, both these figures were due to rise significantly in 1985. Potential for greatly increased hydroelectricity production still exists in Laos. In conjunction with the UN-sponsored Mekong Committee, the government plans to develop a number of regional small-scale projects during the course of the second five-year plan, together with extension of the rural electrification programme.

Mining is another economic sector which has considerable potential for future development. The LPDR possesses important mineral resources as yet virtually unexploited. Only tin and gypsum were produced during the course of the first five-year plan, the former with Soviet assistance, the latter with Vietnamese help. Tin is extracted at former French mines at Phontiou in Khammouane province, with production running as high as 1,500 tonnes a year by 1985—a return to pre-1975 levels. Gypsum is mined in Savannakhet province (more than 40,000 tonnes a year). Most is exported to Vietnam. In Vientiane province, north of the capital, salt is also extracted by boiling underground water. Some 4,000 tonnes a year are produced, with production planned to more than double during the second five-year plan.

Other major mineral resources include high-grade iron ore deposits (60–70 per cent iron content) located in Xieng Khouang province. These have been the target of preliminary Soviet studies which have established reserves at as much as one billion tonnes. Gold, copper, lead and manganese have all been discovered in small quantities. Coal has been discovered in both northern and southern Laos. It is hoped to exploit potassium deposits in Vientiane province, while plans are underway to make limestone deposits in the Vang Vieng area north of Vientiane city the basis for a major cement works to be financed by the Soviet Union as part of the second five-year plan. In the short term, therefore, mineral production will continue to be negligible in terms of both quantities extracted and value; however, in the longer term minerals offer an important source of potential export income for the Lao government.

Transport and Communications

Transport and communications are 'considered as the leading edge of development' by the Lao government (*LDC Report*, 1983). Transportation of goods and people by road increased significantly during the course of the first five-year plan, but not by the projected figure of 80 to 85 per cent. Poor transportation continues to retard Lao economic development, especially the distribution of manufactured goods and other merchandize, and the movement of agricultural surpluses to deficit areas. Development of forestry and mineral resources also depends critically on improvements to the road network.

The government claims to have more than doubled the total road network since 1975. Much progress has been made in road construction, but even so by 1985 the programme was running behind schedule. Priority was given during the first five-year plan to upgrading routes 9 and 13, the former running from Savannakhet to the Vietnamese port of Danang, the latter running the north–south length of the country from Luang Prabang to the Kampuchean border. Together these form the backbone of the national road network. Route 13 is asphalted for only short sections of its 1,294 kilometre length. It crosses more than 200 bridges, including major spans constructed with Soviet assistance over the Nam Ngum and Nam Cading rivers. Route 9 has also required construction of a large number of bridges and culverts. Work due for completion by the end of 1986 was behind schedule at the end of the first five-year plan. Three other priority roads (routes 6, 7 and 14) link Laos with Vietnam, as do routes 8 and 12, both in a very poor state of repair. Fully 2,344 kilometres have been designated part of the Asian Highway network (as routes A3, A11, A12 and A14), but the condition of these sections still leaves much to be desired. The northern, most mountainous parts of the country are particularly poorly served by roads, especially the provinces of Luang Prabang, Oudomsay and Sayaboury. Luang Namtha, Bokeo and Phong Saly are served by narrow, all-weather roads constructed by Chinese engineers between 1966 and 1978, but these are poorly connected with the rest of the national road network.

Maintenance of the road network is a constant problem in a monsoon environment. The LPDR lacks equipment and materials for repair, not to mention a desperate shortage of civil engineers, technicians, equipment operators and mechanics. The poor state of most roads reduces average traffic speed to around 30–40 kilometres per hour on most sections. Transportation is also affected by a shortage of trucks in good mechanical condition and shortages of fuel and spare parts. In 1981, 61 per cent of all road transport in both the public and private sectors was inadequately maintained: only 212 vehicles in the entire country were judged to be in good mechanical condition (*LDC Report*, 1983).

Laos is better served by river transportation. The Mekong River flows through Lao territory or forms the frontier with Thailand for 1,805 kilometres, 1,148 kilometres of which are navigable without interruption most of the year (from Ban Houei Sai in the north to the river port of Keng Kabao upstream from Savannakhet in the south). Of a further 2,400 kilometres of tributaries, approximately 875 kilometres are navigable by shallow-draft river boats for six or more months of the year.

Much of the potential for river transportation is under-utilized, however, in part because the Mekong has traditionally served more as a means of connecting Laos with Thailand than for north–south trade, and in part because of the low capacity and poor condition of the Lao river fleet (fifty-seven vessels of not much more than 3,000 tonnes total capacity in 1983; a 220-passenger vessel began service in 1985). The importance of river transport will increase steadily, however, with the effective utilization of Keng Kabao as a transit port for goods trucked in from the Vietnamese port of Danang and then transported by river to Thakhek, Paksane, Vientiane and Luang Prabang. Projections are that the volume of traffic will more than triple between 1980 and the year 2000.

The only railway ever built in Laos was a five-kilometre stretch constructed by the French administration in the late nineteenth century, bypassing Khone rapids in the far south. Plans drawn up as early as 1889 to link Laos to the Vietnamese rail network never materialized. Recent feasibility studies indicate that costs of constructing a line from the coast of Vietnam to the Mekong would be high—too high to attract the necessary foreign finance for such a project. Laos is therefore likely to remain without a rail system for the foreseeable future.

Poor land communications increase the importance of air transportation in the LPDR. In fact the state company Lao Aviation provides the only means of communication with a number of remote provincial capitals—providing weather conditions permit aircraft to fly. Apart from a few principal routes, however, flights are irregular and it is not uncommon for officials to have to wait weeks for a flight in or out of some centres. Apart from traffic on the two international routes to Bangkok and Hanoi, both the number of passengers and tonnage of freight was still significantly lower in 1985 than it had been under the previous regime. In 1983, Lao Aviation possessed fourteen Antonov aircraft (An-2s, An-24s, and AN-26s) and three helicopters which, given maintenance problems, were barely enough to sustain services. In fact every aspect of aviation in Laos, from the training of pilots and mechanics to the upgrading of facilities and runways, was in need of improvement during the second five-year plan.

Despite a decade of attempts to increase the transportation of goods via Vietnam, by 1985 Laos still remained largely dependent on the transit of imports and exports through Thailand. No adequate road system linked Vientiane, the largest population centre and only industrial area in the LPDR, with the nearest Vietnamese port of Vinh. The distance from Vientiane to Danang, via Savannakhet by road or via Keng Kabao by river then road (necessitating time consuming and costly transhipment) 'amounts to 982 kilometres, as compared with the 610 kilometres from Vientiane to Bangkok (with the added advantage of the Nongkhai–Bangkok rail link). The economic reality, therefore, was that, despite political difficulties, transportation via Thailand remained vital to the Lao economy, and would for years to come.

Telecommunications and postal services could both be described as rudimentary in the LPDR, especially outside Vientiane. While international communications with Moscow (by satellite), Hanoi and Hong Kong (high frequency) and Bangkok (microwave) are just adequate, the government has described the state of internal communications as 'critical'. In 1985 there existed fewer than 5,000 telephones in the entire country, more than 80 per cent of them in Vientiane and the remainder in only four out of sixteen provincial capitals. This means that Laos has 1.2 telephones per thousand inhabitants, or less than one tenth the average number for developing countries in Asia. Most of the equipment is obsolete and dilapidated, and frequently breaks down.

Postal services function marginally better than does the telephone system, thanks in part to administrative reorganization during the first five-year plan. There is, however, a continuing need for better training of postal personnel and for equipment and buildings in outlying areas. The volume of mail handled has shown a steady increase since the early years of the regime, but the suspicion remains widespread that mail is often censored or tampered with in some way, and many people are reluctant to use the postal services for important or sensitive communications or financial transactions.

Transport and internal communications are a priority for the second five-year plan. The present poor state of inter-provincial communications only reinforces regional fragmentation and reduces national economic integration. This only encourages the provincialism that has plagued the country ever since the break-up of the unitary Lao state at the end of the seventeenth century. A degree of provincial autonomy may be a necessity given present conditions, but must not be allowed to develop too far. Improved communications and transportation are clearly essential to the construction of a strong and unified Lao state.

Trade and Commerce

Paucity of statistics and widespread undercover trading make it impossible to quantify the level of internal trade in Laos. According to government figures, however, the 'state trade network' increased its dealings by 110 per cent over the course of the first five-year plan, while 'local people's collective activity' increased 97 per cent for the same period, and the value of commercial goods distributed rose by 146 per cent (FBIS, 17 July 1985). Much of this trade takes place within provinces, as the second figure indicates. Inter-provincial trade is not high, due to the poor state of roads, lack of adequate means of transportation and recurrent security problems. These also affect the level of external trade, along with high costs due to the LPDR's geographic situation and the chronic adverse balance between imports and exports. The deficit in the commercial balance fell in 1984, but only as a result of decreases in both imports and exports. Total exports were reported to be up 81 per cent for the period 1980–5.

In theory the State Trading Company has a monopoly on all foreign trade. In practice, however, not only do provincial administrations conduct trade with neighbouring states, but certain state enterprises and the army too have the right to enter into direct negotiations with foreign companies and/or states. In addition, apart from certain designated exports and imports, private individuals and companies may be granted a licence to engage in foreign trade. Finally, a certain amount of smuggling occurs across the Mekong with Thailand, principally of exports such as benzoin, sticklack and timber, in return for consumer imports. Official figures for foreign trade must be taken therefore as approximate only.

Government monopolies apply in principle to the following products: unsawn logs, sawn timber, wooden furniture, minerals, rice, coffee and forest products such as sticklack and benzoin. Import monopolies cover machinery, vehicles, cement, reinforcing iron, petroleum products, rice, salt and sugar. Joint state–private import–export companies can, however, obtain licences to deal in some of these products. Licences must also be obtained to trade in other products, such as food supplies, textiles, shoes, confectionery, stationery, medicines, tools, spare parts, construction materials and equipment, electrical implements, household appliances and luxury items.

Apart from electricity, exports to the 'convertible zone' remained stagnant throughout the period of the first five-year plan. By contrast, exports to the 'non-convertible zone', primarily to Vietnam and the Soviet Union, increased by 140 per cent between 1981 and 1983, before falling back in 1984. Total exports declined by 15.7 per cent in 1984 compared to the previous year, due to reductions of 38.5 per cent to the non-convertible zone and of 5.4 per cent to the convertible zone. The difference between these figures reflects the fact not only that exports to the Soviet bloc had previously rapidly increased relative to exports to the convertible zone, but also that the contractual export of electricity to Thailand, which accounts for as much as two-thirds of total Lao exports, can under normal circumstances be neither redirected nor reduced.

Imports have shown similar trends, with increases in imports from the non-convertible zone increasing far more rapidly than those from the convertible zone for the period 1981–3. However, the decline registered in 1984 affected imports from both zones approximately equally. Imports in the form of aid also fell between 1981 and 1984. Petroleum products, machinery and raw materials constitute the major import items from the convertible zone. No breakdown of imports from the Soviet bloc is available, though machinery, vehicles and consumer goods constitute a substantial proportion of the total amount.

Living Standards

Given the paucity of accurate statistics, it is extremely difficult to quantify the standard of living in Laos. Estimates of per capita national income range between US$98 and US$184 per annum (cf. *LDCReport*, 1983 and *IMFReport*, 1985). These figures place the LPDR among the poorest countries in the world. By far the majority of the 85 per cent of the population who live in the rural areas are self-sufficient, subsistence level peasant farmers who produce just sufficient to meet their own needs. Some grow cash crops such as coffee or opium, but only those villages in the vicinity of larger towns can be said to be integrated into the market economy.

The economic reforms ushered in by the Seventh Resolution at the end of 1979 encouraged peasants to sell their excess produce in open markets where prices were set by supply and demand. As a result, farmers especially in the vicinity of Vientiane were soon making incomes well in excess of those of most industrial workers or civil servants. By 1985, this disparity had become particularly marked. In the middle of the year best quality white rice was selling for as much as 80 kip per kilogramme, pork for 300 kip per kilogramme, and beef for 400 kip per kilogramme. (The official exchange rate was then 108 kip to US$1; while the free market was three times as much.) Overall, food prices had increased by up to 50 per cent over the previous six months. The prices of imported consumer items were even more expensive—40 kip for a ballpoint pen, 200 for a tin of sweetened condensed milk, 500 for an electric torch. Blackmarket petrol sold for 60 kip per litre, five times the official price for rationed petrol.

At the same time cash payments to civil servants ranged from 150 to 600 kip per month. In addition, each person had the right to purchase with coupons basic items at state shops at heavily subsidized prices: 20 kilogrammes of rice a month, plus 10 for each child, at 3 kip per kilogramme, 1 kilogramme of sugar for 8 kip, meat when available at variable but comparably low prices, and so on. Each family as a matter of course grew their own vegetables and most raised poultry and pigs. Even so, it was literally impossible for a family to survive on an official salary unless one member at least was producing and selling on the free market. A husband and wife could both work for the government only with support from other family members, parents or working children, or by drawing on financial assistance from relatives abroad. In many cases people have left government employment altogether, or taken time off to moonlight on another job, or indulged in petty corruption, simply to make ends meet.

In 1985, the government introduced a modified salary structure. Salaries were increased considerably and a variety of levels included to provide incentives through opportunities for promotion. In 1985 government employees were given two kinds of coupon, one for food, the other for consumer goods such as cloth, soap, toothpaste, shoes, petrol, etc. (5 litres per month for a motorcycle, 20 litres for a car). These coupons could only be spent in government shops, where supplies were erratic, to say the least, but unspent coupons could be saved to purchase consumer durables such as fans and even refrigerators. However, employees still continued to receive only the same small amounts of cash (up to 600 kip per month). By contrast, a peasant with a regular stall at the Vientiane market could make ten to twenty times as much—though a peasant family had to purchase all their needs at free market rates. Those entrepreneurs who had set up small industries or commercial enterprises, either individually or in state-private partnership were even better off.

Ten years after a socialist regime was installed in Laos, therefore, great disparities of income and living standards remain. Urban living standards have undoubtedly fallen on average since the period before 1975 when relatively massive American aid was readily available. But after the initial collapse from 1976 to 1979, urban living standards slowly improved for most sectors of the community, except perhaps government servants. In the countryside little has changed. Material standards of living remain extremely low. Improvements in the quality of life consist almost entirely in improved access to education (of a low standard), and limited health care. Otherwise government services have hardly improved over what was provided by the previous regime—and in some cases have deteriorated due to lack of trained personnel. In more remote areas the availability of both goods and services remains what it always was, virtually nil. Overall there is widespread disappointment at the failure of the regime to improve standards of living. Comparisons with even the impoverished northeast of Thailand show up the LPDR in a poor light. Only in comparison with the Vietnamese are most Lao well off—and that is a comparison made relatively frequently in Laos, at times in grateful recognition of Vietnamese aid, but often with an air of smug superiority.

Industrial Relations

There is very little that can be said about industrial relations in Laos. The industrial sector is minute, employing, as noted, only 0.8 per cent of the workforce. Half these workers are represented by the Federation of Lao Trade Unions which theoretically negotiates wage levels with the government (NL, November and December, 1985). During the years 1976-9, despite erosion of wages by massive inflation, anyone was lucky to have a job at all and no industrial unrest was reported. Since 1980, as inflation continued and the free market became established, dissatisfaction increasingly came to be expressed over wage levels, both in the civil service and in state industries. Complaints have been dealt with within the Party, however, rather than being given alternative expression. In the case of civil servants, salary increases have not kept pace with inflation partly because the government has had no funds available and partly because it wanted to encourage people to resign from government service in order to cut costs, particularly expensive food and consumer subsidies. In order to maintain manning levels in industry, however, the government gave state enterprises the right to set salary levels in relation to performance, subject to ministerial approval. As a result, the disposable cash income of workers in state enterprises averaged about three times that of civil servants by 1985. This together with food and consumer subsidies for workers and their children provided an income sufficient to prevent widespread industrial discontent.

5 The Regime's Domestic Policies

Ethnic Affairs

Policies towards ethnic minorities in Laos have a potential importance far greater than in most Marxist states because of the ethnic composition of the population and the strategic location of minority groups along the country's borders. This is particularly so as those minority groups which played a significant part in bringing about the Lao revolution developed certain expectations as to the benefits their support would bring. That many of the promised benefits have not been realized during the initial decade of communist government is a cause for official concern, since it has serious implications both for economic development and for the internal security of the state.

Throughout the Thirty-Year Struggle, the Lao communist movement drew on the support of ethnic minority groups, both in the northeast of the country and in the south on the Bolovens plateau and along the Ho Chi Minh trail. In return the minorities were promised not their own autonomous areas as in China or North Vietnam, but integration into the greater Lao polity and the opportunity to play a role in the political life of the country. This was clearly stated in the Action Programme of the Lao Patriotic Front drawn up in October 1956 and was repeated in subsequent documents. Thus the 1968 twelve-point programme of the Front promised:

To actively assist all nationalities, especially the minorities, in developing [their] economy, in study, in improving their material and cultural life, in preserving their own customs and traditional culture, and in combating dangerous diseases detrimental to the national progeny so as to help increase the country's population. To actively form a contingent of cadres and intellectuals of minority origins, thus enabling the national minorities to build a more and more advanced life and join in the management of the country. [Zasloff, 1973, p. 124.]

A significant number of Lao Theung, Lao Soung and hill Tai representatives served on the Central Committee of the Front. As much as 60 per cent of the membership of the LPRP before 1975 is reported to have come from minority groups. At all times minority recruits made up the bulk of the Pathet Lao armed forces. Areas inhabited by minority tribes suffered worst from the American bombing of Laos.

Clearly the Lao revolutionary elite which came to power in 1975 owed much to the support they had received from minority groups. Yet it should be noted that both the Central Committee of the LPRP and the government of the LPDR were overwhelmingly ethnic Lao in composition. Only in the Supreme People's Assembly, where the four vice-presidents were Lao Theung (Sithon Kommadan, since deceased), Lao Soung (Faydang Lobliayao), hill Tai (Sisomphone Lovansay, the only minority representative in the Politburo of the LPRP) and lowland Lao (Khamsouk Keola), were the minorities somewhat more proportionally represented. The subsequent expansion of the LPRP Central Committee and reorganization of the government following the Third Congress of the Party in April 1982 slightly improved minority representation: eleven of the fifty-four members and alternate members of the LPRP Central Committee were from ethnic minorities. The government, however, remained firmly in the hands of ethnic Lao.

At the provincial and local levels of both party and government minority representation is more pronounced. In all the far northern provinces, including Luang Prabang and Houa Phan, members of ethnic minorities hold one or both of the two most powerful positions, as Secretary of the Party Committee or as Chairman of the People's Administrative Committee. The same is true of the southern provinces of Saravane, Sekong and Attopeu, covering the area of the Bolovens plateau. At the local level in minority areas, local Party branches and the local administration are often entirely in the hands of minority cadres. The stated policy of effectively integrating minority groups into the political life of the country can thus be said to be well underway, at least where local administration is concerned. No previous Lao government ever made as serious an attempt to include the ethnic minorities in the national political culture. Ethnic Lao monopoly of political power at the national level remains intact, but at least a start has been made. As more minority cadres receive higher education, their involvement in politics at the national level can be expected to increase.

The importance of 'all-people unity and unity among the people of all nationalities' as 'fundamental factors deciding the complete victory of the national-democratic revolution' that brought the LPRP to power was freely admitted by Kaysone in his speech to the Supreme People's Assembly introducing the nation's first five-year plan. Its continuing significance was said to be 'of paramount importance in defending and building our socialist fatherland', and a key factor in the successful implementation of the five-year plan. To this end, Kaysone told the SPA,

We must strive to educate and train the people of all nationalities to clearly understand the great strategic significance of the strengthening of all-people unity and unity among the people of all nationalities. We must expose the schemes of the big-nation expansionists and hegemonists [China] and the imperialists [the United States] to divide and pit the various Lao nationalities against each other. We must increase our efforts to educate and train ourselves, examine the implementation of the Party's policy on nationality solidarity and adopt a strict attitude towards activities which harm unity among nationalities. We must positively introduce culture, education, science and public health into nationalities areas in order to free our nationality brothers from backward customs and traditions and supernatural beliefs so they can build a new, modern life. [FBIS, 13 February 1981.]

This statement sums up both the security concerns of the government with reference to the ethnic minority population, and the policies to be adopted towards them. These policies were to be given practical effect both by striving to overcome traditional Lao attitudes of condescension and superiority and by example through creation of

economic, political, cultural and social models in nationality areas so that they can be imitated by our fraternal ethnic minority people in building the villages and in enabling the mountainous areas to gradually catch up with the plains areas, thereby creating conditions for achieving true equality among our fraternal nationalities. We must step up the Front [LFNC] work in various localities in order to use this Front to truly unite the people of various strata and nationalities to carry out the programme of action of the Lao Front for National Construction aimed at mobilizing the people of all nationalities and strata to effectively implement the Party and State line, policies and plans. [FBIS, 13 February 1981.]

The need for an effective minorities policy has consistently been tied to the strategic task of national defence in Laos. Since the break with China following the Sino–Vietnamese border war, the Lao have consistently charged Beijing with fomenting discontent among minority groups in the north of the country—in particular among Lao Soung tribes such as the Hmong and Yao also inhabiting southern China. Much of the Lao concern stems from the fact that the border is so porous. Besides, any attempt to close the border would cause popular dissatisfaction. The traditional cross–border trade by Chinese merchants and minority tribes straddling the frontier provides most of the consumer goods available in the area, goods that the government in Vientiane does not have the resources to replace.

The government has attempted to mobilize the mountain minorities in the cause of national security, especially in the north of the country, by a number of means. Propaganda teams have been sent to minority villages in an attempt to raise the political consciousness of the inhabitants, explain government policies, and warn against the machinations of the 'enemy'. Networks of informants have been established to report on the movements of strangers in an area. The government appears to have had some success in mobilizing and politicizing the northern minorities thus containing Chinese influence in the area, a probable factor in inducing the Chinese to adopt a more constructive policy towards Laos.

The government has also appealed to the minority tribes by respecting their cultural, particularly religious, traditions, by providing economic assistance and advice, and through social welfare measures, notably in the fields of education and health. Increased official tolerance for tribal customs and beliefs came about largely as a result of tribal opposition to earlier policies. From 1976 to 1979, attempts were made to suppress those traditional customs and practices which were considered 'backward' and economically wasteful. These included in particular the slaughter of buffaloes at animistic feasts at a time when there existed a shortage of draught animals, and traditional slash-and-burn agriculture which destroyed valuable forests. Readers of the Party journal *Sieng Pasason* were called upon to help eradicate the 'obscure superstitions' and 'individualistic tribal ways of life' of tribal minorities (KPL/BQ, 29 December 1978). Wherever possible, agriculture was to be collectivized by abandoning slash-and-burn techniques and constructing paddies for wet rice cultivation—a programme which entailed either extensive terracing, or resettlement at lower altitudes along river valleys, neither of which appealed to the mountain minorities. Opposition to these policies increased as a result of the coercive means used by over-zealous cadres during the accelerated cooperativization drive of 1978 and early 1979. This took various forms, from sullen non-cooperation to migration to Thailand or China. Tribespeople objected to working in collective labour gangs, disliked living at lower altitudes where they were susceptible to malaria and other diseases and resented close government supervision and control.

Discontent among tribal minorities was one of the factors which led the government to change tactics and ushered in the liberalization of 1980. Criticism of 'superstitious' minority beliefs was muted; dancing, handicrafts and other aspects of traditional culture were encouraged; and persuasion rather than coercion was used to convince minorities to resettle or abandon destructive agricultural practices. As a result, during the period of the first five-year plan opposition to government policies among minority groups subsided, but the pace of change in the highlands slowed. Emphasis was placed on increasing the extremely low productivity of upland agriculture rather than on collectivization and resettlement, and on improving the diet and living conditions of minority groups. An attempt was made to provide necessary consumer goods such as agricultural tools, shoes and clothing, salt and medicines through state trading outlets (even when such goods could only be obtained from southern China). This does not mean that in the long term the government's aim to settle the highland minorities in permanent villages and curtail slash-and-burn has been abandoned. Protection of the country's forests remains a priority. So too does the need to improve the standard of living of the ethnic minorities and to integrate them into the national economy.

In two fields the government has made a special effort to assist the minority groups: in education and in public health. Despite problems of transport and communication, and the remoteness of many mountain villages, primary schools have been set up in most villages and an effort made to reduce adult illiteracy. But all education for children of ethnic minorities is in Lao, a language many minority people do not even speak, let alone read. No provision is made for literacy in a minority language, even where, as in the case of some hill Tai, traditional scripts already exist, or where, for some Lao Theung their languages have been transcribed using Roman script. This educational policy is in line with the slogan: 'Take the Lao language as the common language; use Lao writing as the official writing', and is one of the means by which the government is pursuing its goal of national unity and the 'unity of all nationalities' in the multi-ethnic Lao state. The danger is, of course, that such a policy will be seen as 'Laoization' and resented by minority groups determined to preserve their own linguistic and cultural identity. Education in Lao at the primary level is essential, however, if members of ethnic minorities are to take advantage of the opportunity for higher education. Special provision is made at some regional centres for minority children from remote villages to attend as boarders at middle and high schools with all costs paid by the state. The best students then progress to technical secondary schools (particularly in agriculture), to teachers' training college or even to study abroad.

A genuine attempt has been made to improve public health at the village level. Health teams teach methods of simple hygiene. Village nurses are trained to dispense elementary health care often using traditional herbal remedies. All services are nominally free, though a charge may be made for Western medicines—if and when they are available. As a result of these measures, the government claims to have brought about a net improvement, difficult to quantify, in infant mortality rates and life expectancy for minority groups.

Opportunities for education and improved health care have been welcomed by the ethnic minorities. Education in particular is seen by minority groups as the key to economic progress and political influence. By the government it is seen as the principal means of generating a sense of national unity and identity, both through common use of the Lao language to teach a single national history and through contacts at all levels between different ethnic groups as a means of breaking down ethnic prejudice. All children are taught that Laos is a multi-ethnic state and learn something about the customs and culture of other ethnic groups. All learn of the role minority groups played both in opposing French colonization (Kommadan of the Lao Theung and Ba-Chay of the Lao Soung have become revolutionary heroes), and during the Thirty-Year Struggle to bring about a communist regime. A persistent problem that is more difficult to overcome is ethnic prejudice. Ethnic Lao traditionally called all Lao Theung *kha*, meaning slaves, and often made pejorative remarks about Lao Soung and Lao Theung alike. These attitudes have been consistently criticized by communist authorities, but persist despite official condemnation. Minority students sent to study in Vientiane, and other Lao Loum dominated areas, encounter ethnic prejudice and suffer accordingly. Such prejudice is likely to remain one of the last barriers to be overcome in creating a unified Lao state (cf. Chagnon & Rumpf, in Stuart-Fox, 1982a).

The present policies of the LPDR towards the country's ethnic minorities represent the first concerted attempt made by any Lao government to create a national consensus and identity. The most sensitive test of the success of these policies will almost certainly be how readily Lao Soung tribes accept the regime, particularly the Hmong. Hmong resistance to the new regime was not destroyed until 1979, leaving a legacy of ill-feeling and suspicion. The government then called for reconciliation. On the occasion of the Hmong New Year in November 1979, Souphanouvong addressed an open letter to all 'Hmong patriots' calling for ethnic solidarity under the leadershp of the LPRP in order to defeat 'reactionaries, imperialists, reactionary exiles, and the traitors of Vang Pao'. The following day, the veteran Hmong leader Faydang Lobliayao appealed to young Hmong not to leave their families to become mere mercenaries for anti-government resistance groups (KPL/BQ, 12 and 13 November 1979). Displaced Hmong have been resettled in Xieng Khouang and south of the Plain of Jars, and encouraged to take up wet rice cultivation. Those who returned to their mountain villages have continued growing opium which is purchased by the state. Problems evidently persisted, however, for in 1981 the Politburo decided to examine the whole question of how best government personnel could work with the Hmong. A conference in June discussed a series of recommendations which applied to all minority groups. Since then, by all accounts, relations between the Hmong and the government have improved. The presence of some 40,000 strongly anti-communist Hmong refugees just across the border from Sayaboury province in northern Thailand remains, however, a constant source of concern to the regime.

Defence and Internal Security

Militarily Laos is the weakest state in mainland Southeast Asia. Recent estimates place the size of its regular armed forces at 53,700, of which 50,000 are in the army, 1,700 in the navy, and 2,000 in the air force (*The Military Balance*, 1985). The army comprises four infantry and one artillery division, plus seven independent infantry, one engineering and two construction regiments, and five independent artillery and nine anti-aircraft battalions. The army is equipped with a variety of American and Soviet weapons from tanks (T-34, T-54) and armoured personnel carriers (BTR-60) to howitzers, mortars and recoiless rifles. Laos also possesses SA-7 surface to air missiles. The navy is poorly equipped with twenty river patrol craft; while the air force has one squadron of twenty MIG-21s and a squadron of assorted transport aircraft. Conscription into the armed forces is for a minimum period of eighteen months. The country is divided into four military regions within each of which regional forces and local village self-defence militia are recruited and operate.

Lao policies on internal security and national defence are related to perceptions of the strategic environment in which the country finds itself and of the limited options open to the regime. The LPDR's geopolitical vulnerability poses a number of specific problems for the defence of the country's borders and maintenance of its internal security. This is because for each of the LPDR's three most powerful neighbours—China, Thailand and Vietnam—control over Laos has potentially important strategic advantages. For China, it would mean the extension of Beijing's influence into mainland Southeast Asia in such a way as effectively to limit Vietnamese ambitions; for Thailand, it would provide a useful buffer against both China and Vietnam; and for Vietnam, the country which has succeeded in establishing a dominant influence over the LPDR, it provides protection for Vietnam's long and vulnerable western border, as well as a means of extending Vietnamese influence further afield (cf. Stuart-Fox, in Stuart-Fox, 1982a, on which much of this section is based).

Other reasons for Laos' vulnerability include the size, composition and location of its population and the undeveloped nature of its economy. The population of Laos is too small to deter any aggressor. Also, lack of ethnic homogeneity makes it always possible to exploit ethnic prejudice and antagonisms, especially since many minority groups extend across the LPDR's frontiers into neighbouring states. Poor communications and limited means of transportation are another reason for the LPDR's vulnerability, for they make it difficult for defence forces to respond to guerrilla activity— especially when this is mounted from bases in neighbouring states. The LPA's inability to threaten guerrilla bases beyond the country's frontiers leaves support for such activity as a perennial option by which neighbouring states may interfere in Lao internal affairs.

By the end of 1975, with the continued outflow of refugees, the main outlines of the combined defence and security problem which would face the new regime were already apparent. The refugee camps of Thailand held thousands of bitter Lao and Hmong exiles, a ready source of recruits for either political agitation or military action against the new regime. The threat this presented to the nation's internal security was greatly increased, in the estimation of the Pathet Lao, by Thai collusion with rightist exiles and hostility towards the new regime.

Lao defence and security forces were reorganized early in 1976 both to meet the double threat posed by Thai 'reactionaries' and Lao 'counter-revolutionaries' and to deal with problems that had arisen from the use of PL troops to police the urban civilian population during the latter half of 1975. Pathet Lao guerrillas trained for jungle warfare were unprepared to take up police duties. Most were young, uneducated Lao Theung, who were jealous of the wealth and living standards of the lowland Lao and resentful of their assumed racial and cultural superiority. Incidents of looting and disputes between guerrillas and townspeople were not infrequent. The government responded by setting up an independently trained and organized police force under the control of the Ministry of the Interior and municipal authorities and by reorganizing the army, instituting tighter discipline and stepping up political indoctrination. Soviet and Vietnamese instructors were brought in to train Pathet Lao recruits at the American-built Police Academy outside Vientiane.

Reorganization of the armed forces was carried out with Vietnamese assistance, in accordance with five major principles: unification of organization; standardization of manpower; systematic implementation of policy decisions; standardization of political education and training; and standardization of logistics. However, the basic structure of the Pathet Lao armed forces that had proved so effective during the Thirty-Year Struggle remained unchanged. This consisted of three levels of organization derived from the wartime structure of main force units and regional and local guerrillas. The Lao Peoples's Army was similarly organized with regular forces under a central military command, regionally recruited units and a local village militia made up of part-time self-defence volunteers.

The first test for the LPA came from rightist guerrillas operating from Thailand and from the Hmong resistance in the Phou Bia region which gained ground during 1976 and became a serious threat in 1977. Plans for a coordinated anti-government uprising were reportedly discovered in December 1976. In March 1977, rightist insurgents captured and briefly held the village of Muong Nam, some fifty kilometres south of Luang Prabang. The government, fearing a concerted move by rightist guerrillas with Thai support in conjunction with Hmong rebels already operating in Laos, took no chances. Vietnamese military assistance was requested to put an end to the Hmong insurgency. Thus little more than three years after they had been partially withdrawn as part of the 1973 cease-fire agreement, Vietnamese troops returned in force to Laos. The LPA had proved incapable of assuring the defence and security of the state.

Official concern over the ineffectiveness of the armed forces in countering rightist insurgency, especially at the village level, was evident in criticism expressed in *Sieng Pasason* in mid-1977. Local militia forces, the journal noted, often failed to understand their task of suppressing counter-revolutionaries.

They do not yet know how to distinguish friends from foes. In addition, some local guerrillas have even been bought off by the enemy, who has carried out deceitful schemes ... others have violated the rights and interests of the people. More seriously still, they have even touched [*sic*] the masses' rights of collective mastership, thereby creating an opportunity for the enemy to carry out deceitful propaganda, distorting facts with a view to impairing the prestige of our party and state. [FBIS, 17 August 1977.]

These were serious charges. At the local level, in villages along the Mekong, discipline tended to be poor and morale low. Extortion, corruption and petty oppression by often newly recruited village militias were widespread enough to be exploited effectively by anti-government propaganda.

Also in 1977 another factor began to play a role in the defence considerations of Lao military leaders and their Vietnamese advisers—deteriorating relations betwen Vietnam and Kampuchea. Lao-Vietnamese relations, by contrast, were formalized through a twenty-five year Treaty of Friendship and Cooperation, which included provisions for the stationing of Vietnamese troops in Laos. The Kampuchean–Lao border was effectively closed when the Kampucheans cut route 13. Throughout 1978 a number of incidents occurred along the frontier in which Khmer Rouge troops violated Lao territory, often in pursuit of refugees. The Lao did not publicize these violations at the time, but indignantly resurrected them after the Khmer Rouge regime was overthrown.

Early in 1978, the decision was taken to use the army as 'a dictatorial force of the proletariat class, a sharp tool of the party and a core force of revolution' (FBIS, 25 January 1978). Thus in addition to its military role, the army was charged with a political role in pursuing the twin tasks of socialist construction and national defence. In order to perform their new duties, the regular armed forces were increased under close Vietnamese supervision, while the efficiency and training of regional and local forces were improved. The local and regional command structure of the armed forces was strengthened so that 'regional military work' could serve as 'a basis for the success of socialist construction' by turning provinces and districts into 'strong combat units' (FBIS, 1 May 1978).

The Vietnamese invasion of Kampuchea in December 1978, and the subsequent Sino–Vietnamese border war, introduced a new strategic dimension into Lao defence planning. The carefully nurtured Lao policy of friendship towards all her neighbours—symbolized by the signing of agreements with Thailand in January and April 1979—was left in tatters as the Lao leadership, after some slight hesitation, backed Vietnam against China. The Chinese response was measured, but left no doubt that Beijing viewed the Vietnamese presence in Laos in much the same light as they viewed Vietnam's occupation of Kampuchea. Soon the Lao were accusing Beijing of training Lao reactionaries in southern China and of conducting a campaign of anti-government propaganda.

By the end of 1979, therefore, the outlines of the defence and security problems that would face Laos in the coming decade were already clear. With the change of government in Bangkok that brought General Prem Tinsulanond to power, Chinese-Thai collusion became more overt, and more overtly anti-Vietnamese. Chinese and Thai support for Lao anti-government insurgents was stepped up, with the covert backing of the United States. A new coordinated Thai-based resistance movement, the National United Front for the Liberation of the Lao People, was established, which was soon reported to be in liaison with the Khmer Rouge and to be receiving Chinese weapons. The LPDR thus faced a new and ominous threat to its internal security.

Just how seriously the regime viewed the situation was evident from Kaysone's speech to the annual joint sitting of the Supreme People's Assembly and Council of Government on 26 December 1979 when he announced that Laos was engaged in a new war, 'a war of national defence' against those who sought to overthrow the regime.

We are facing dangerous enemies who maintain a close alliance with various imperialist forces and other reactionaries as well as with the exiled reactionaries and reactionary remnants in the country. The enemies have colluded in implementing many subtle, brutal schemes and tricks in the economic, political, military, cultural, ideological and other fields. They have combined schemes of spying . . . and psychological warfare with schemes aimed at disrupting the unity of the country and at sowing division between Laos, Vietnam and Kampuchea. They have misled and bought off Lao cadres into serving them while infiltrating . . . our offices, organizations, enterprises and mass organizations with a view to sabotaging, destroying and controlling the economy, creating disturbances, inciting uprisings, carrying out assassinations, and subversive activities in the country, putting pressure on and weakening our country in order to proceed to swallowing up our country in the end. [FBIS, Supplement, 8 February 1980.]

The Lao response to this security threat took a number of forms. On the diplomatic front Indochinese solidarity and the 'special relationship' with Vietnam were constantly stressed, while every Chinese and Thai action was shrilly denounced. Militarily, however, Lao policy was careful and controlled and aimed at preventing any outbreak of hostilities either with the PRC or with Thailand. Essentially Lao policy consisted in relying on the presence of some 50,000 Vietnamese troops stationed in Laos as a deterrent to outright invasion, while using Lao forces primarily to ensure internal security. Vietnamese units in northern Laos were kept well away from the border area, while Vietnamese advisers and/or observers with Lao border troops wore Lao military uniforms. When Chinese soldiers happened to cross the ill-defined frontier into Lao territory, Lao forces generally avoided armed confrontation. Interestingly in 1981 on one occasion when an armed clash did occur, the Chinese produced photographic evidence that those responsible had been Vietnamese in Lao uniforms. A similar policy of avoiding both armed confrontation and the provocative use of Vietnamese troops has also been pursued *vis-à-vis* Thailand. This was particularly evident during the long-running dispute over three border villages in Sayaboury province. An initial series of contacts in April and May 1984 between Thai border police and Lao troops was followed by Thai army seizure of the three villages a month later. Instead of replying in force, however, the Lao adopted a diplomatic approach. Neither Vietnamese nor Lao forces were used to dislodge Thai troops from what by all accounts (and certainly in the eyes of the Lao leadership) was Lao territory.

Internally, in contrast to the moderation shown towards external provocation, the government at all times has pursued a policy of unremitting hostility towards all forms of insurgency. Most of the responsibility for combating anti-government insurgency devolves on local militia forces which are responsible both for protecting the village and for patrolling the countryside. Once a group of insurgents is located, the militia patrol may engage it immediately or call for assistance from regional forces or from a nearby regular army unit. Vietnamese troops may also be called upon to assist if the insurgents are numerous and well armed. The effectiveness of militia forces is variable, however. Motivation and morale often leave much to be desired. Some village militia are reluctant to patrol: some have come to a tacit understanding with the guerrillas. Overall though, it is probably fair to say that local militia forces have been relatively effective in combating anti-government insurgents, both in the north of the country, and along the Thai border. Thus in strategically vulnerable Sayaboury province in 1984 'local guerillas and public security forces' in conjunction with regular army troops reportedly clashed with insurgents on twenty-two occasions, killing twenty-two, wounding thirty-three and capturing eighteen weapons (FBIS, 15 January 1985). As these figures indicate, while insurgency against the regime continued to be of concern, it nevertheless remained at a manageable level. At no time during the first decade of communist government in Laos has it ever constituted a severe threat to the existence of the regime.

In the north of Laos, intelligence on the movements of strangers has proved remarkably effective in limiting the activity of agents smuggled into Laos from southern China. Knowledge that their presence has been reported to the Lao authorities is often enough to convince agitprop teams to move back across the border. By mid-1985, the situation on the Lao-Chinese border had reached a state of wary co-existence. Armed incidents had entirely ceased. Chinese propaganda broadcasts had been toned down, cross-border trade had increased and both mail and people were apparently moving freely. Relations between the respective armies were correct and even, on occasions, cordial.

The Chinese-Thai security threat has had the effect of increasing the importance of the army in Lao national life. The regime quickly realized that national security could not be left in the hands of the masses. A professional army was required, but one which would at the same time be ideologically sound and active in the socialist construction of the country. The increased political influence of the army became apparent at the Third Congress of the

LPRP in April 1982. As noted already, army representation on the Central Committee was increased to twelve, not including former officers such as Phoune Sipaseuth likely to be sympathetic to the military. Five ministries are headed by regular officers, two more, Finance and Foreign Affairs, by former generals. The powerful Interior Ministry with responsibility for the security police and political police is in the hands of General Sisavath Keobounphan, concurrently Chief of the General Staff of the LPA. This is in line with the LPRP's military policy which is, in Kaysone's words, 'to build the security force into a pure and seasoned one closely united and coordinated with the Armed Forces' (FBIS, 27 March 1985).

In 1985 two measures were announced which had the effect both of strengthening the political power of the LPA and of increasing its organizational autonomy. The first of these measures was modification of the command structure of the army, which had the effect of streamlining decision-making. The former system under which military and political officers jointly took decisions was replaced by a 'one-man command system', which relegated political cadres to subordinate positions at each level. The changes were 'aimed at ensuring unified party leadership, promoting and developing the responsibilities of a commander' and had to be understood 'in an objective and scientific way' by displaced political cadres (FBIS, 18 April 1985). The net effect of the changes was both to strengthen the role of the armed forces within the Party, since every army officer was also a member of the Party, and to reinforce the autonomy of the army as an organization with its own specific interests to pursue.

The army's autonomy was further augmented by the second measure introduced in 1985, granting the army the right to set up its own timber exploration and marketing organization. The significance of this decision was greater than might appear. Although the army had for some time been running its own farms and workshops, these had not been for commercial exploitation. Production had gone to meet the army's own needs. By obtaining not only potentially valuable timber concessions in central Laos, but also the right to deal directly with foreign buyers and thus obtain its own foreign exchange, the army has effectively ensured an independent source of finance for its various projects. The rationale for this entry of the army into the field of commerce and international trade is twofold: it is consistent with the decentralization of economic management that has progressively taken place in Laos and it permits effective pursuit of the army's two strategic tasks—'to defend and build the country, [and so] coordinate economic construction with national defence'. Thus in principle, foreign exchange gained through timber sales is to be used to finance construction projects allotted to the army under the second five-year plan to run from 1986 to 1990. In practice, however, the potential for mismanagement, misapplication of funds and outright corruption is considerably increased.

The oft-repeated goal of the LPRP's military policy is 'to build the LPA into a model modern and well-disciplined revolutionary army'. Increasingly, however, the army has been called upon to shoulder additional responsibilities, mainly because it constitutes the only really efficient and disciplined organization in the country. Army cadres have been sent to work at the village level, not only to improve the performance of local militia and security forces but also to promulgate the Party line. In addition, the army has been called upon to play an ever-increasing economic role,

Our Army must continue boosting production of foodstuffs, essential goods, and goods for export; contributing to producing resources for society; building local logistics supply sources; and improving its own living conditions by itself. . . . It must try to participate in building the local economy and certain important state enterprises. [FBIS, 11 February 1985.]

To this end, certain units 'have been transformed into services carrying out economic construction duties'. These have, however, in many cases experienced 'a lack of technical & scientific know-how and sound economic management'. Worse still, 'a line of administrative favoritism still prevails', resulting in low productivity. Also, it was admitted that 'The act of misusing equipment and materials still remains prevalent. The quality of products and manufacturing . . . still remains uneven. Factories in certain areas fail to fulfil targets' (FBIS, 11 February 1985). Whether these problems can be overcome, or whether the burden placed on the army is too great remains to be seen. What seems certain, however, is that the LPA will continue to play an ever more important political and economic role in the future of the LPDR.

Education

Education has consistently received high priority in the LPDR. Particular attention has been given to primary education at the village level, technical education, and the abolition of adult illiteracy for those between the ages of 15 and 45. Together these represent a major shift of emphasis in educational policy compared to that of the previous regime. Whereas the Royal Lao government followed French precedent by giving greater emphasis to quality education for an elite group than to universal education for the mass of the population, the educational policy of the LPRP has been just the reverse. In addition, whereas the former regime retained French as the language of instruction for higher education, the present government has made a concerted effort to 'Laoicize' the educational system in its entirety. While the results of these changes have not been uniformly positive, at least the present educational system offers previously unavailable opportunities for education to a much wider cross-section of the population than was formerly the case.

The educational system in the LPDR consists of five levels. These are pre-school (*anuban*), primary school (*pathom*), middle school (*mathanyom*), high school (*udom*) and university-level education of one kind or another (*mahavitanyalay*). The aim is to provide two years at the pre-school level (equivalent to kindergarten and pre-school proper) in order to free working mothers and provide an educational environment for children at an early age. This level of education is not well developed, however, and where *anuban* facilities do exist, they tend to be little more than child minding centres. The goal of increasing *anuban* attendance to between 30 and 40 per cent of pre-school age children during the course of the first five-year plan was not achieved.

Traditionally, primary education at the village level in lowland Lao areas was provided by Buddhist monks in the village *wat*. Apart from inculcating Buddhist moral values through the use of popular stories and Buddhist legends, the monks taught children to read and write. Depending on the capacities of individual teachers, some Lao history and geography or elementary mathematics might also be taught. The monks were responsible for transmitting the traditional Lao view of the world and saw themselves as guardians of Lao culture and values. Those ethnic groups which were not Buddhist previously had no formal education, even at the primary level. Where a writing system did exist as in the case of some hill Tai tribes, literacy was limited and tuition informal.

Maximum emphasis has been placed by the present regime on establishing schools at the primary level in every village in the country, including those of all ethnic minority groups. More than 90 per cent of school-age children now attend primary school. Primary education in Laos lasts for five years, but in a number of villages only a three-year *pathom* programme exists. All education is in the Lao language, which means that children of minority groups are at an immediate disadvantage, especially in more remote areas where contact with Lao-speakers is minimal. A continuing shortage exists of Lao-speaking primary school teachers among most minority groups. Some minority teachers have been trained in place by ethnic Lao volunteers who teach for a few years in minority villages. But the problem of language has retarded establishment of universal primary education of a similar standard.

Lao Loum children completing primary school generally have a net advantage in terms of language ability and literary skills over the children of minority ethnic groups. Whereas in the past, however, the acquisition of French as the necessary prerequisite for all higher education was virtually impossible for minority children, now at least some facilities are available for the equally indispensable acquisition of Lao.

The massive increase in education at the primary level during the first ten years of the LPDR was accomplished with a minimum of educational equipment and financial support. Wherever necessary, Buddhist *wats* continued to serve as schools. Monks receive additional education and ideological training in Marxism–Leninism and the policies of the LPRP before being sent out to teach. Emphasis was placed initially on self-help, community-based education. Anyone who could read or write was expected to teach, some at the primary level, others in adult literacy classes. Not surprisingly, the quality of education was often very low. In the urban areas, educational standards fell dramatically in the early days of the regime, as many teachers fearful of being sent for long terms of political re-education joined the exodus of refugees. Declining educational standards then contributed to the decision of families to leave to seek better opportunities for their children overseas.

Apart from a chronic shortage of trained and qualified teachers at the primary level, shortages of everything from chalk and pencils to textbooks and teaching aids have had an equally adverse effect. UNICEF has provided assistance for primary education through improved teacher training, provision of essential school supplies and the production and printing of textbooks. Inadequate means of distribution has been another problem: remote schools often lack even the most basic facilities. The capacity and efficiency of printing works have been inadequate to meet the demand for textbooks in Lao. The shortage of cadres, excessive centralization of decision-making and need for ideological orthodoxy have all reduced textbook production, particularly for middle- and high-school levels. An ideologically acceptable brief history of Laos for use in schools was not produced until 1984, after it had been cleared by the Secretariat of the Party. The only Lao geography text had to be replaced when the number of provinces was increased from thirteen to sixteen.

Secondary education is divided into two levels, known as middle school and high school, each lasting for three years, which together are said to constitute 'the focal point of educational development' in Laos. Middle schools, *mathanyom*, are usually located at the sub-district (*tasseng*) level; while high schools, *udom*, are located in the larger centres which serve as the capitals of districts (*muong*). Here again, at both levels, there exist shortages of qualified teachers and textbooks. Class sizes tend to be large and specialist facilities such as science laboratories, audiovisual equipment or resource centres all but non-existent. A number of serious structural problems also exist at the secondary level. Because of low population density and difficulties in transportation, middle and high schools are often situated too far away for students to attend. Few facilities exist for boarding, except in the case of some specialist technical middle and high schools with a selected intake. Difficulties in attending secondary schools tend to disadvantage two groups in particular: ethnic minorities and girls. Even in larger centres where middle and high schools are available notable reductions occur in the numbers of girls and ethnic minority children attending (cf. Chagnon & Rumpf, in Stuart-Fox, 1982a). Another problem is that of low academic standards. After 1975 most high school teachers joined the refugee outflow to Thailand. Replacements were often inadequately trained primary teachers who were rapidly promoted. A vicious circle thus began to operate in which standards progressively declined further year by year throughout the early years of the regime.

An important innovation was introduced in secondary education during the course of the first five-year plan. A new category of 'technical secondary schools' was established for vocational training of students in practical skills of value in improving technology and raising living standards. These schools have mostly been set up in provincial and district towns to teach new agricultural techniques and mechanical and engineering skills. Students learn about agricultural methods, care of livestock, forestry management and maintenance of agricultural and other mechanical equipment, skills that they can then apply when they return to their villages. Since students usually live communally at these schools, minority students from remote villages can more easily attend. The oldest and largest such technical school in Laos is the Pacpasak vocational school in Vientiane (previously known as the Vientiane Industrial School, founded by the French in 1936). The school now has eleven departments teaching everything from car repair and carpentry to food processing and factory management. It is staffed by ninety-five teachers and graduates more than two hundred students per year (*Vietnam Courier*, January 1985).

Tertiary education remains strictly limited in Laos. There exist only five institutions: the Teacher Training College at Dong Dok on the outskirts of Vientiane, the School of Civil Engineering, the Medical School, the School of Agriculture and Forestry and the newly formed National Polytechnic Institute in Vientiane. Only the first and last of these are under the control of the Ministry of Education: the others are controlled by the appropriate ministries. Courses commenced at the Polytechnic only in 1985 with the first intake of students in electronics and engineering. Other branches of study will be added as needed. Instruction at all five institutions is entirely in Lao: foreign lecturers use Lao interpreters when teaching. In the case of medical terminology, however, many terms have been borrowed from French, and medical students are still encouraged to learn to read a foreign language. At the Teachers' Training College five languages are taught—Russian, English, French, German and Spanish—but surprisingly not Vietnamese. Language teaching in secondary schools is important for students who hope to obtain a scholarship to study in a foreign country. There is a serious shortage of language teachers, especially in Russian, and standards are low.

Tertiary level education in Laos has to compete with the attraction of education abroad. Most of the best students are chosen to study in Vietnam, the Soviet Union or Eastern Europe. Probably the most popular tertiary institution in Laos is the Medical School. As of 1984, the School began graduating 100 students a year as six-year trained doctors, and over 300 as auxiliary doctors with three years' training. This compares with nine doctors graduated in 1976, and 118 auxiliaries. The School also provides 'recycling' or 'supplementary' courses which permit anyone in medical or pharmaceutical studies—including nurses and mid-wives—to improve their qualifications. In 1984, such courses attracted over 500 students (figures provided during interviews, August 1985).

Similar courses to upgrade professional competence are held for teachers, engineers and agricultural technicians. Improving the quality of teachers was described as 'the fundamental issue' in education for the period of the first five-year plan. Full courses last four years for secondary school teachers, but upgrading courses have to be fitted into vacations. The standard of new trainees is sometimes disappointingly low, in part because there is now less incentive to become a teacher in the LPDR due to the profession's reduced prestige and low salary levels. In addition students entering Teachers' Training College are often poorly motivated and have poor study habits. Similar problems were evident with the first small intake for the Polytechnic Institute. Fully half the students had to be given a year-long supplementary course to bring them up to the minimal entry standard. Many of the estimated 10,000 Lao students studying in Soviet Bloc states have also had to undertake supplementary courses to meet minimal entry standards.

It was in the field of adult education that the regime claimed its greatest success during the first five-year plan. The goal of abolishing illiteracy for all adults between the ages of 15 and 45 was officially said to have been achieved by the end of 1984—even among ethnic minority groups. This compares with an estimated literacy rate of between 35 and 40 per cent for this age group among Lao Loum alone in 1975. A little consideration, however, is enough to cast serious doubts on the government's claim to have abolished illiteracy. It is possible that illiteracy has been all but abolished among lowland Lao, and even among all Lao Loum. Certainly a considerable effort was made in most Lao villages to hold classes and get people to attend. It is quite another thing to assert that a large, illiterate population of tribal peoples has learned to read a language many of them do not even speak.

There is an additional reason to doubt the claim that illiteracy was abolished in 1984 and that is the phenomenon of regression through disuse. Reading is a skill that has to be maintained: it is not enough to learn to recognize letters, and then never to read. Laos is a country where very little reading matter exists and very few people bother to read. Few books are printed in Lao. The National Library contains mainly French literature and is not open to the public. The two bookshops in Vientiane contain virtually nothing but the communist classics and magazines from the Soviet Union and Eastern Europe. It is extremely rare even in Vientiane to see anyone reading. Newspapers have a low circulation, and many people cannot afford even the small cost involved. No reading matter is handed out in political seminars as the government cannot afford printing costs. Thus despite the claims of the universal literacy, many Lao do not read because they have no occasion to read: they revert to a state of functional illiteracy.

The educational policy of the LPRP is not simply to build more schools and teach more children: education is to play a significant role in forming the new Lao socialist man or woman. In Kaysone's words: 'Education of children and youths must be considered a significant tool of proletarian dictatorship to build a new generation, new men and the country'. Education has been seen as a principal means of raising political consciousness, especially among minority groups. To this end, political education has an important place in the curriculum at all educational levels. Politics pervades the teaching of Lao history, geography and literature, particularly at the middle and high school levels, but even primary school teachers are expected to carry out 'information and propaganda activities' in order to publicize Party policies. Political studies (*kan meuang*) are usually held at the beginning of each school year, to coincide with important anniversaries or events (such as the Third Congress of the LPRP), or at times of crisis (such as the dispute with Thailand over the three border villages). Sessions may last from as little as a couple of hours to a full week, during which students discuss political events and policies under the direction of an official from the Ministry of Education or a member of the

LPRP. Students complain that these political meetings, known as *saminar* in Lao, often tend to be too long, repetitive and boring; but they have become part of school life in modern Laos.

Socialist morality is given practical expression in schools through encouragement of cooperative learning, and through a system of student-teacher committees (known as *bamlun*, caring and helping, committees). Students are divided into small groups of twelve to fifteen which work together to help each other with difficult problems. Each group usually meets once a week to discuss problems and carry out self-criticism. Group leaders meet with teachers to discuss any difficulties which have arisen, request additional lessons where necessary and plan future school work projects (Chagnon & Rumpf, in Stuart-Fox, 1982a).

In summary, therefore, it would be fair to say that educational policies of the new regime are promising and progressive. It is their application which remains disappointingly defective.

Public Health and Social Welfare

Public health has been another area of primary concern in the LPDP. Laos has one of the lowest life expectancies at birth of any Asian country, estimated at 46 years. In 1976, the first year in power of the new regime, the infant mortality rate stood at the shockingly high figure of 284 per 1,000. The death rate of between 23 and 25 per thousand was also one of the highest for Asia. A high birth rate of around 47 per thousand, however, ensured a population increase of around 2.9 per cent for the first ten years of the new regime, a figure which is unlikely to fall as infant mortality and the overall death rate are reduced. Other public health statistics were as bad. The country had fewer than ninety doctors for a population of more than three million; the few hospital beds were concentrated in major centres; and much of the population had no access to primary health care of any kind. Malaria, tuberculosis, dysentery and other diseases were endemic; leprosy and cholera not uncommon. General levels of health were low due to poor nutrition and lack of sanitation.

The priorities of the new regime lay in the area of mass education in the practice of elementary hygiene and sanitation as a preventative measure, extension of public health care to remote villages, especially in minority areas, and the training of medical personnel. Teams of 'public health cadres' were sent out to explain simple hygienic measures necessary to reduce intestinal disease and parasitic infection. Basic health education took the form of a 'Three Cleans' campaign—clean food, clean water and clean houses. In 1985, contaminated water was described as the principal problem encountered by the Public Health authorities in improving the general standard of health of the population. In 1976, only 1 per cent of Lao villages had access to a supply of fresh potable water. By 1985, the figure had risen to 18 per cent—which still left 82 per cent of all Lao villages without potable water. Nevertheless, the Ministry of Public Health estimated that improvements to water supplies over a ten-year period had reduced intestinal disorders by half. (This section is largely based on an interview with Khamlieng Pholsena, Minister of Public Health, August 1985.)

Work has also gone ahead on eradicating other endemic and contagious diseases, in particular malaria and tuberculosis, and intestinal and parasite diseases. The malaria eradication programme undertaken with American assistance prior to 1975 had to be curtailed for lack of funds. Nevertheless spraying with DDT did continue in certain districts, notably in Vientiane and Champassak provinces. In 1976 blood samples from Champassak showed an 18.6 per cent rate of contamination with the Plasmodium organism responsible for malaria. By 1985, this had been reduced to 2.8 per cent and the government claimed that malaria had been completely eradicated among children in the province. Similar programmes have been commenced in Luang Prabang, Sayaboury and Savannakhet provinces, though malaria still remains a major scourge. Other diseases have registered a slow rate of improvement and the government's health programme does seem to be having some effect.

Another area of particular attention has been childhood diseases responsible for the high child mortality rate. Here intestinal diseases have been the principal target. Women health workers have been sent out to villages to conduct classes in maternal and child health. From 1975 to 1980, the government claimed to have trained almost 6,000 public health cadres and paramedical personnel, a figure that was to be more than doubled during the course of the first five-year plan. Most of these health cadres were volunteers who were given a few weeks' training and sent back to their villages.

Extension of medical facilities down to the grassroots level has taken the form of establishing so-called 'health stations' in as many villages as possible. These consist of little more than first-aid posts, staffed by a part-time public health worker or nurse. By the beginning of the first five-year plan, health stations had been set up in one third of Laos' 11,424 villages, a figure due to be considerably increased during the period of the plan itself. At the sub-district (*tasseng*) level, dispensaries have been established staffed by trained nurses. In 1976, there were dispensaries in 294 of the 950 *tassengs*. By 1985, this number had increased to 706, many of which have between two and seven beds. Small hospitals have also been established in all of the country's 112 district towns (*muong*), containing altogether some 3,000 beds. Each of the sixteen province capitals has a larger hospital, of which those built in Xieng Khouang (by the Mongolians), Oudomsay (by the Vietnamese) and one of the three hospitals in Vientiane (by the Russians) are newly constructed. The total number of hospital beds was put at 8,970 in the last year of the first five-year plan (compared with 6,178 beds in 1976).

Another priority has been the extensive training programme inaugurated for full-time medical personnel. The previous government's programme of training both fully qualified doctors (six years of study) and auxiliary doctors (three years of study) was continued, and the intake increased to cope with the shortage of doctors, a shortage soon exacerbated by the decision of many doctors to leave the country as refugees. In 1976, Laos had only one doctor for approximately 35,000 people. By 1984, even after the loss of more trained doctors abroad, the number of doctors had increaesd to 418, or one for every 8,576 people—still an unacceptably high figure, but a considerable improvement none the less. Over the same period the number of auxiliary doctors increased from 371 to 1,892 or one for every 1,700. This meant that by the end of 1984, Laos had between seven and eight doctors or auxiliary doctors for every 10,000 people. At the same time there has been a much slighter increase in the number of full time nurses. In 1976, these numbered 15,476, according to Public Health Ministry figures, whereas in 1984, there were 17,943 nurses. These were backed up, however, by thousands of part-time nurses, known as 'public health activists and propagandists', who have undergone brief training courses. Overall the total number of health workers is said to have increased by 67.5 per cent between 1976 and 1985.

The medical training programme in the LPDR has been systematized and integrated in such a way as to permit medical personnel to upgrade their qualifications. Thus full time nurses can elect to become auxiliary doctors, or even six-year trained doctors, by taking an upgrading course whose length depends on previous qualifications and experience. Auxiliary doctors can upgrade their qualifications to the level of doctor by studying a further one to three years, again depending on experience and previous training. Auxiliary doctors with some years of experience who have attended a number of additional specialized seminars and training sessions might only have to complete one additional year of formal study: one recently graduated would have to study for a further three years to become a doctor.

The statistics for the increase in the intake of medical students speak for themselves. In 1976, only 127 students were studying medicine in Laos, nine of whom graduated. In 1984–5, 1,020 students were studying to be six-year trained doctors, and 104 graduated. There was thus a 700 per cent increase in the number of full-time medical students. Over the same period, the number of auxiliary doctors increased from 360 (118 graduates) to 1,122 (with 313 graduates). In 1976, 211 students were enrolled in the new upgrading courses, many of them from previous Pathet Lao controlled areas. By the 1984–5 academic year, the number had increased to 511. Just over 3,000 medical personnel enrolled in such courses over the period 1976 to 1984.

This rapid expansion in the training of medical personnel has not been without its problems. One has been the shortage of textbooks and the problem of language. Many of the new generation of students do not speak French, or indeed any foreign language. All courses have therefore had to be translated into Lao. Russian and Cuban doctors teaching in the Medical School have difficulties in communicating with students. Translation has sometimes been first into French, then into Lao. Also existing facilities have been pushed to their limits to accommodate increased enrolments. The Medical School has only 'the minimum necessary equipment' to enable it to graduate 100 six-year trained doctors a year. As a result of these problems, standards have suffered, though it is difficult to determine to what extent. Young doctors have therefore had to learn 'on the job', especially those sent directly to remote areas where they are out of contact with older and more experienced colleagues.

An important part of medical training in the LPDR consists in political education and the inculcation of a spirit of service. In the words of Health Minister Khamlieng Pholsena: 'Political education is necessary to provide the incentive for doctors to serve the people.' Medical students study Marxism-Leninism for three hours a week, particularly the way in which socialist theory and morality applies to medical practice. According to Khamlieng, political education has been particularly effective in changing pre-revolutionary attitudes. No longer do doctors adopt 'mandarin' attitudes towards their patients, or treat only those who can pay. Thanks to their political training, and a compulsory period of three months practical work in the countryside as fifth-year students, graduate doctors readily volunteer to work in remote areas. Not all medical personnel, however, develop a proper socialist morality. Many still prefer to practise in Vientiane, or one of the larger towns. Also, although some of the worst abuses under the old regime (such as the selling of unanalysed blood taken from prisoners to the highest bidder) no longer occur, the fact that patients usually have to pay something towards the cost of medicines opens the way to abuses, especially since many medicines are in short supply.

Problems have also been encountered in the distribution and supply of medicines. Most medicines and pharmaceuticals are supplied by United Nations agencies (UNICEF, WHO) or by other international and humanitarian organizations. All stocks are held in the central medical store in Vientiane prior to distribution. But distribution is often slow and new medicines arrive before the previous batch has been sent out. Due to poor stacking procedures, older medicines get pushed behind those recently arrived, and disappear from view until their expiry date is past. The problem is exacerbated because there is a reluctance to throw out expired medicines: in part because people believe that they must still be of *some* value, and in part because no one has the authority to destroy them. Medicines are state property, and it requires a group decision at the highest relevant administrative level to throw them away. Party leaders are called upon to take the decision, rather than qualified pharmacists, and it is a decision they are often reluctant to take.

Because of the cost of imported medicines, Laos has made a virtue of encouraging the use of traditional herbal remedies. One of the public health goals of the first five-year plan was, in Kaysone's words, to

maintain, promote and expand the fine tradition of curing patients with herbal medicines, which is regarded as one of the strong points in the public health field.... We must take steps to expand the planting of herbs and to make full use of the roots of these precious plants. We must learn how to cure patients by using traditional herbal medicines in combination with modern medicines in various hospitals. [FBIS, 26 January 1981.]

Herbal remedies are most used at the village level where their cultivation and use is usually the responsibility of Buddhist monks. Traditional medicine is also encouraged in minority areas, but in conjunction with modern scientific medicine which it is hoped will have the effect of limiting superstitious practices.

The health of minority groups is of particular concern to the government. Despite ideological education, however, ethnic Lao medical personnnel do not readily volunteer to work in minority areas. To overcome the shortage of trained minority health workers, therefore, a form of positive discrimination is practised, particularly in upgrading courses. Minority students are given special help to cope with the course work, and then sent back to their own areas. Standards may suffer, but even partly trained minority medical personnel are in a much better position than are ethnic Lao to administer a judicious mixture of traditional and Western medicine to their own people.

Information and Propaganda

Responsibility for information and propaganda in the LPDR is shared between the Central Propaganda Committee (CPC) answerable to the LPDR Central Committee and the State Committee for Propaganda, the Press, Radio and Television which is a government body. Acting chairman of the State Committee, Sone Khamvanvongsa, is concurrently vice-chairman of the Party's Central Propaganda Committee and serves as the liaison between the two organizations. In fact the responsibilities of each body are not clearly differentiated.

The State Committee is in charge of disseminating local, national, and international news through the Lao News Agency, Khaosan Pathet Lao. Daily bulletins are produced in Lao, French and English (as of 1985). The Committee also publishes the Party journal *Pasason* (previously *Sieng Pasason*), meaning 'The People'. It is published six times a week in Lao. In 1985, the Committee also assumed responsibility for publishing the Party's new theoretical journal *Alum Mai* (New Dawn). The national radio network consists of a 150 kilowatt station at Vientiane, built with Soviet aid to replace the previous 25 kilowatt station, and seven regional stations at Luang Prabang, Oudomsay, Xieng Khouang, Sam Neua, Thakhek, Savannakhet and Pakse. Programmes are broadcast in Lao, Vietnamese, Khmer, Thai, English and French. No broadcasts are made in minority languages from Vientiane but regional stations do broadcast such programmes. For example, both Luang Prabang and Xieng Khouang broadcast programmes in Hmong. Broadcasting in minority languages is due to be increased in future, especially in northern Laos, in an effort to counter Chinese propaganda. Chinese radio stations in Yunnan beam a number of programmes to Laos in minority languages.

The State Committee is also responsible for Lao television. Broadcasts began on an experimental basis on 1 December 1983 using a 100 kilowatt transmitter with a range of 25 to 30 kms. Broadcasts were thrice weekly during 1984, but were increased to five times a week from 7.30 p.m. to 10 p.m. or 11. p.m. depending on programmes in 1985. Plans were underway to increase broadcasting to seven days a week by the end of 1985. Vientiane has a Soviet satellite reception station which enables the television channel to tune into and transmit inter-Sputnik network programmes. Other programmes include news, folkdancing and music, films, children's programmes and sport. Broadcasts are in colour, but the quality of reception remains poor.

Lao television attempts to compete with Thai TV broadcast from Nongkhai, just across the Mekong from Vientiane. Thai TV has the

attraction of broadcasting for more hours with better quality and of pro-
gramming popular Chinese and Thai drama and opera interspersed with
commercials. Lao authorities in Vientiane make no attempt to prevent those
few residents lucky enough to possess TV sets from watching Thai
programmes. These are 'neither forbidden, nor encouraged'. Some programmes, on agricultural techniques for example, are considered useful;
others are considered 'very bad'. The position of the Lao authorities is that
people must decide for themselves; if they possess a developed political
consciousness, they will be discriminating. Lao television claims to have
received letters from Thai viewers saying how nice it was to see films without
the interruption of advertisements. The Lao also claim that Thai boy scouts
patrol at night to check that Thais in Nongkhai are not watching Lao TV.
(This section is largely based on an interview with Bouabane Volakhoun,
vice-chairman of the State Propaganda Committee, August 1985.)

Most Lao provincial towns are out of range of Thai television. Only those
close to the Thai frontier can receive programmes. In Thakhek and
Savannakhet, both situated, like Vientiane, just across the river from sizeable
Thai towns relaying Thai TV, authorities take no action against those
watching Thai programmes. At Pakse, however, local authorities have
consistently banned the watching of Thai TV. Any resident caught doing so
faces confiscation of his set and a period of political re-education.

Extension of the national TV network depends on regional priorities. A
province may, like Savannakhet, include provision of a TV relay and
transmission station as part of the next provincial five-year plan or, like
Pakse, decide against it. Provinces will relay central programmes, but in time
will be able to add local news and eventually produce their own local
programmes. During the course of the second plan transmission facilities in
Vientiane are due to be improved and new studios built. Other plans include
the upgrading of regional radio stations under the auspices of the International Telecommunications Union.

The most important task allotted to the State Committee which it shares
with the Central Propaganda Committee is to act as ideological watch dog on
all publications produced in Laos or brought into the country. Permission for
publication can be given by the State Committee, or by the CPC. Editors of
regular publications, such as the popular magazine *Vannasin* produced by the
Minsitry of Culture, are responsible for maintaining editorial policies in line
with those of the Party. The State Committee chairman or vice-chairmen can
call in editors and instruct them to publicize a particular Party policy or
government directive, or reprimand them for failing to do so. So too can the
CPC chairmen. Permission may also be granted by either organization for the

publication of Lao novels, poems and short stories in book form (manuscripts are checked for ideological error) and for foreign literature to be translated and published in Lao. Actual publication rests with the Ministry of Culture, or the Ministry of Education or with some organization such as the Lao People's Revolutionary Youth or the Union of Lao Women.

When it comes to granting permission to import foreign publications or take out subscriptions to foreign periodicals, there exists a further overlap of authority for permission can be given not only by the State Committee or the CPC, but also by the Press Department of the Foreign Ministry. Which organization to approach thus often depends on what category of publication is involved and who one knows, or is related to, on which examining body. Technical publications may more easily obtain clearance from the Foreign Ministry, for example, than from the CPC. In some cases the lack of clear lines of demarcation of responsibility leads to a degree of confusion. Thus in 1985, video cassettes were, in the words of one official, 'pouring into the country' without official clearance because the CPC and the State Committee could not agree on whose responsibility it was to control them.

Taken together, however, controls on the free flow of information in Laos are stringent and effective. Customs officials confiscate all foreign reading matter. Even children's books in English or French brought into the country by foreigners resident in Laos are confiscated, and can only be obtained after written applications which may take months to process. The Lao population is systematically restricted in what it can find out about the world. The country has very few printing facilities, all under government control. Publications in Lao are thus limited entirely to what is permitted by the Party. Libraries are almost non-existent. Despite the increase in adult literacy, therefore, there is remarkably little to read in Lao, and strict controls over what can be read in foreign languages.

Information is circulated in Laos primarily by word of mouth. So-called 'seminars' are regularly held in neighbourhoods, villages, offices, enterprises and associations during which the political line of the Party is explained and justified. Differences of interpretation, and even probing questions, are not encouraged. In the early years of the regime seminars even for villagers lasted up to several hours. Often meetings were held in the evening after work. Cadres sometimes spoke for four or five hours on end in a boring, repetitive and often ill-informed stream. So unpopular did seminars become, so constant the complaints, that in 1982 meetings were limited to two hours duration, with the opening speech by visiting cadres limited to half an hour. Longer courses in Marxism-Leninism and party policies may last from one to two days to several weeks. Attendance is compulsory and all work in the ministry or enterprise comes to a standstill. Seminar topics may include not only Party policies, but also security matters, foreign affairs (such as events in Nicaragua or Afghanistan), or the Soviet position on some matter of international concern. A constantly reiterated theme is the need for Indochinese solidarity with the peoples of Vietnam and Kampuchea against Chinese great-power hegemonism.

More effective, and certainly more popular, as a means of communicating government propaganda are the film shows and song and dance troupes which make periodic tours of the villages. So starved are people of any kind of popular entertainment that the whole village will congregate willingly to watch films on hygiene or agriculture. Live performances are also very popular, especially of a traditional nature or on traditional themes. The authorities are well aware of the impact of such performances. Kaysone warned delegates of the Supreme People's Assembly when launching the first five-year plan that

Close and careful censoring must be carried out with regard to the themes of all performances staged by state and popular art troupes before they are presented to the public. The themes of such performances must be of an educational, patriotic and mass nature, and must be easy to understand. [FBIS, 26 January 1981.]

Satire at the expense of the regime is out of the question.

Law and Justice

The lack of an adequate system of justice must be counted as a major failing of the LPDR. No code of socialist law was promulgated during the first decade of the regime. Crimes against persons (such as murder or assault) or against personal property (theft, receiving stolen goods) are, of course, understood, for they are just as much part of Buddhist as of socialist morality. Far less consensus exists, however, over what constitutes a crime against socialist morality, or against the Party, or the state. Much depends on interpretation, which can lead to all but arbitrary punishments. As one Vientiane resident put it: 'we know there are limits, but we do not know what the limits are until we come to them. Then we are arrested' (in conversation with the author, July 1985).

The first act of revolutionary justice perpetrated by the new regime was the 'people's trial' *in absentia* of a number of prominent right-wing government ministers and army officers in September 1975, before the proclamation of the LPDR. A prepared list of names was submitted, various crimes were detailed, no one spoke in defence of the accused, guilt was established by popular acclaim and judgment passed—death or imprisonment—according to decisions previously taken at the highest levels of the Party.

The judgment came as a shock to many Lao. Even before the arrival of the French, Lao justice was administered in accordance with a written code. Under the French, rules of evidence and legal defence prevailed and similar safeguards were incorporated in the legal system of the Royal Lao government. Those arrested by Pathet Lao authorities in Vientiane and other cities in 1975 and subsequently enjoyed no legal safeguards at all. Arrests were often made at night; no information would be given as to why the arrest was being made or where the prisoner was being taken. Soon a climate of fear and suspicion prevailed in which few had the courage to speak out in favour of anyone arrested for fear that they would be arrested in turn. Many were arrested after an anonymous denunciation made out of personal animosity, professional jealousy or in order to settle old scores. A charge of being an enemy of the state, or a threat to internal security was enough to have the accused sent off to a re-education camp. So too were allegations of prostitution, drug addiction or of being unduly influenced by decadent Western culture.

Almost all of those arrested underwent no trial at all. Those considered a political risk were sent to re-education camps in Houa Phan, Attopeu and other provinces. Many politically active students who had been involved in demonstrations against the former regime were also sent to work camps, even after volunteering to continue their studies in Soviet bloc states. Unemployed, Western-influenced youths and girls were rounded up and trucked off to rehabilitation camps on two islands in the Nam Ngum reservoir: one for men (Done Thao) and one for women (Done Nang). Suspected opponents of the regime often underwent questioning at the Ministry of the Interior before being consigned to re-education camps. Those accused of more specific crimes, such as assault, theft, sabotage or destruction of state property were sent to the prison of Sam Khe outside Vientiane, a new wing of which was built to house political prisoners.

Not until October 1978 was an ordinance circulated within the Party, though never officially published, outlining procedures to be followed in the case of arrests, and warning against excessive zealousness on the part of the arresting authorities. How this ordinance was applied, however, depended on local Party officials. It did little to alleviate the problem of the arbitrary exercise of power since no formal system of defence and appeals procedures was introduced. Nor were people informed of their personal rights before the law (cf. *Amnesty International Report*, ASA 26/02/80). Eventually, however, criticism from both outside and inside the Party of the way in which arrests were made and punishments handed down began to have some effect. By the early 1980s, a system was in place to dispense socialist justice even though no legal code was publicly available.

Common forms of crime are dealt with on a series of different levels. At the local village level, cases are examined by a committee consisting usually of the local Party secretary where there is one, the head of the village administrative committee, local representatives of such popular organizations as the LFNC, the ULW or LPRY, perhaps a monk or two and co-opted villagers known for their integrity. Serious or politically contentious cases are referred to higher authorities. Peoples' tribunals exist at the district (*muoung*) level and at the provincial level (including the Prefecture of Vientiane). The presidents, vice-presidents and judges assisting at these tribunals are appointed by the government. So too are the public prosecutors; but at each level two 'people's assessors' are elected by the people's assembly corresponding to that level. (This section is largely based on a written statement given to the author by the Ministry of Justice, August 1985.)

The highest court in the land is the Supreme People's Court (SPC), established by decree of the SPA on 11 January 1983, fully seven years after the founding of the LPDR. The president, who in 1985 was Ounneua Phimmasone, vice-presidents and presiding judges are elected by the Supreme People's Assembly, or by its Standing Committee when the Assembly is not in session. The Supreme People's Court acts both as a court of first instance in important cases, as an appeal court and to determine commutation or remission of sentences. Its plenary council consists not only of the president, vice-president and judges of the SPC, but also the presidents of provincial courts and of the court of the Prefecture of Vientiane and presidents of superior military courts. Panels of judges may be drawn to constitute civil, criminal or military courts (NL, No. 5, November 1985).

The Lao penal procedure, according to the Justice Ministry, requires provision of an arrest warrant signed by the public prosecutor at the appropriate level of government. This follows preliminary police enquiries to establish a prima-facie case against the accused. If the prosecutor decides there is sufficient evidence, the case goes before the tribunal. It is judged in public 'except in such cases where it is necessary to guard a state secret or good national traditions'. Otherwise all evidence, including statements by the accused, by the victim of the crime, by witnesses, by the police or by any experts called is open to public scrutiny. The accused must always be present, except where he or she 'has left the country, evaded justice, or in some exceptional cases covered by the law'. Judgment is according to evidence provided by the police enquiry in conformity with the case put by the public prosecutor. It must be based on 'sufficient proof', not suppositions. A verdict of 'not guilty' is passed 'in cases of insufficient proof, mental incapacity, legitimate defence, necessity or of other reasons covered by the law'.

Judgments are passed 'according to socialist humanism in conformity with Lao penal law'. Sentences range from the death sentence, to imprisonment, internal exile, confiscation of goods or public rebuke when the accused is sternly warned to mend his or her ways. Before sentence is passed, the accused has the right of appeal to the next higher level, and theoretically on up to the Supreme People's Court. For his part, the prosecutor can also appeal to a higher court against an aquittal by a lower court which he considers illegitimate or without foundation (Ministry of Justice statement, August 1985).

The legal system as outlined above has the appearance of being both logical and effective. It works best, however, in straightforward criminal cases. Social and political 'crimes' are far less clear cut. Indeed, whether certain behaviour constitutes a 'crime' at all often depends on circumstances. Nowhere, for example, is it stated that an unmarried girl may not go out with a young man alone. But if a girl remains unmarried and goes out with a number of young men at different times she risks being arrested on a charge of immorality and sent to Done Nang rehabilitation centre. How many times a girl may go out with a different man is entirely arbitrary, and depends on local authorities, on who her family and friends are, on whom she may have offended—perhaps by refusing to go out—and so on.

The same kind of uncertainty applies in the area of ideological 'crime', such as unacceptable criticism of Party policies. Criticism is permitted, within certain limits which are nowhere specified, during self-criticism sessions in different ministries, departments and enterprises. But criticism taken too far, made to persons who are not entitled to hear it—such as Western diplomats, United Nations' officials, visiting journalists, etc.—can lead to a course of re-education. Criticism of the Party line which is unacceptable at one time may become acceptable once policies change, though it must be remembered that the Party line is always correct at the moment it is formulated; it changes in response to objective conditions, but at all times it constitutes the correct response to those conditions!

Periods of punishment are equally uncertain. An offender is not given a time to serve in prison or in a re-education camp, for this depends not on the 'crime' committed, but on the attitude of the person who has committed it. The prisoner or camp inmate must show signs of contrition and determination to mend his ways. He or she must become a model prisoner, and 'show progress'. What constitutes progress is again somewhat arbitrary, but roughly it means recognizing the omniscience of the Party, and conducting oneself at all times in strict conformity with the Party line. In practice this requires the prisoner to adopt an attitude of fawning docility towards all persons of authority, to be alert in seminars, to question nothing and respond always in the prescribed way, and to take an active part in all physical labour. The power of prison or camp authorities is absolute, however, for no matter how an inmate behaves they can always report that in their estimation the prisoner has not shown sufficient 'progress' to be released. Inmates of correctional institutions of all kinds in Laos never know how long a sentence they will have to serve. The psychological effect of this is to weaken resistance, and hasten 'progress'.

The open-ended nature of corrective sentences in part explains the persistence of re-education camps in the vicinity of Viengsai in northeastern Laos and in Attopeu province in the south, for members of the civil administration and military officers of the former regime (see *Amnesty International Reports* ASA 26/04/85 and ASA 26/01/86). Those who agreed to attend 'seminars' in 1975, either voluntarily, or under duress, believed they would be gone for a period of weeks or months at most. When none had returned by the end of the year, popular concern became so great that the authorities announced that the courses would be terminated. As the new regime established its authority, however, quite the reverse occurred. More former officials were despatched to the camps. At the same time, lower-ranking civil servants were sent for short courses of instruction in Marxism-Leninism, and the policies of the new regime, from which they soon returned. The hope was kept alive, therefore, that higher-ranking officials and army officers would also return in due time, after longer courses of rehabilitation. When by 1978, the third year of the regime, none had yet returned, many families gave up hope and, their resources exhausted, crossed to Thailand.

Towards the end of 1980, the first small groups of rehabilitated officials and officers were brought back to Vientiane and given subordinate positions in the new administration. To the disappointment of the authorities, however, many of these returnees crossed to Thailand at the first opportunity. Five years of physical labour and socialist instruction seemed to have had little effect. More were released in 1981 but with similar results. Since then small groups have occasionally returned, but the massive release which had previously been hinted at of all remaining political prisoners still held in various camps never occurred. Evidently the 'progress' made was not considered sufficient to permit their complete rehabilitation as willing workers for the LPDR—especially when most of their families and friends were already in the United States, France or Australia.

In 1984, at a time when Amnesty International estimated that there remained as many as 6,000 to 7,000 political prisoners in Laos, the government claimed that all re-education camps for members of the former regime had been abolished. Former inmates who remained in remote areas did so, it was claimed, of their own free will. This may well be so in a few cases. LPDR authorities encouraged the families of prisoners to settle in the area of the camps, and a few did take up the invitation—if sometimes only to secure the conditional release of a husband and then flee the country. Prisoners whose wives had left the country without them were permitted, even encouraged, to take a second wife from the local population. Some inmates with particular skills were co-opted into working for the provincial administration. Others were assigned to live in villages as a form of internal exile. Those who remained in the camps became members of cooperative work brigades through the simple expedient of converting re-education camps into state farming enterprises. Thus while it may be true in a sense that re-education camps as corrective institutions for former members of the Royal Lao government and army have ceased to exist as such, it is still the case that some thousands of former inmates do not have freedom of movement, and cannot elect to join relatives abroad. Unlike Vietnam, Laos has no orderly departure programme with countries of ultimate asylum for Indochinese refugees.

Laos still has an undisclosed number of political prisoners in the sense that Amnesty understands the term; that is, people imprisoned for their political or religious or ideological beliefs. To begin with, there is no confirmation that anyone has been released from the special prison camp numbered O5 situated near Viengsai that was set aside for high-ranking members of the former regime accused of war crimes for their activities during the Thirty-Year Struggle. To this camp were sent as many as 500 senior generals, former cabinet ministers, leading civil servants, and right-wing politicians who had consistently collaborated with the United States in the war against the Pathet Lao. Many of these were old men when they were interned, unused either to physical labour or the harsh climate of northern Laos. Many are reported to have died, others to be in poor health. Also still under house arrest are members of the former royal family imprisoned in 1977 under suspicion of being in contact with anti-government insurgents. Both the former King Savang Vatthana and Crown Prince Vong Savang are believed to be dead, though the Lao authorities have steadfastly refused to confirm this, or to provide any information as to their fate. The former queen was reportedly still alive in 1985.

Conventional criminals who have committed serious crimes are usually sent to prisons such as Sam Khe, near Vientiane. Those guilty of petty offences of 'social crimes' may be sent to the island rehabilitation camps of Done Thao or Done Nang. Important persons charged with corruption or a crime against the state usually await trial at Sam Khe (bail is unknown). Those guilty of political 'crimes' such as excessive and injurious criticism of the Party line, of expressing 'pro-Chinese' sentiments, or of 'narrow nationalism' and failing to understand the need for 'Indochinese solidarity' or the 'special relationship' between Vietnam and Laos, are usually sent to Houa Phan province for a period of physical labour and ideological remoulding. There thus exist four categories of detention in Laos: prisons for criminals, re-education camps for former RLG officials, rehabilitation camps for social deviants and remoulding centres for ideological deviants.

In 1983 and 1984, a series of arrests took place of senior government officials on unspecified charges. The subsequent release of some, and their rehabilitation to previously held positions does indicate that an appeal system of sorts was operating. These arrests and releases (which have already been discussed from a political point of view) do, however, point up weaknesses in the Lao legal system. Arrests were made on the basis of denunciations which were not adequately investigated. Evidence was circumstantial and in some cases appears to have been fabricated. Appeal against sentences came from pressure mounted by families and friends of the accused rather than by qualified legal representatives in accordance with recognized procedures. Thus although some attempt has been made, especially since 1983, to set up a formal system of justice in the LPDR, there is still much room for improvement. Further changes are unlikely, however, before the new constitution is promulgated, probably in 1986.

Religion

Pathet Lao policies towards Buddhism have undergone certain transformations over the period 1955–85. As early as the first coalition government in 1957, when present Politburo member Phoumi Vongvichit was Minister for Religious Affairs, the Pathet Lao recognized the potential value of gaining support of the Buddhist *Sangha* (community of monks). At the same time they recognized the need to politicize the *Sangha* progressively if it were to become an instrument of Pathet Lao policy (Stuart-Fox & Bucknell, 1982). Particularly effective use was made of the *Sangha* as a vehicle for the propagation of Pathet Lao policies during 1974 and 1975 in creating conditions for the seizure of political power and subsequently in legitimizing the political authority of the new regime (Stuart-Fox, 1983).

Since 1975, two phases can be discerned in the policies pursued by the new regime towards Buddhism. During the first phase, the accent was on political consolidation of the regime, and legitimization of the right of the LPRP to exercise a monopoly of political power. The Party set out to reorganize the *Sangha* in such a way as to destroy it as an autonomous hierarchical social organization and to subordinate Buddhist teachings to the political ideology of the LPRP. During this phase, the traditional relationship between the *Sangha* and the Lao lay community was consistently undermined in order to reduce the possibility of popular support for any resistance the *Sangha* might offer. Only when the reorganization of the *Sangha* was complete were these pressures reduced. In the second phase since 1980, a more liberal policy has been pursued towards Buddhism, which has experienced something of a revival as measured by popular attendance at festivals and membership of the *Sangha*. These phases are worth briefly examining before present policies towards Buddhism are discussed.

On the theoretical level, the Pathet Lao have consistently claimed that Buddhism and socialism are compatible systems of belief. During special seminars in 1975 and 1976, monks were told that Buddhism and socialism had much in common: both taught the equality of all men and women; both renounced individual, but accepted communal ownership of property; both sought to alleviate human suffering. The socialist monk Khamtan Thepbuali argued that Buddhism had in the past proved itself compatible with various different political and social systems and could do so again. However, in the process of adapting to socialism, Buddhism in Laos would have to rid itself of those superstitious accretions which had served the old order by keeping people in the bondage of ignorance. In their place should be taught those truths which promote social progress and socialist morality (Stuart-Fox and Bucknell, 1982).

On the level of popular belief, however, Pathet Lao criticism of Buddhist rituals and practices actively sought to undermine the Buddhist world-view. Cadres ridiculed the Buddhist cosmology of tiered heavens and hells, the existence of nature spirits (*phi*) and the notions of transference of merit. More importantly, they criticized the non-materialism of Buddhism, and urged instead the crucial importance of material accumulation for social progress and the alleviation of want. The surplus wealth that peasants directed to the *Sangha* in order to obtain religious merit should instead be directed to the state, where it could be put to better use.

More important from the Pathet Lao point of view than the challenge offered by Buddhist beliefs to the implementation of socialism was that offered by the *Sangha* to LPRP monopolization of social influence and political power. Traditionally, Buddhism provided the primary focus of cohesion in Lao village society. This was symbolized by the village *wat*, the site not only of religious rituals and ceremonies, but also of community meetings called to discuss the secular affairs of the village. Monks often played a moderating role in such discussions and were invariably listened to with respect. In order for the LPRP to impose its will, the social influence of the *Sangha* had to be replaced by the Party itself. From 1975 on, Party controlled village administrative committees took all important decisions. Monks might be co-opted to serve on these committees, but only if prepared to follow the Party line—in which case, in the eyes of many villagers, they lost the prestige associated with their supposedly uncommitted detachment from worldly affairs.

During 1975 and in the early years of the regime, the LPRP pursued a deliberate policy aimed at identifying the *Sangha* with the propagation of socialism. Monks, accompanied by PL officials, were used to spread the Party line. As Phoumi Vongvichit stated in a speech to Buddhist monks in Vientiane in October 1976,

the policy of this party and government is . . . to request Buddhist monks to give sermons to teach the people and encourage them to understand that all policies and lines of the party and government are in line with the teachings of the Lord Buddha so that the people will be willing to follow them. Thus, there will be no lazy people, thieves, or liars in our country. Instead, there will be only diligent people working for the prosperity of the country. If our Buddhist monks can do this, it means that they are contributing to economic construction. [FBIS, 28 October 1976.]

Monks reluctant to include political material in their sermons were forced to attend re-education seminars. At the same time as the *Sangha* came increasingly to be used as an instrument of Party policy, its structure as an independently organized hierarchy offering an alternative path to social advancement and prestige was effectively subordinated to the Party. The *Sangha* was restructured under close Party supervision as the Lao United Buddhists Association (LUBA), in which elected committees at each level replaced individual leaders, and all appointees to executive positions required Party approval. Abolition of the former *Sangha* hierarchy was symbolically effected by smashing the large ceremonial fans that higher grades of monks carried as emblems of their rank.

As a result of these measures, many monks fled to Thailand. Others left the *Sangha* and returned to lay life. Those who remained accepted the role the

Party assigned them. The *Sangha* thus became a vehicle of government policy for the building of socialism. All monks had to study Marxism–Leninism and the pronouncements of the Party in order to perform their social duty of educating children to become good citizens in a socialist state. In addition they were to care for the sick by administering traditional medicines and to assist in the socialist construction of the country by working to produce their own livelihood—by growing their own vegetables and no longer relying solely on donations from the lay community. A monk was only eligible for a government rice ration provided he worked at such socially productive tasks. The traditional dawn alms-round was never abolished, however—at least not in Vientiane—though with the economic downturn of 1976–8, few could afford to give much. Also fewer people visited *wats* for fear of being branded religious. The key relationship between monks and the lay community was thus progressively weakened.

The political use made of Buddhism had a positive aspect, however: since the regime was deliberately using Buddhism to advance its own ends, it had necessarily to grant it official recognition. Monks attended all secular celebrations, while government representatives attended major Buddhist festivals. The official news media carried occasional reports of Buddhist activities, and the government even provided some assistance in recon-structing damaged or dilapidated Buddhist *wats*. After the liberalization of policy introduced by the Seventh Resolution in December 1979, Buddhism came increasingly to be accepted as integral to the Lao cultural identity, and thus to be officially condoned, and even encouraged. The number of novices, after falling sharply, began to increase; lay attendance at Buddhist ceremonies picked up; and the ban which prevented Party members from participating in religious rituals was relaxed. By 1985, Party members could even enter the *Sangha* for the brief period necessary to perform funerary rites for close relatives, and even members of the Politburo and their wives began regularly attending major Buddhist festivals.

According to LUBA President, Maha Thongkhoune Anantasounthoṇe, in August 1985 there were 6,897 monks and 9,415 novices in Laos living in 2,812 *wats*, 373 of which had been restored since 1975 (interview, August 1985). Of the total number of monks and novices, over 3,000, or close on 20 per cent lived in Vientiane. To become a novice parental agreement is of course necessary, together with permission from the village administrative committee, while to take full ordination as a monk requires the permission of district (*tasseng*) authorities, and of the local *tasseng* committee of the LUBA. Many novices still join the *Sangha* to obtain an education and free board and lodging in a larger urban centre. Their studies include the usual school subjects together with instruction in Buddhist precepts and socialist politics. Political instruction is necessary, according to the Venerable Thongkhoune, because in contemporary Làos Buddhism and politics go together: monks are citizens of the LPDR and have to understand the situation in their country, The principal tasks for all monks were, he said, as follows; to educate the people in the Buddhist religion; to teach people to read and write; to care for the sick and promote use of traditional medicines; to assist in self-help projects such as construction of village roads, wells, and *wats*; and to take part in the international movement for peace. (Laos hosted the Seventh Asian Buddhist Conference for Peace in February 1986, with 200 delegates from twenty countries.)

Monks are free in Laos to pursue traditional Buddhist activities. The dawn alms-round is a regular feature of life in Vientiane. In addition to their studies and work programme, monks meditate for two hours daily. During the Buddhist lent (the three months of the rainy season) special courses for young monks are given to inculcate Buddhist principles. Pali studies are pursued in Vientiane and the LUBA has applied for advanced students to be again permitted to study in India, as under the previous regime. (Between 1975 and 1985, no Lao Buddhists were permitted to pursue Buddhist studies abroad.)

After a decade of socialism in Laos an acceptable *modus vivendi* has been arrived at between the Party and the *Sangha*. The earlier repressive phase has been replaced by a more liberal recognition of the continuing importance of Buddhism in defining the Lao national cultural identity. The annual cycle of twelve major Buddhist festivals is regularly performed with Party representatives in attendance. All major Party functions are attended by senior monks. In addition, several monks were members of the Lao Front for National Construction at various levels, with five serving on the LFNC Central Committee in 1985. Buddhism, it would appear, seems assured of a continuing place in the life of the LPDR.

Culture

The cultural policy of the LPRP has had two overriding concerns: the first has been to destroy the baleful influence of imperialist culture, mainly that of the United States; the second has been to develop a socialist Lao culture, purged of all backward and superstitious accretions. To this end the regime initially waged a relentless struggle against such 'decadent' Western cultural influences as drugs, gambling, pornography and rock music. The worst offenders were rounded up and sent off for rehabilitation in re-education camps. In place of the 'rotten, depraved and reactionary' culture that characterized the former regime, the Party set out to develop a modern socialist culture which would both create and be created by new Lao socialist men and women. In a major speech delivered to the 1984 annual conference on culture, Phoumi Vongvichit defined culture as 'the material and mental values built by mankind in the process of the evolution of their history'. And since the history of mankind is the history of classes, 'culture has to possess class characteristics'. As such, 'culture is revolution, and this revolution must correctly advance . . . in accordance with the policy and line of the Party and state' (FBIS, 12 December 1984). That line, Phoumi told conference delegates, had been defined in the Third Resolution of the Party CC outlining the three revolutions. The cultural and ideological revolution had to stay a step in advance in order to build a socialist culture that would be 'a fragrant flower and delicious food feeding the labouring people's happy morale' (ibid.). Such a culture could only be built by resolutely opposing the 'rotten culture' of Western capitalist countries. But, Phoumi warned, 'we have lowered our guard in many cultural domains', and young people were again being poisoned 'with liquor, girls, and rock music'. Many older people, on the other hand, had reverted to 'backward traditions' that were equally inimical to the building of a modern socialist culture.

The Party has had to move carefully with respect to these 'backward traditions', especially those religious rites and ceremonies which stand at the centre of both Lao Buddhist and minority cultures. Party policy is to 'keep the good traditions and reject the bad', good traditions being those which contribute to the socio-cultural goals of the Party; bad traditions those infused with either superstition or brutality, or which give rise to anti-social behaviour. Popular Buddhism has come under Party scrutiny for its superstitious beliefs (in demons, heavens and hells, etc.), for its anti-social practices (such as pursuit of the state of *upekkha*, inward-looking equanimity which takes no active interest in social problems), and for its tacit encouragement of crude and unseemly behaviour (during the rocket festival, for example, with its overt fertility symbolism). Even classical Buddhist texts have been re-edited to eliminate unacceptable anti-social or superstitious references.

One traditional Lao ceremony which has been fully accepted by the new regime is the *baci*. This ancient, characteristically Lao ceremony is non-Buddhist in origin (Zago, 1972), and probably dates back to the time when the Lao tribes were animist. In theory it is performed to ensure the return of a person's thirty-two souls in preparation for some important occasion. In practice it has become a semi-secular ceremony of welcome or farewell for honoured guests, or to mark some auspicious occasion. All communist leaders in Laos take part in *baci* ceremonies which are regularly performed in honour of foreign dignitaries and delegations.

The Party has been circumspect in its treatment of the culture of minority tribes. Ceremonies have been criticized for their brutal animal sacrifices, or for their superstitious worship of a variety of spirits (*phi*). Initial attempts to curb such practices and beliefs met with concerted tribal opposition, however, and have subsequently been relaxed. As Vice-Minister of Culture, Somsi Desakhampou admitted, minority beliefs were deeply held and difficult to change: the government could not prevent people from continuing to hold their beliefs (interview in Vientiane, August 1985). What he did not say, but clearly implied, was that the problem is a political one, for the cultural identity of tribal groups centres upon traditional ceremonial and to threaten that identity opens the government to charges of attempting to assimilate minorities into a dominant lowland Lao culture.

The long-term goal is to draw both lowland Lao and minority cultures into a unified evolving Lao socialist culture in which all ethnic groups can participate on a basis of cultural equality. To this end, the government has taken measures to preserve certain aspects of minority culture, such as traditional dress, handicrafts, music and dance. Minority dances are taught at the National School of Dance and Music in Vientiane, at which some of the best Lao classical dancers from the former Natasingh School of Dancing continue to teach. About a hundred students attend the school: most specialize in traditional Lao music, or classical dancing.

At the forefront of the struggle to create a modern Lao socialist culture incorporating all that is best from the traditional cultures of the different ethnic groups is the National Institute for Artistic and Literary Research, an institution within the Ministry of Culture. The Institute encourages cultural debate by, among other things, publication of the literary journal *Vannasin*. It is a measure of the popular thirst for cultural expression in the LPDR that *Vannasin*, which sells for ten times the price of any other monthly journal, has the highest circulation (8,000 at the end of 1985). The journal regularly holds literary competitions which draw hundreds of entries. The winning short stories and poems are published in the journal or in anthologies. Letters to the editor and unsolicited contributions arrive in a steady stream. The Institute is also responsible for cataloguing and preserving an estimated 5,000 Buddhist manuscripts in Vientiane, and another 3,500 in Luang Prabang, with the help of the Ecole Française d'Extrême Orient.

The goal of creating a new Lao socialist culture, like that of creating new Lao socialist men and women, is likely to take a considerable period of time. It was not long before the regime was forced to relax its puritan restrictions on popular culture, whether in the form of Buddhist *boums* (pagoda fairs or festivals) with their gambling and dancing, or in the form of amateur theatre troupes performing at private functions such as weddings or parties (Stuart-Fox, 1984). Since then the Lao have in some measure reverted to their characteristic selves: pleasure is sought in convivial company; *boums* flourish again; the 'graying' of Lao society has to some extent been reversed (cf. *New York Times Magazine*, 20 May 1979). If the present trend is anything to go by, future Lao socialist culture will take more account of traditional Lao cultural values than seemed likely during the early years of the regime.

6 The Regime's Foreign Policy

Because of its economic and political weakness on the one hand, and its strategic situation on the other, the LPDR faces particular problems in the formulation of its foreign policy. During the first ten years of its existence, the communist regime in Laos had to contend not only with Thai antagonism and the barely concealed hostility of the United States, but also, because of its alignment with Vietnam, with the active displeasure of the People's Republic of China. Since 1979, the keystone of Lao foreign policy has been the 'militant solidarity and multi-faceted cooperation' between the three countries of Indochina—Laos, Vietnam and Kampuchea—supported by the Soviet Union and other Soviet Bloc states. Chinese and Thai policies have been vigorously denounced, but at the same time, the LPDR has sought a measure of accommodation with both states on the level of day-to-day relations. Recognition of the country's continuing need for development aid has led the leaders of the LPDR not only to establish cordial relations with a number of capitalist states, but also recently to attempt to improve relations with the United States. The net effect of these policies has been to move Laos towards *de facto* non-aligned status without, however, impairing its standing within the Soviet Bloc as a faithful ally of both the Soviet Union and Vietnam.

The foreign policy of the LPDR can thus best be examined under five headings: the 'special relationship' with Vietnam which serves as the basis for relations within the 'Indochina Solidarity Bloc'; relations with the Soviet Union and Eastern Europe; relations with the People's Republic of China; relations with Thailand and the other Asean states; and relations with the rest of the capitalist world, particularly with the United States. In conclusion an attempt will be made to sum up the logic and direction of Lao foreign policy and to assess the future prospects of the LPDR.

The 'Special Relationship' with Vietnam

Vietnamese writers have attempted to discover deep historical roots for the special relationship that now exists between Laos and Vietnam (Ky Son, 1980a). In reality, however, the present relationship was only forged in opposition to French colonial rule after the founding of the Indochinese Communist Party in 1930; and not until 1945 did a pattern of systematic cooperation between revolutionary elites in both countries develop. The basis of this cooperation was spelled out in a document entitled 'Viet-Lao Cooperation' rather hastily drawn up in August 1945 immediately following the Japanese surrender. This called for a popular seizure of power in Laos, under the leadership of the Lao branch of the ICP, whose membership was then very largely drawn from the 100,000 strong Vietnamese community in Laos. In other words, Vietnamese communists were to assist in creating a revolutionary government in Laos which would be responsive to Vietnamese national and strategic interests—a broad policy goal which the revolutionary leadership in Vietnam consistently pursued over the next thirty years. (This section is largely based on Stuart-Fox, 1986c.)

The history of Lao–Vietnamese cooperation during the Thirty-Year Struggle has already been traced. This long period of common commitment to a common cause and shared revolutionary experience forms the historical basis for the 'special relationship' as it presently exists. Both the LPRP and the Vietnamese Communist Party trace their history back to a common origin, the ICP, and a common founder, Ho Chi Minh. Thus Phoune Sipaseuth could describe the LPRP as 'pursuing the glorious historic cause of the Indochinese Communist Party—which was founded, trained and tempered by great Comrade Ho Chi Minh' (FBIS, 19 March 1985). During those thirty years, a close personal relationship developed between the revolutionary leadership of the LPRP and the VCP. Common ways of thinking developed which led to the adoption of common approaches to similar problems. The leaders of both countries have a similar ideological perception of the historic roles of their respective parties and revolutions. They share a commitment to proletarian internationalism and to promotion of the world socialist revolution for which Indochina as a whole, and Laos in particular, must serve as the 'advance post'.

A further important basis for the 'special relationship' between Laos and Vietnam has been the close and continuing military cooperation between their respective armed forces. From the arrival of Souphanouvong in Savannakhet in September 1946 with a Vietnamese 'personal guard' to the involvement of Vietnamese 'volunteer' forces in Laos during the 'anti-US resistance' prior to the cease-fire agreement of February 1973, the full extent of this military cooperation was consistently concealed. Only since the formation of the LPDR has the military role Vietnamese forces played during the course of the Lao revolution been fully recognized ('Vietnam: The Anti-U.S. Resistance War', JPRS 80968, 3 June 1982). The often expressed militant solidarity which grew up between the Vietnamese People's Army and the Lao People's Liberation Army during this long period continues to characterize the military collaboration which exists between the two states.

Military cooperation during the Thirty-Year Struggle is not seen by the Lao as having been a purely one-way process. The strategic importance of Laos was especially evident during the Second Indochina War. The Ho Chi Minh trail, for example, ran almost entirely through Lao territory. Writing in November 1975, Kaysone described the revolutionary relationship between Laos and Vietnam as follows:

The revolution(s) of the two nations—Laos and Vietnam—have special interrelationships and mutual influence. For the Lao revolution, the contribution of Vietnam is indispensable, and for the Vietnamese revolution the contribution of Laos is indispensable . . .

And he went on to add:

The Lao people have the obligation of continuing to strengthen their solidarity with Vietnam, so that those two peoples can continue to carry out their revolutions and continue to assist each other in developing and defending their countries. [JPRS 609, 21 January 1976.]

Two months later, after the final victory of the Lao revolution and establishment of the LPDR, a joint Lao–Vietnamese communiqué issued on the occasion of the visit to Vietnam of a high level Lao delegation, endorsed the concept of a 'special relationship' between the countries in the following terms:

The two sides greatly rejoice at and we are proud of the splendid development of the special relationship which has closely bound the Vietnam Worker's Party with the Lao People's Revolutionary Party, and the Vietnamese people with the Lao people . . . [VNA, 11 February 1976, cited by Thayer, in Stuart-Fox, 1982a.]

The communiqué was of particular importance, both because it marked the first official use of the term 'special relationship', and because in the Vietnamese view, it 'laid down the general principles governing the relations of mutual assistance and cooperation between the two countries' (Ky Son, 1980b, p. 26). The two sides agreed, *inter alia*,

to consolidate and enhance the solidarity, long-term cooperation and mutual assistance between the two parties and the two countries in a spirit of correctly combining genuine patriotism with proletarian internationalism in the interest of each nation. [VNA, 11 February 1976.]

The communiqué also foreshadowed a number of measures aimed at reinforcing the 'special relationship'. These included the regular exchange of party and state delegations, training of Lao cadres in Vietnam, and cooperation in everything from economic development to culture, education and information under the auspices of national committees set up for these purposes.

In August the same year, Lao Finance Minister Nouhak Phoumsavanh led a delegation to Hanoi to negotiate a series of agreements on Vietnamese financial aid to Laos, training of Lao technicians, trade and transit rights for Lao imports passing through Vietnamese ports. At the same time, a joint Vietnam–Laos Economic, Cultural, Scientific and Technical Co-operation Commission was established to co-ordinate all non-military cooperation between the two countries. This opened the way for as many as 5–6,000 Vietnamese advisers to be stationed in Laos.

The last step in the process of formalizing the 'special relationship' came with signing in July 1977 of a twenty-five year Treaty of Friendship and Co-operation between the two countries. The treaty itself comprises six brief articles, but includes in addition three secret protocols covering joint defence arrangements, delineation of the Lao–Vietnamese frontier and Vietnamese economic aid to Laos. Article Two of the treaty states simply that both sides agree

to wholeheartedly support and assist each other and carry out a close co-operation aimed at reinforcing the defence capacity, preserving the independence, sovereignty and territorial integrity [of each state] . . . against all schemes and acts of sabotage by imperialism and foreign reactionary forces. [This translation is taken from FBIS, 19 July 1977, as quoted in Brown & Zasloff, 1986. For the French translation, see BN no. 26, 16 April 1983.]

Agreement on the stationing of Vietnamese forces in Laos, secondment of Vietnamese advisers to the Lao army, political and military training of Lao military personnel and provision of military equipment to the Lao army were all relegated to the relevant protocol, and remain a close secret. Suffice it to say that the close military cooperation that existed between the armies of the two countries during the Thirty-Year Struggle has continued into the post-1975 period. Vietnamese influence in the Lao army remains strong and pervasive. Vietnamese advisers are attached to Lao units down to the battalion level, or below (company level) in specialist units. Vietnamese logistics, communications and engineering personnel are stationed in Laos. The reorganization of the Lao People's Army in 1976 was carried out under Vietnamese guidance and supervision. More importantly, Vietnamese political cadres assist in the political training of Lao officers and influence the appointment and promotion of Lao military personnel. The military dimension of the Lao–Vietnamese 'special relationship' is thus of central importance in any estimation of the nature of this relationship.

Article Three of the Treaty outlines the full extent of non-military cooperation between the two countries. Both sides agreed to

strengthen their relations of socialist cooperation of mutual benefit in agriculture, forestry, industry, communications and transport, the exploitation of natural resources and other economic fields; wholeheartedly assist each other economically and technically; help each other to train cadres, exchange economic, cultural, scientific and technical specialists and broaden the trade relations according to a regime of special privileges.

The two sides will widen scientific and technical exchanges and cooperation in the domains of culture, arts, education, public health, information, press, radio broadcasting, cinematography, physical culture and sports, and other cultural fields.

Over subsequent years the extent of this cooperation has become evident. Meetings of the joint Vietnam–Laos Cooperation Commission take place roughly once a year to plan policy and review progress. In addition, on an average more than a dozen major delegations are exchanged annually in each direction from ministries and state committees of the governments of both countries—not to mention innumerable lower-level delegations. These visits have resulted in literally dozens of different agreements covering particularly financial assistance, communications, public works such as bridge construction projects and road building, agriculture, forestry, irrigation, mining, transportation, education, public health, publishing, information, culture, sport and even tourism. Almost without exception these are one-way agreements under which Vietnam provides assistance to Laos, either in the form of training of Lao technical cadres or through the provision of Vietnamese experts to work in Laos.

Vietnam also provides considerable economic assistance to Laos. A number of interest-free loans have been made available to finance Lao projects. The Vietnamese port of Danang charges no duties on goods for trans-shipment to Laos. Vietnam is assisting the Soviet Union in building an oil pipeline from the coast to the Mekong to supply Lao fuel needs. As one Vietnamese publication noted, Vietnam has assisted Laos

in the fields of agriculture and forestry in particular, focusing on a survey of Laos's agricultural, forestry, and stockbreeding potentials. Vietnam has helped Laos conduct basic surveys, then build a series of production and experimental establishments such as plant and animal nurseries, State farms, afforestation centres and logging camps, roads for the transportation of timber and forestry products, sawmills, turpentine and shellac extraction factories and factories manufacturing such production means as farm implements, fertilizers, insecticides and animal feed.

Vietnam also helped in the survey and construction of small- and medium-sized hydraulic, irrigation and hydro-electric projects....

In industry, Vietnam supplies to Laos raw materials, fuel and equipment to expand and build a number of industrial establishments to produce tools, cement and building materials, engineering factories for the postal and communications and transport services, a number of consumer goods factories as well as some mining enterprises, tin and gypsum.

Vietnam is also helping in the repair and upgrading of old roads and in the building of new roads and bridges, in improving the navigability of . . . rivers, the building of ferries, and vehicle repair shops. A major joint project is being undertaken by Vietnam and Laos: to build roads from Laos to the Vietnamese ports of Vinh-Ben Thuy and Da Nang across the Truong Son Range [the Annamite Cordillera] . . .

Vietnam's assistance and cooperation in the domain of culture and education has helped Laos shoot a number of documentary films, provide vocational training for Laos's art troupes and build the first material and technical bases for cultural and artistic work including a film studio and expand information and exhibition work [*sic*]. Many Lao students have been sent to study in Vietnam. Vietnamese cadres have also helped Laos to carry out an educational reform, improve school curricula, compile text-books, and open vocational schools and a teachers' college. [Ky Son, 1980b, pp. 26, 30.]

This is the most complete summary available of the range of Vietnamese economic assistance to Laos. No value has ever been placed by the Vietnamese on their aid to Laos. The only figure has been provided by the Lao who revealed that Vietnamese aid had totalled US$133.4 million to finance some two hundred economic projects during the decade 1975–85 (FBIS, 8 November 1985).

Article Four of the Treaty of Friendship and Cooperation refers to the 1,650 km. long border between the two countries. It states 'The two sides affirm their determination to build the Vietnamese–Lao border into a border of lasting friendship and fraternity between the two countries.' This was no more than a signal of intent. The protocol on the border remains unpublished, as does the subsequent 'rectification' of the frontier. Presumably, however, the protocol established certain guidelines to be followed in delineating the new frontier. The agreement was said by the Vietnamese to provide 'a model for relations of good neighbourliness and friendship between two countries'. On this basis, a joint border commission from both countries 'conducted a series of investigations and surveys to delimit the national borders, planted border markers, discussed the setting up of border posts and laid down principles for the operation of border crossing points' (Ky Son, 1980b, p. 26). By all accounts, however, the seven years of negotiations that followed were hard-fought and at times heated. Vietnamese demands that the frontier be 'rectified' in their favour met with determined resistance from Lao negotiators. Shouted accusations were exchanged, and at one point the Lao delegation broke off the negotiations. There are even unconfirmed reports that Lao troops fired on a Vietnamese team moving border markers.

On 24 February 1986, a border agreement was eventually signed, though its contents have not yet been published. Nor has either side notified the United Nations of changes to their frontiers as required under the Charter. The agreement was accompanied by a protocol covering on-the-spot delimitation and placing of a final set of border markers. That some 'rectification' of the frontier has already occurred seems certain, however. Vietnam is reported to have gained some territory southeast of Sam Neua, and some strategic points of access to, and sections of, the old Ho Chi Minh trail. In return the Lao have been given some territory in the south in what is now Sekong Province. Until the border between the two countries is published, however, the suspicion will exist that the Lao were forced by the Vietnamese, despite their opposition, to concede more than they gained.

Article Five of the Treaty obliged each side to respect the foreign policy of the other. This is particularly significant in view of subsequent events which drew Laos into conflict with the People's Republic of China in support of Vietnam. Consultations on foreign policy were unofficial and sporadic until the inaugural meeting in January 1980 in the series of biannual meetings between the foreign ministers of Vietnam, Laos and Kampuchea. These are held in Vientiane, Ho Chi Minh city and Phnom Penh in rotation to establish a coordinated foreign policy for the three states. The last article of the Treaty committed both states to a regular exchange of views on their mutual relationship.

The formal provisions of the Vietnam–Lao Treaty of Friendship and Cooperation established the legal basis for the stationing of Vietnamese troops in Laos, for Vietnamese military advisers to be attached to the Lao army, and for the whole spectrum of Vietnamese economic assistance to Laos. These provisions do not, however, exhaust the avenues of Vietnamese influence in Laos. Other avenues include province-to-province relations and relations between mass organizations. But by far the most important avenue of influence not mentioned in the treaty is through party-to-party relations.

Province-to-province relations provide for contact between Vietnamese and Lao administrative officials and Party members at the provincial level. The basis for such exchanges is the so-called 'sisterhood relationship' which links all sixteen Lao provinces with at least one corresponding province in the

SRV. For example, Lai Chau province in Vietnam is twinned with Phong Saly; Thanh Hoa with Houa Phan; Binh Tri Thien with Savavane and so on. Some provinces in Vietnam have a 'special relationship' at the local level with a particular district; others, such as Nghe Tinh, have relations with more than one Lao province (Bolikhamsai, Xieng Khouang, and Khammouane). Vietnamese provinces assist their Lao counterparts in small-scale construction projects, such as a village school or dispensary, in projects to increase agricultural production or improve public health, and in training personnel.

Province-to-province trade is also important in Vietnamese–Lao contacts at this level, especially given the considerable degree of provincial autonomy which pertains in Laos. The political and economic reasons for this autonomy have already been discussed. What is important in the present context is that trade between sister provinces in Laos and Vietnam not only is of economic importance, it also effectively reinforces provincial autonomy, weakens central Lao government control and potentially increases Vietnamese influence over Lao affairs.

Relations between corresponding mass organizations, including trade-union federations, women's unions and youth associations from each country provide additional avenues of contact and influence. Delegations are regularly exchanged between the Lao Front for National Construction and the Vietnamese Fatherland Front and between respective Lao–Vietnamese Friendship Associations. Such visits assist in breaking down Lao suspicion or resentment and help increase mutual understanding. Assistance is given in organization and political mobilization.

Examination of party-to-party relations is also of crucial importance for understanding the nature of the Lao–Vietnamese 'special relationship'. Relations between the two parties are particularly close, for reasons given above. Most leading Lao Party cadres have studied in Vietnam at the Nguyen Ai Quoc School outside Hanoi. Those with the rank of vice-minister or department head in the government who have not yet attended continue to be sent off in small groups for courses which last from nine months to a year. Instruction is in Lao on the theory of Marxism–Leninism and its application to conditions in Indochina. Within the LPRP the 'special relationship' with Vietnam is constantly stressed. For as Kaysone stated in the March 1985 issue of the Vietnamese journal *Tap Chi Cong San*:

To unite with Vietnam has always been a policy of strategic significance, a sacred sentiment and glorious obligation of the Lao party, administration and people, and also a guiding principal for all activities of all party, administrative and mass organizations and a criterion for fostering the revolutionary qualities of all party members and cadres at all levels. [FBIS, 27 March 1985.]

Vietnamese advisers also assist in planning the curriculum of the Lao Party and State School for Political Theory run by the relevant committee of the LPRP Central Committee, which lower ranking Lao cadres attend in Vientiane. There thus exists close correlation between the respective socialist ideologies taught in each country.

Vietnamese advisers and experts have been active in assisting the LPRP in a number of critical areas. These include the organization and administration of the Party; the work of the Party through propaganda and political education; and the organization and development of mass organizations. Delegations at various levels specializing in all these areas are regularly exchanged between the two countries. These have the nature of inspection missions when the Vietnamese visit Laos, and instruction missions when Lao delegations visit Vietnam. Party delegations are also exchanged on the local level, between towns or provinces.

It is at the highest level, however, that party-to-party relations are most effective as an avenue for the exercise of Vietnamese influence on Laos. Formal party-to-party relations are reportedly handled by the Secretariat of the Central Committee, but these are probably of less importance than informal relations between Vietnamese and Lao party leaders. Kaysone is said to consult regularly with members of the Vietnamese revolutionary elite who act as his advisers, most of whom he has known personally for decades. Discussions take place either at Kaysone's well-guarded headquarters compound just outside Vientiane where senior Vietnamese advisers also reside, or during occasional unpublicized visits to Hanoi. Among such old comrades, the need for a close and continuing 'special relationship' between Laos and Vietnam is taken for granted. After all, the present Lao leadership owes its position almost entirely to Vietnamese support, both past and present. Any reduction of that support could jeopardize the monopoly of political power enjoyed by present leaders.

The Vietnamese have not been content to base their country's relationship with the LPDR on personal relations between individual leaders, no matter how firmly founded these may be. An elaborate organizational structure reportedly exists, known as the Working Committee for the West, designated simply as CP-38. Whether this is actually its name is immaterial, however. So too is its actual membership, previously placed at 140 cadres, all experts on Lao affairs (FEER, 26 March 1982). What is important is that this organization, headquartered in Vietnam, reports directly to a representative of the VCP Politburo on matters of policy coordination between Laos and Vietnam.

Last but not least must be mentioned the presence of Vietnamese intelligence and security cadres in Laos. A contingent of Vietnamese political police is reported to train and advise their Lao counterparts (FEER, 24 August 1979). Vietnamese advisers are attached to the Lao Ministry of the Interior. Vietnamese instructors teach at the Lao police academy at Don Noon, six kilometres to the east of Vientiane. A Vietnamese security unit is said to have been assigned to guard senior Lao leaders after a series of unsuccessful assassination attempts against Kaysone in 1976 and 1977. Vietnamese advice, based on secret police reports, is believed to have played a part in purgng the LPRP of anti-Chinese elements in 1979 (FEER, 26 March 1982). How effective Vietnamese intelligence operations are in Laos is, of course, impossible to assess. What can be said is that the Vietnamese intelligence network is widely believed in Laos to be most efficient, to have developed excellent Lao contacts, and to be extremely well informed on what goes on in the LPDR.

The relationship between Laos and Vietnam has been described by the Vietnamese as closer than lips and teeth. The Lao refer to the mutual affection between the two peoples as 'deeper than the water of the Mekong River', season unspecified. For both sides their relationship is said to constitute a 'law of development' of their respective revolutions. Foreign observers have pointed out the inequality of the relationship, and charac- terized Laos variously as a 'colony', or 'puppet' of Vietnam (e.g., Pasakhom, 1985; cf. Dommen, 1979). Others conceive of Laos as forming part of a *de facto* Vietnamese-dominated federation of the three Indochinese states. At the other extreme, some authors believe that Lao decision-making is all but independent of Vietnamese influence (Evans & Rowley, 1984). Thayer has argued that Vietnam enjoys an 'influence relationship' with Laos, by which he means that Vietnam employs 'non-coercive means' such as diplomacy and economic assistance to ensure that Lao policies are favourable to Vietnam (Thayer, in Stuart-Fox, 1982a). The nature of the 'special relationship' between Laos and Vietnam is not simply a matter for academic dispute: it is central to any appreciation of the constraints operating on Lao foreign policy. It is essential therefore to understand by what means Vietnamese influence is exerted.

Clearly the relationship between Vietnam and Laos is not one between metropole and colony: Vietnamese officials do not form the administration of Laos. Nor does an Indochinese federation exist: it is unnecessarily misleading therefore to make reference to such a form of relationship between states. Equally, it is naïve to believe that Vietnam is at once the dominant partner in the relationship with Laos, but chooses not to exercise that dominance to dominate (Evans & Rowley, 1984, p. 82). Vietnam has nurtured its relationship with Laos with great care over many years, but hardly out of a spirit of pure altruism. For Vietnam, Laos is essential to its strategic defence. It is only to be expected, therefore, that the Vietnamese would want to protect and prolong the close and friendly relations they now enjoy with the leaders of Laos. The measure of the degree of control that Vietnam has over Laos is the extent to which the Vietnamese can ensure that the government in Laos remains staunchly pro-Vietnamese.

Vietnamese influence in Laos is, as outlined above, exercised in a variety of ways. The economic relationship is important but not crucial. Laos could obtain aid from other donors. Even the road links with Vietnam, the oil pipeline and use of Vietnamese ports are not enough to establish Lao economic dependency on Vietnam: supplies can always be brought through Thailand. Nor is Vietnamese influence exercised primarily through economic experts working in Laos, or through advisers attached to Lao ministries, though these do offer political as well as technical guidance. Vietnamese experts do direct particular projects—but then other foreign experts exercise similar direction over 'their' projects. Vietnamese working in the areas of education, culture and propaganda do exert considerable political influence, but in all cases such influence derives not from the advisers and technicians *per se*, but from the political backing they receive from the leadership of the Lao People's Revolutionary Party.

Vietnamese political influence in Laos is principally exercised through two channels: the LPRP, and the Lao People's Army. As noted above, liaison between the LPRP and the VCP takes place at the highest level, both informally between members of the respective Politburos, and formally through special Party organizations. So pervasive is the Vietnamese presence in Laos, so extensive their contacts at all levels of the LPRP and so accurate their sources of information, that no one in the Lao Party can afford to so much as voice any position which would be interpreted as anti-Vietnamese. Indeed, access to power within the LPRP depends upon overcoming entirely all sentiments of 'narrow nationalism', and endorsing fully the necessity for 'Indochinese solidarity'. To suggest any other policy would be to invite a period of political re-education. Cooperation with Vietnamese cadres at all levels is thus a prerequisite for political survival in Laos. To do otherwise would be to open oneself to criticism and censure and to destroy all political prospects, as every Lao cadre well knows.

The army, however, constitutes an equally strong focus of Vietnamese influence. As outlined above, Vietnamese influence in the LPA constitutes a high degree of control, so ubiquitous is it. Only in the numerically small and politically unimportant air force is there any comparable countervailing

Soviet influence. Promotion in the LPA depends upon political reliability as determined by the same criterion of devotion to Indochinese solidarity as applies in the Party. In the army, however, the Vietnamese presence is more pervasive than in the LPRP. Vietnamese cadres are not members of the LPRP; but Vietnamese advisers are permanently attached to the LPA. Once again, however, influence is not exercised primarily at the level of logistics or weapons supply—it is political. If the need arose, the army could always be used to exert control over the Party—from within the Party—much as Soviet influence was exercised in Poland. And in Laos, too, as in Poland, there is always an ultimate means available of enforcing the will of the dominant power—the presence of 50,000 Vietnamese troops. This, too, all Lao cadres recognize as a crucial component of their political environment. Through these means, therefore, through the Party and the army, the Vietnamese exert not an influence over the day to day affairs of the Lao state, but ultimate control over the governance and policies of Laos in all areas that impinge upon Vietnamese interests. Only within the limits set by these Vietnamese interests do the Lao have freedom of action, either in the internal development of their country, or in their external relations. Clearly Vietnamese strategic interests impinge more on the latter than on the former.

The 'special relationship' between Laos and Vietnam forms a model for the relationship between Vietnam and Kampuchea. On 18 February 1979, less than six weeks after the fall of Phnom Penh to invading Vietnamese forces, Vietnam signed a twenty-five-year Treaty of Friendship and Co-operation with the new People's Republic of Kampuchea remarkably similar to that signed with Laos eighteen months before. No such treaty exists, however, between Laos and Kampuchea; only an Agreement on Economic, Cultural, Scientific and Technical Cooperation signed in March 1979. These two agreements did, however, extend the solidarity relationship which existed between Vietnam and Laos to include Kampuchea. In a declaration accompanying the signing of the Lao–Kampuchean agreement, Presidents Souphanouvong and Heng Samrin 'expressed their determination to reinforce the militant solidarity and the great, pure and healthy friendship between Laos, Kampuchea and Vietnam'. For, in the words of the Lao Party journal: 'The ties between Laos, Vietnam and Kampuchea constitute a factor in, and an objective law for the existence and development of these three nations sharing common frontiers and the same common destiny' (KPL/BQ, 15 August 1980).

The 'great friendship, special militant solidarity and all-round cooperation' between the three countries were formally endorsed at the first summit conference of the leaders of the three Indochinese states held in Vientiane in

February 1983. Frequent trilateral meetings take place on an increasing range of concerns of interest to all three states. The most important are the regular semi-annual meetings of the foreign ministers of the three states, and of the committees set up to coordinate economic cooperation. It is clear, however, that the third link in the 'Indochinese solidarity bloc', between Laos and Kampuchea, is very much less substantial than the two involving Vietnam. The Lao do have a few technicians working in the adjoining Kampuchean provinces of Stung Treng and Monkolgiri. There has been some cooperation between Laos and Kampuchean forces in the border region against remnants of the Khmer Rouge. Delegations are exchanged, but far less frequently than with Vietnam. Laos and Kampuchea have important interests in common, however, not least their relations with Vietnam. It seems logical, therefore, that the two countries should develop closer relations in the future—Vietnam permitting.

The Soviet Union and Eastern Europe

Relations between Laos and the Soviet Union have steadily gained in importance since 1975. The Soviet Union supplies Laos with around 60 per cent of the total value of its annual economic aid package. Lao gratitude is expressed in terms hardly less effusive than those used to describe the relationship with Vietnam. Lao leaders take every opportunity to express their 'close solidarity and all-round cooperation' with the Soviet Union, which is recognized as undisputed leader of the Soviet Bloc. Soviet anniversaries, such as the sixtieth anniversary of the founding of the Soviet Union, and the fortieth anniversary of the victory against fascism, are regularly commemorated with amicable gatherings and mass meetings. Soviet initiatives in the pursuit of world peace, and Soviet policies on everything from disarmament to Afghanistan are enthusiastically endorsed. In October 1985, the twenty-fifth anniversary of the establishment of Lao-Soviet diplomatic relations was 'joyfully celebrated by the entire Lao people' (FBIS, 9 October 1985).

The stream of Party, state, army and 'friendship' delegations exchanged between Laos and the Soviet Union is second only to the number exchanged between Laos and Vietnam. A Lao delegation dutifully attends every important Soviet occasion. Kaysone himself led the Lao delegation to the 26th Congress of the Communist Party of the Soviet Union in 1981. In return, a high ranking Soviet delegation led by Politburo member Grigorii Romanov attended the Third Congress of the LPRP in 1982. Kaysone regularly spends an annual vacation in the Soviet Union, at the end of which he meets with top Soviet leaders. In August 1985, Kaysone was summoned to Moscow on what was called 'a friendly working visit' to meet with Mikhail Gorbachëv. The visit was lauded as 'an event of historical importance', which could only strengthen 'the relations of fraternal friendship, militant solidarity and cooperation on all levels betwen Laos and the USSR, relations which no enemy can destroy' (KPL/BQ, 31 August 1985). The joint communiqué issued after the meeting noted Soviet support for Lao attempts to improve relations with Thailand and Lao support for Soviet foreign policy initiatives, including normalization of relations with China, 'normalization which would not be conditional upon any prejudice to any third country' (KPL/BQ, 29 August 1985).

Soviet aid to Laos takes a variety of forms. As many as 1,500 Soviet political, economic and military advisers plus their dependents reside in the LPDR, a total of around 5,000 Soviet citizens. Soviet political advisers assist in Party organization and Soviet experts teach Marxism-Leninism at the Lao Party and State School for Political Theory. In terms of military aid, the Soviet Union has supplied Laos with artillery pieces, mortars and other light weapons for the army and with MIG-21 jet fighters, Antonov 24 and 26 transport planes, and helicopters for the Air Force. It has also provided civilian aircraft for Lao Aviation. Soviet experts train Lao pilots and Soviets assist in air traffic control, logistics and communications. The Soviet Union has built a satellite reception station and radar facilities at Vientiane, an airport at Xieng Khouang on the Plain of Jars and new military installations at the former French base of Seno. On the economic side, six Soviet experts are permanently attached to the Lao Planning Committee and high powered delegations from the Soviet Planning Committee (Gosplan) visited Laos to assist in formulating both the first and second five-year plans. Other experts work in broadcasting, public health, communications, agriculture, mining and public works. The Soviets have built an oil pipeline from Vietnam to Laos, a 150-bed hospital at Vientiane, a polytechnic institute, a car-repair workshop, and major bridges over the Nam Ngum and Nam Ca Dinh rivers, among the fifty-four projects scheduled for completion during the first Lao five-year plan. More than 1,000 Lao students are undergoing education at any one time in the Soviet Union. A number of long-term economic and financial agreements have also been signed between the two countries, the details of which have not been released, but which among other things commit the Soviet Union to help meet the chronic deficit in the Lao budget. Trade between the Soviet Union and Laos under bilateral commodity exchange agreements has steadily increased though detailed figures are not available.

As the principal aid donor to Laos, the Soviet Union wields considerable influence in Vientiane. Given the Lao–Vietnamese 'special relationship', from the Lao point of view the Soviet Union represents the only possible alternative pole of influence which might be used to offset Vietnam. Although there is no indication that the Soviet Union would be prepared to displace the Vietnamese in Laos, it is true to say that the Russians have effectively built up a bilateral relationship with Laos which could serve as the basis for increased Soviet influence at the expense of Vietnam. It is at least worth noting in this regard that in a booklet produced in Moscow by Soviet writer Youri Mikhéev celebrating the tenth anniversary of the LPDR, no mention was made of a 'special relationship' between Laos and Vietnam (Mikhéev, 1985).

Lao relations with other states of the Soviet Bloc are warm, but not as close as with Vietnam or the Soviet Union. All except Poland and Romania have on-going aid programmes in Laos. East Germany and Czechoslovakia provide scholarships for up to 300 Lao students a year. East Germany has also established a number of small workshops and assists in forestry and coffee production. Hungary has built a seventy-bed maternity hospital in Vientiane. Bulgaria has experts working in oilseed production and vegetable gardening. Cuba has established a livestock and dairy farm. Mongolia has built a sixty-bed hospital at Phonesavan on the Plain of Jars. Hungary and Czechoslovakia have built road bridges. Altogether well over a hundred Soviet Bloc experts are resident in the LPDR at any one time.

The People's Republic of China

The PRC greeted the formation of the LPDR with enthusiasm, even though it must already have been apparent to Chinese leaders in Beijing that the new communist state on China's southern frontier lay firmly in Vietnam's rather than China's sphere of influence. Chinese assistance to Laos throughout the Thirty-Year Struggle had been considerable, but Chinese influence was limited to the northern provinces where major Chinese aid projects, especially a ten-year road building programme, were concentrated. After December 1975, the LPDR invited the Chinese to continue their aid programme, though only in the north of the country, as far south as Luang Prabang. A priority was to complete the section of road from Nam Bac to Luang Prabang in order to link Vientiane with the northern road network running south from the Chinese border.

Initially the Lao attempted to maintain a balance in their relations with the

PRC, but with the signing of the Lao-Vietnam Treaty of Friendship and Cooperation, it became clear that Vietnamese and Soviet influence was on the increase. Beijing muted criticism of the treaty and continued its policy of friendly relations with Vientiane. But as relations between Hanoi and Pol Pot's Democratic Kampuchea worsened after Lao attempts at mediation failed in December 1977, and as the war of words between Hanoi and Beijing increased in intensity, Laos was inevitably drawn into the developing conflict. Lao attempts to maintain a semblance of neutrality between Vietnam and China came to an end in July 1978 when Kaysone denounced the Chinese as 'international reactionaries', Vietnam's term of abuse for the Chinese leadership and accused them of sowing dissension among the ethnic minorities of northern Laos. The Chinese were requested to close down the coordination centre for their aid programme, situated in Oudomsay, which they did later in the year.

As tensions in Indochina rose and Lao–Chinese relations cooled during the second half of 1978, there is evidence to suggest that not all members of the Lao Politburo were in agreement over how the LPDR should respond to the developing crisis in Sino–Vietnamese relations. In October 1978, Souphanouvong reportedly told a meeting of senior civil servants that certain reactionaries and bad elements had spread the rumour that 'Lao traitors in exile' were receiving aid from China. This, he said, was 'very wicked and dangerous propaganda aimed at sowing bedevilment and anxiety among our people to make them lose confidence in the line and policies of our party and state, to sow division between the Lao people and the Chinese people, and finally to sabotage our revolution' (FBIS, 18 October 1978). Coming after Kaysone's accusations, this could only mean that differences existed over the wisdom of alienating Beijing by siding openly with Hanoi (Stuart-Fox, 1980a). Within a week, however, Souphanouvong was quoted as encouraging a visiting Vietnamese delegation to overcome all difficulties caused by the 'international reactionaries'. From this point on Laos was to remain a loyal supporter of Vietnam.

The Lao authorities were quick to commend the Vietnamese invasion of Kampuchea. Within a week of the Vietnamese capture of Phnom Penh, a Lao ambassador to the new Heng Samrin regime was named and a Lao Party and government delegation left for the Kampuchean capital. The Lao response to the outbreak of fighting between China and Vietnam was rather more cautious. A government statement called for the immediate withdrawal of Chinese forces but refrained from condemning Beijing. Lao concern was evident. The statement read, in part: 'the Lao government and people feel great anxiety with respect to this new and undesirable situation' (KPL/BQ,

19 February 1979). Subsequent Lao statements reiterated the need for negotiations to end the conflict.

Not until early March did Lao authorities bow to concerted Soviet and Vietnamese pressure to adopt a more overtly anti-Chinese position. This followed Soviet and Vietnamese reports that Chinese troops were massing on the Lao border. Four days after the initial report, and the day after Beijing announced its forces were withdrawing from Vietnam, an emergency joint sitting of the Lao Supreme People's Assembly and Council of Government met to consider the Chinese 'threat'. There the decision was taken to back Vietnam, and to demand the withdrawal of all Chinese road construction workers from northern Laos. A note from the Lao Foreign Ministry explained that the decision had been taken 'to ensure the safety of these workers and to safeguard the ancient tradition of friendship between the Lao and Chinese peoples'. The resumption of aid would be discussed 'when the situation has improved'. (This note was not published until 12 March 1979 in KPL/BQ.) The next day the Lao Politburo met and committed Laos totally to the Vietnamese side: the 'adventuristic and bellicose policies' of the Chinese power-holders were roundly denounced as 'most dangerous and full of execrable crimes'. The attack on Vietnam was described as 'a ferocious and very barbarous' example of 'great Han hegemonistic policies' (KPL/BQ, 9 March 1979).

The Politburo statement marked an important shift in the Lao position. Reaction from the Chinese was predictable. Lao accusations 'viciously attacking China' were rejected as fabrications. The Chinese government expressed 'great indignation' over the way in which Lao actions were 'poisoning the relations between the two countries', but hinted that the Chinese realized that Laos was 'acting under pressure from certain quarters' (*Beijing Review*, 16 March 1979). Nevertheless, Beijing warned that 'criminal' Vietnamese schemes of intensifying control over Laos only invited 'stronger opposition from the Lao people', and called for the immediate withdrawal of Vietnamese forces. Not to be outdone, Lao spokesmen referred to China's 'dark and extremely cruel schemes against Laos', and accused Beijing of conniving with Lao reactionaries and Hmong insurgents to destroy the country's internal security and overthrow the Lao regime (FBIS, 16 March 1979; cf. Stuart-Fox, 1980a). Chinese forces were also said to be occupying a small area of Lao territory, a charge which Beijing rejected.

As the war of words and accusations between Vientiane and Beijing mounted during 1979, the Chinese were requested to reduce their embassy personnel to twelve, the number allowed the United States. Relations were reduced to the level of chargé d'affairs, but were not broken. Later in the year, the LPRP carried out a purge of pro-Chinese cadres, a number of whom fled to Thailand. In October, the PRC offered to accept 10,000 Lao refugees for resettlement in southern China, much to the consternation of authorities in Vientiane who feared they would be given guerrilla training and sent back into Laos. When Chinese officials visited the Thai refugee camps, however, they made it clear that preference would be given to ethnic Chinese. Few volunteers were found, and the quota was never filled. Most who did go were settled on Hainan island. The Lao did have cause for concern, however, for during 1979 the Chinese began providing military training for Lao insurgents in Yunnan province. By the end of the year, Kaysone admitted in his report to the SPA that relations with China were a cause of 'great concern'. Laos, he said, was engaged in a 'war of national defence' with a power which sought the overthrow of the state. 'The acts of the Chinese side threaten the independence, sovereignty, territorial integrity and political security of our country', Kaysone told assembled delegates (FBIS, 18 January 1980; see also Stuart-Fox, 1981d).

By 1980, a pattern of relationships had developed which persisted over the following years. From the Lao point of view, the most disturbing aspect of these relations was Chinese-Thai collusion in support of Khmer Rouge guerrillas in Kampuchea in order to force the withdrawal of Vietnamese forces. This led Vientiane to interpret Thai intransigence over a shooting incident on the Mekong in mid-1980 and subsequent closure of the border as part of a plot orchestrated by Beijing. The meeting of Lao, Vietnamese and Kampuchean foreign ministers in Vientiane in July that year directly accused the Chinese of being 'the motor stimulating the Thai side to commit acts of provocation on the frontier [with Laos]' (KPL/BQ, 18 and 19 July 1980). The Chinese were thereafter held to be behind every difficulty the Lao experienced in their relations with Thailand.

In June 1981, Vientiane accused Chinese troops of pursuing a Lao patrol four kilometres into Lao territory. The Chinese responded by claiming that Vietnamese soldiers in Lao army uniforms had attacked Chinese border guards, and warned that the flames of 'anti-Vietnam guerrilla warfare' were 'blazing up' everywhere in Laos (FEER Yearbook, 1982). Relations between the two states appeared to have reached a new low. Despite Chinese support, however, the insurgency in both the northern and southern theatres during 1981 and 1982 never reached a level that posed any real threat to the existence of the regime. Incidents along the Chinese-Lao border, far from increasing as might have been expected, decreased to one or two a year and were quickly settled.

In 1983, a curious disparity had become evident between the rhetoric of

Lao accusations and the level of insurgency in northern Laos. China continued to be ritually denounced as the principal enemy of the peoples of Indochina, but primarily on the grounds of its policies towards Vietnam and Kampuchea. China was held responsible not only for military provocations on the border with Vietnam, but also for keeping tension high on the Thai–Kampuchean border and for preventing any solution to the Kampuchean problem. By contrast, the Lao–Chinese border was all but free of incidents. Vientiane objected to Chinese radio broadcasts containing interviews with Lao exiles critical of the regime's dependence on Vietnam, but had few other complaints.

Evidence of improved relations between the two states was contained in some of the messages exchanged. The Chinese sent 'wholehearted greetings' on Laos' national day, and maintained that 'the Chinese government and people sincerely hope to see Chinese–Lao relations of friendship restored and developed on the basis of the five principles of peaceful coexistence, and are pleased to make active efforts [to this end]' (*Asian Almanac*, 1983, p. 11671). In their congratulations on the conclusion of the Chinese National People's Congress in June, the Lao expressed the hope that 'the time-honoured traditional relations of friendship between the two countries ... will be consolidated and normalized in the common interests of the peoples of Laos and China ...' (FBIS, 30 June 1983). A commentary in the LPRP official organ *Pasason* noted the change in tone of the Chinese approach towards Laos, but warned that this was only 'a device' in Beijing's 'all-round notorious and cunning war against the Lao revolution' (FBIS, 26 August 1983).

By early 1985 Lao relations with China had settled into a new pattern. Vientiane continued to denounce Chinese intentions not towards Laos but towards 'the three Indochinese countries' taken together. Meanwhile the actual situation along the Lao–Chinese border was remarkably peaceful. Kaysone, writing in the Vietnamese journal *Tap Chi Cong San* on the occasion of the thirtieth anniversary of the LPRP, stated that

the direct and most dangerous enemy of the three countries's revolutions at this new stage is Chinese big-nation expansionism which is colluding with the U.S. imperialists and other ultra-rightist reactionary forces to oppose the revolutions of the three Indochinese countries—a main obstacle to China's scheme of conquering all of Southeast Asia. [FBIS, 27 March 1985.]

Lao radio broadcasts purporting to expose Beijing's reactionary nature said next to nothing in 1985 about Lao–Chinese relations, but a great deal about Chinese-American and Chinese-Thai collusion against 'the three Indochinese countries' and about Chinese schemes to subvert attempts to resolve the Kampuchean problem.

By 1985 the situation along the Lao–Chinese border had returned to something approaching pre-1977 conditions. Relations between Chinese and Lao border forces had improved to the point where the Chinese requested permission to send a delegation to take part in local celebrations for Lao army day. The offer was turned down as 'premature', but contacts between the two sides continued. (Vietnamese forces in northern Laos were stationed well away from the frontier.) Movement across the border was also reportedly freer than it had been for years. Chinese consumer goods were again widely available in northern Laos and the security situation had improved. Lao officials at the highest levels confirmed in Vientiane in August 1985 that Lao–Chinese relations were no longer a problem though minor incidents were still occasionally reported.

The official explanation for improved relations between Laos and the PRC is that it is part of a subtle Chinese scheme to differentiate between policies towards Vietnam and Laos, and thus to drive a wedge beween the two states and undermine Indochinese solidarity. In fact the improvement seems to be due to both sides. The Chinese have accepted that Lao freedom of action in the field of foreign relations is limited and are prepared to disregard statements critical of Beijing. In return the Lao have pragmatically accepted Chinese advances where these count most—at the local level along the common border of the two states. By this means the Lao have managed to improve relations with China while simultaneously preserving the 'special relationship' with Vietnam. Officially Laos would like to restore normal relations with the PRC—but only provided 'the reactionaries in the Beijing ruling circles' end their 'hostile policy' of 'striving to sabotage our people's revolutionary cause' (Kaysone, Speech to SPA, FBIS, 29 January 1985). In the meantime, Laos has probably gone as far as is possible in improving relations with the PRC until such times as Sino–Vietnamese relations improve.

Thailand and ASEAN

Except for a brief interlude in 1979, during the prime ministership of Kriangsak Chamanand, Thai–Lao relations have oscillated between strain and crisis. On three occasions since 1975, for varying periods, Thailand unilaterally closed the border with Laos. On each occasion Laos suffered economic dislocation, shortages in consumer goods and unnecessary social hardships. Thailand has also enforced an economic blockade on a long list of 'strategic' items. Even more serious, from the Lao point of view, has been continued Thai sanctuary and support, at a local level, if not by the government in Bangkok, for Lao insurgents. Both economic pressures and support for insurgency have consistently been interpreted by Vientiane as part of a systematic policy to destabilize and weaken the LPDR. Since 1980 at least, the Lao have claimed to discern the hand of Beijing behind every incident between Thailand and Laos. Thai occupation in June 1984 of three border villages claimed by Laos has resuscitated old fears of pan-Thai expansionism in Vientiane (*Livre Blanc*, 1984).

The pattern of Lao–Thai relations over the decade 1975–85 reflects changing power relations in the region: it also notably reflects changes in the political complexion of successive governments in Bangkok. Even before the formation of the LPDR during the second half of 1975 relations along the Thai–Lao border were tense, especially in the vicinity of Vientiane. The border was briefly closed in November and remained partly closed until the following July when the Thai took steps to normalize relations with the LPDR. The visit of Thai Foreign Minister, Pichai Rattakul, placed relations on a formally correct, if not friendly, basis. The Mekong was to become 'a river of true peace and friendship', and a mechanism for provincial level contacts was established to resolve frontier incidents. Hopes for continuing improvement in Lao–Thai relations were dashed, however, by the Thai military coup of October 1976 which brought the strongly anti-communist Thanin Kraivichien government to power. In the following months a continuing series of border incidents strained relations between the two states, but with the change of government in Bangkok in October 1977 relations began to improve. In March 1978, Lao Foreign Minister Phoune Sipaseuth visited Bangkok and the two sides reaffirmed the principles agreed upon in August 1976. In June a new trade agreement was signed.

During the first six months of 1979, Thai–Lao relations were warmer than at any other time during the decade 1975–85. In January, despite a recent border incident, and despite the fact that Vietnamese forces were at the time pushing ever deeper into Kampuchea, Thai Prime Minister Kriangsak Chamanand paid an official visit to Vientiane. Kaysone reciprocated with a visit to Bangkok in April. The joint communiques issued at the end of these two visits affirmed a number of important points: respect for each other's independence, sovereignty and territorial integrity; respect for the right of each country to direct its own affairs free of foreign interference; refusal to permit the territory of either country to serve as a military base for interference, threat or aggression against the other, or to mount subversive activities of any kind against the other. Since the signing of these communiqués, the Lao have consistently argued that they form the best possible basis for relations between the two countries, but that subsequent Thai governments, for their own various reasons, have chosen to ignore them.

This period of friendly relations did not outlast the Kriangsak government. After Kriangsak was deposed early in 1980 in favour of Prem Tinsulanond, relations rapidly deteriorated. A new shooting incident on the Mekong in June led to closure of the border in July. Both sides blamed the other after negotiations failed to resolve the matter. For the Thai, Lao intransigence in refusing even to express regret over the shooting incident was part of a Vietnamese orchestrated attempt to bring pressure to bear on Bangkok. For the Lao, Thai refusal to open the border was part of a Chinese orchestrated attempt to weaken the 'Indochinese solidarity bloc', and the LPDR in particular. At the end of August the Thai reopened two posts after the Lao ambassador appealed directly to the King of Thailand, but relations remained strained, mutual accusations continued, and the border was closed again for a month early in 1981.

For the next two years relations followed the familiar pattern: slow improvement of relations until another frontier shooting incident brought mutual accusations and again soured relations. The Lao took the opportunity of a 1982 visit to Vientiane by the Thai Minister for Commerce to request and eventually obtain the opening of two more border posts. In January 1983, the Lao were incensed when Thai troops used heavy weapons in an exchange of fire which damaged the Lan Xang Hotel just at a time when an international Mekong Committee meeting was in progress. When Kriangsak Chamanand led a Thai parliamentary delegation to Laos in August 1983, the Lao used the occasion to recall the Kriangsak–Kaysone communiqués of 1979 and reiterate their belief that these formed the best basis for improved relations.

Then in June 1984 came the most serious incident of all in Lao eyes when Thai troops occupied three border villages in Laos' Sayaboury province. Earlier Lao troops had prevented extension of a Thai strategic road into the area of the villages. Negotiations over the incident broke down in August, though Thai troops evacuated the villages in October, taking most of the local population with them. However Thai frontier forces took up positions on surrounding ridges which the Lao claimed were still up to half a kilometre inside Lao territory. Occasional shooting incidents continued as each side accused the other of failing to negotiate in good faith. Lao news media in the latter part of 1984 and the first few months of 1985 whipped up a veritable storm of criticism of Thailand and Thai policies. Articles revealed 'the dark side of Thai society'—including Bangkok slums, rural poverty, and child labour, and blamed Thai military spending for Thailand's 'social-economic crisis'. Lao criticism of Thailand centered on the alleged pan-Thai hegemonism and expansionism of the 'reactionaries in power' in Bangkok, Thai support for Lao insurgents, and Thai subservience to their 'Chinese masters'. The White Paper on Thai-Lao relations made the same point, if more diplomatically: 'It is necessary to stress that the activities of the reactionaries in Thailand aimed at creating tension on the Thai-Lao frontier are carried out in coordination with the activities of China.' (*Livre Blanc*, 1984, p. 43.)

Thai criticism of Laos is remarkably similar in content—accusations of dependency on Vietnam, of harbouring 'pan-Lao' designs on the northeastern Isan provinces of Thailand and of providing sanctuary for Thai communist insurgents. At various times since mid-1979, the Thai have accused the Lao of giving assistance to a 'Thai Isan Liberation Party', a 'Democratic Alliance of Thailand' (whose manifesto was broadcast over Radio Vientiane in August 1980, but which has not been heard of since), and the 'Pak Mai', or New Party, supposedly a pro-Vietnamese splinter group which has broken away from the pro-Chinese Communist Party of Thailand.

The barrage of Lao criticism of the Thai leadership and their policies eased slightly by mid-1985 when Lao Foreign Minister Phoune Sipaseuth proposed a new round of negotiations to resolve outstanding difficulties between the two states. Despite publicly voiced doubts about the sincerity of the Lao proposal, the Thais sent a delegation to Vientiane to talk about talks—but to no avail. The Lao wanted talks to be held at the highest level in order to resolve not only the 'three villages' dispute, but also trade relations and refugees, both matters of great importance to the Lao. The Thais responded by suggesting talks be held only at the local level to resolve the problem of the 'three villages', a suggestion which the Lao angrily rejected as inadequate.

Officials at the Lao Foreign Ministry insisted Laos was entirely sincere in wanting to resolve all outstanding problems and improve relations with Thailand, as it was obviously in the Lao national interest to do so. Even though the value of Thai exports to Laos decreased by as much as 65 per cent in 1984–5 compared to previous years, they still amounted to an average of 30 million baht per month (about US$17 million per year) (FBIS, 14 June 1985). More important from the Lao point of view was the fact that despite improved communications with Vietnam, more than half of total Lao imports still arrived via Thailand. The Thai, however, maintained controls on the 273 items supposedly of 'strategic significance' for which special permits are required—including even such items as bicycles, medicines, needles and thread. Asphalt provided under the Japanese aid programme to surface

Vientiane's deteriorating roads in preparation for the tenth anniversary celebrations of the LPDR was held up in Thailand on the grounds that it might be used to build military airstrips. Such interference and intransigence merely convinced the Lao of the need to channel more goods through Vietnam. (For alternative views on Thai–Lao relations, see Ngaosyvathn, 1985, and Viraphol, 1985.)

The other major problems bedevilling Lao–Thai relations in 1985 were Thai support for Lao insurgents, and Thai refugee policies. The effect of the outflow of refugees on Lao social structure and on economic development has already been discussed. The Thai (and American) policy of accepting everyone who crossed the Mekong as a political refugee has had the effect of steadily draining Laos of virtually all its educated class—a loss from which the country will take years, perhaps decades, to recover. Only as of July 1985 did the Thai begin to treat Lao as illegal immigrants in cases where economic motives alone had induced them to leave. Thai support for Lao insurgents has often been furnished by local officials, or army commanders acting for their own motives, without central government approval or direction. The Lao want tighter controls to be placed on such activities and an end to the provision of Chinese weapons to southern Lao insurgents via Thailand.

There is no doubt that the Lao would like to maintain neighbourly relations with Thailand. Not only does Thailand remain an important trading partner, but access to the sea via Bangkok is both more convenient and less expensive than via Vietnamese ports. For the Lao, the basis for improved Lao–Thai relations exists already in the Kriangsak–Kaysone joint communiqués of 1979. Given goodwill on both sides, the Lao believe that outstanding problems can be resolved by negotiations at the national level, backed up by regular local level contacts. Privately the Lao cannot understand what the Thai have to gain by pursuing a policy which destroys Lao freedom of movement and forces Laos to become ever more dependent on Vietnam, even though publicly Lao statements confirm Thai fears that this is in any case what is happening.

Lao relations with the other members of the Association of Southeast Asian Nations (ASEAN) have been determined almost entirely by relations with Thailand. Lao criticism of ASEAN at the Fifth Non-aligned Summit Conference in Colombo, Sri Lanka, in August 1976, was toned down subsequently, especially after ASEAN reacted angrily to the Vietnamese invasion of Kampuchea. In January 1981 Laos was designated to represent the three Indochina countries in consultations with ASEAN aimed at finding a solution to the Kampuchean problem. Various high-level contacts followed, both in the region and at the United Nations, but without result. Lao relations with ASEAN member states remain cordial (with the exception of Singapore), but not close. Any improvement in relations is dependent on a settlement in Kampuchea.

The United States and Other Capitalist Countries

Since the foundation of the LPDR, Laos has managed to maintan better overall relations with capitalist states than have either Kampuchea or Vietnam. In mid-1975 the USAID mission to Laos was withdrawn, but diplomatic relations were maintained. United States' representation in Vientiane was reduced to the level of chargé d'affairs, with, at Lao request, a maximum staff of twelve and no military attaché. Other Western embassies also remained open. A number of Western aid programmes continued, and new ones were undertaken, especially by Sweden, Japan, the Netherlands and Australia. American aid was not resumed, however, as Laos was listed, along with Vietnam, as an 'enemy' country.

For the first five years of the new regime, Lao–American relations were cool and correct. The Lao demonstrated a pragmatic lack of ideological hostility by directly appealing to the United States for food aid after the disastrous harvests of 1977. Washington obliged by providing 10,000 tonnes of grain valued at US$5 million in 1978. In 1981, US$100,000 worth of medical aid was quietly handed over to a Vientiane hospital. The first real improvement in Lao–American relations came in 1982, however, when hints from Vientiane that improved relations might be in the interests of both countries led in September to the visit to Laos of a delegation from the National League of Families of United States' Servicemen Missing in-Action in Indochina, a lobby group representing the families of MIAs. The four delegates were given a sympathetic reception which contrasted with their cool welcome in Hanoi, and their visit was followed up by an American State Department official (FEER/YB, 1983).

Relations suffered a temporary set-back in 1983 when a former American Special Forces officer mounted a private MIA search mission into Laos. The venture was a fiasco. The group clashed with anti-government guerrillas, and members were arrested on their return to Thailand. The raid was denounced by Vientiane as 'arrogant and open interference in the internal affairs of Laos', and as 'a serious encroachment on the sovereignty of an independent state', which had 'adversely affected relations between the two countries' (FBIS, 8 April 1983). This was relatively mild criticism, however, and the Lao seemed mollified when the United States categorically denied that the mission had any official backing. In December 1983, a survey team from the Joint Casualty Resolution Center in Hawaii visited the 1972 crash site of an AC-130 aircraft some forty kilometres northeast of Pakse, and negotiations began for a joint Lao–American mission to excavate the site and exhume the bodies. In 1984, the United States provided a further gift of 5,000 tonnes of rice when bad weather again reduced harvests.

The actual crash site excavation did not get underway until February 1985 but was entirely successful. The remains of thirteen MIAs killed in the crash were identified. The joint mission was followed up by Lao agreement to send a team to the United States' Central Identification Laboratory in Hawaii. Vientiane announced that a second crash site would be visited, and let it be known that Laos hoped for reciprocal concessions from the United States. The Reagan administration promptly asked Congress to remove Laos from the list of enemy states. Both the House of Representatives and the Senate agreed, thus opening the way for direct American aid. In September, after spending four days in Hawaii, a Lao delegation was received at the State Department in Washington, and a further round of meetings took place in New York between senior American officials and Lao Foreign Minister Phoune Sipaseuth. In January 1986 a return visit brought a high ranking United States' delegation to Vientiane jointly led by Assistant Secretaries of the State and Defense Departments.

By the beginning of 1986, therefore, Lao–American relations were warmer than they had been for a decade and the way lay open for American participation at the next international conference of aid donors to Laos due to be held in 1986. Relations with other capitalist states, however, varied from warm to distant. Laos has enjoyed excellent relations with Sweden, Japan and Australia, but relations with Britain and France have been somewhat less cordial. Japan and Sweden both have extensive aid programmes: Japan providing electrical and water filtration equipment, Sweden providing assistance in forestry, truck maintenance and the production of industrial gases. Australia and the Netherlands also have limited aid programmes. Britain, by contrast, after long association with Laos as former co-chairman of the 1962 Geneva conference closed its embassy in Vientiane at the end of 1984, much to the displeasure of the Lao government. The British ambassador to Thailand is presently accredited to the LPDR.

Lao relations with France have not been particularly smooth since 1975. After French embassy personnel were implicated in assisting former RLG officials to flee the country, Laos broke diplomatic relations with France in August 1978 and demanded that some fifty French teachers and six doctors leave the country. Relations were not re-established until five years later, still without resolution of the problem of debts accrued by the former regime which the present government is unwilling to pay. The sum involved is 100 million francs, 70 per cent in government loans, and 30 per cent in compensatory payments paid to expropriated French companies. Vientiane would like both claims cancelled as a 'gesture' in order to place Franco–Lao relations on a new and friendly footing (*Humanité*, 23 August 1985). So far the French have refused, and French aid to Laos has been negligible since relations were re-established.

The Logic of Lao Foreign Policy

When the first decade of the foreign relations of the LPDR is surveyed as a whole, some interesting trends become evident. The period can be divided into three phases. From 1975 to early 1979 Laos, although a member of the Soviet bloc, pursued what might be termed a traditional foreign policy of friendship towards and acceptance of aid from any state prepared to reciprocate and donate. Relations were maintained with the United States and a careful balance was struck between China on one hand and Vietnam and the Soviet Union on the other. The twenty-five year Treaty of Friendship and Cooperation with Vietnam of July 1977 threatened, but did not immediately disrupt this traditional policy. Only in early 1979, following the Vietnamese occupation of Kampuchea and subsequent border war with China did pressures on Laos become so great due to deteriorating inter-state relations in the region that they could no longer be resisted. The first serious move away from the traditional policy came with the request to the PRC to terminate its aid programme—ironically just at a time when the traditional policy was at last bearing fruit in the form of better relations with Thailand.

Since 1979, the LPDR has been closely identified, as a member of the 'Indochinese solidarity bloc', with Vietnamese foreign policy. This was particularly evident during the four years from 1979 to the end of 1982, a period when Laos almost invariably followed the Vietnamese lead. Since 1983, however, Laos has begun to re-activate its traditional policy of cultivating friendly relations with all states. This reversion to what effectively amounts to a more neutral foreign policy has been accomplished slowly and carefully, on the practical level above all, without abandoning the rhetoric of the previous four years. Lao–American relations have been improved through practical action to discover what happened to American MIAs. Lao–Chinese relations have been improved through practical initiatives in the broader area. Despite Thai intransigence, the Lao have attempted to create appropriate conditions for Lao–Thai relations to follow the same pragmatic course.

The logic of Lao foreign policy thus becomes clear. Despite all the glowing claims of economic progress made by the new regime, the fact is that for the foreseeable future Laos will remain chronically dependent on foreign assistance for economic development. Internal sources of revenue are insufficient to meet government expenditures; exports nowhere near cover imports; foreign aid therefore provides the only source of investment funds. It is in the interests of the LPDR that Laos cultivate friendly relations with every country prepared to assist her economic development. At the same time, Vientiane must reassure the Vietnamese that the LPDR remains a loyal member of the 'Indochinese solidarity bloc' and a faithful ally of Hanoi. Such reassurance is given both on the level of rhetoric, and on the level of private undertakings to take Vietnamese interests into consideration. The Lao, therefore, are saying one thing, and doing another, both with Vietnamese concurrence. Actions may tend to speak louder than words, but the success of Lao foreign policy depends on whether other states are prepared to take account of actions, while disregarding the words. Indications were, at the end of 1985, that both the Chinese and the Americans, were prepared to do so. Only the Thai seemed determined not to respond.

7   The Lao Revolution in Context

The geographical frontiers of the state of Laos are the result of historical accidents—of internal division and weakness after the seventeenth century, of the intrusion of French imperialism into Indochina, and of the balance of British, French and Thai interests on mainland Southeast Asia. What remains is a truncated political entity quite unable to withstand the might of powerful neighbouring states. Independent Laos from 1953 to 1975 was never a unified state. The only opportunity to create a neutral and unified Laos was lost with the collapse of the first coalition government in 1957, due mainly to American machinations. Thereafter Laos was subjected to *de facto* division into areas under Vietnamese, Chinese, and American/Thai control. Chinese influence was predominant in the north, Vietnamese along the length of the eastern frontier, and American/Thai in the Mekong Valley.

Given the polarization of forces during the Vietnam war, neutrality was no longer a political option in Laos even in 1962. Divisions ran too deep thereafter to permit reunification under any but one of the principal opposing factions—the right, corrupt, inept, and discredited; or the Pathet Lao with its carefully crafted image of egalitarian nationalism and political moderation. When events in Kampuchea and Vietnam in April 1975 jolted the political balance in Laos, a Pathet Lao take-over became inevitable. Unity was achieved at last—but at the price of acceptance of Vietnamese hegemony as the guarantor of that unity.

In his perceptive analysis of the communist seizure of power in Laos, MacAlister Brown has argued that Laos fits most closely the Czechoslovak model in which a semi-legal take-over occurred with a considerable degree of popular support, backed by the threat of armed force (Brown, in Stuart-Fox, 1982a). The legalism evident both during negotiations leading to formation of coalition governments and in intervening periods to maintain the illegitimacy of all but those governments, was an enduring and characteristically Pathet Lao revolutionary tactic. The popular support received by the Pathet Lao during the third coalition government was the product of a number of factors—war weariness, moral abhorrence of civil conflict, disillusionment with the veniality of many leading rightists, reaction against the less attractive aspects of the American presence, popular perception of the incorruptibility of the Pathet Lao leadership, and genuine support for the moderate political action programme incorporated in the 'eighteen points' advocated by the PL dominated NPCC. This support was effectively mobilized, and brought to bear on rightist politicians and generals alike. But behind such popular pressure stood the threat of armed force, both by LPLA, and by the Vietnamese army.

The crucial role played by Vietnamese communist forces in establishing and maintaining the Lao insurgency from 1953 when the Vietminh thrust into northern Laos to 1973 when the final cease-fire went into effect is no longer a secret. The Vietnamese have taken credit for their exploits; the Lao have decorated Vietnamese units. At all times throughout the thirty-year struggle the Pathet Lao was dependent for military training, equipment and support on the army of the DRV. In part this was to counter the just as total dependency of the Royal Lao Army on American military training, equipment, and support. But in part DRV military involvement in Laos was to assure extension of Pathet Lao influence over eventually four-fifths of the national territory and two-fifths of the population. Without such military support, and the political commitment on which it was based, it is unlikely that the Pathet Lao as a movement would have been successful in seizing power, and certainly not within the period it took. The remote mountains of northern and eastern Laos became formidable military bases only because the LPLA was supplied and equipped, guided and encouraged from across the border.

It is misleading therefore to equate the Pathet Lao victory in Laos with popularly supported, Marxist-inspired revolutions in such places as Cuba, Ethiopia or Nicaragua. The Pathet Lao, like the revolutionary movements in these states, did develop and capitalize upon anti-imperialist nationalism. So too did they stimulate, and so benefit from, the aspirations of minority ethnic groups for access to national political power and improved conditions of life. Where the Pathet Lao differed from almost all other national revolutionary movements (including, be it noted, the Khmer Rouge in Kampuchea) was in the extent to which the movement was at all times dependent for advice and material support on foreign cadres—political, technical and military/advisory—and on foreign military intervention.

Vietnamese involvement in the Lao revolution did not cease once the national democratic phase was completed with the seizure of power and proclamation of the LPDR in December 1975. Although the LPRP took full credit for its 'correct and clear-sighted leadership' of the revolutionary struggle, the assistance of fraternal Vietnamese comrades was readily acknowledged, and their continued assistance during the socialist transformation phase of the revolution welcomed. The closeness and extent of continuing Vietnamese involvement was evident before its formal disclosure with the signing of the Lao–Vietnamese Treaty of Friendship and Cooperation in 1977. It would be true to say, therefore, that Vietnamese involvement has been and will almost certainly continue to be the most salient feature of the Lao revolution. Any assessment of the impact of the Lao revolution and its place in Lao history must take cognizance of this factor.

Perhaps potentially the most important benefit deriving from the LPRP decision to enter into a close and continuing relationship with Vietnam is that the Party has been able to capitalize on Vietnamese protection to unify what remains of the Lao state under indigenous government for the first time since the end of the seventeenth century. The Party thus has the opportunity to generate a sense of Lao national identity, which, also for the first time, can be based not on ethnicity (lowland Lao) or on religion (Theravada Buddhism), but on egalitarian participation in a national polity by all ethnic groups in the 'multi-national' Lao state. The significance of this lies in the opportunity it provides to create an enduring geo-political entity that can withstand attempts to absorb the country into either a greater Vietnamese, or a greater Thai, state.

The Party thus has an opportunity to reinforce its own political legitimacy by acting as the vehicle for such multi-ethnic political participation, as well as by directing and underwriting the social and economic development of the country. It will only be effective in doing so, however, if it can be seen as dedicated to the welfare and interests of the Lao people, and not as subservient to the interests of a foreign power—no matter how pressing the demands of 'proletarian internationalism'.

The close relationship with Vietnam does provide important economic benefits through the SRV's aid programme in Laos. Improved communications with Vietnam and use of Vietnamese port facilities reduce Lao economic dependency on Thailand, and its vulnerability to Thai economic blackmail through closure of the border. The LPRP itself benefits considerably from the Vietnamese connection through assistance it receives in political organization and mobilization, in the training of cadres, and in the formulation and dissemination of propaganda. Finally, Laos also benefits from its military alliance with Vietnam. Laos is unable, with its long and vulnerable borders, to ensure its own security. The stationing of Vietnamese troops in the LPDR effectively discourages military threats from other neighbouring states, and frees Lao forces for counter-insurgency operations.

The benefits of accepting continuing Vietnamese hegemony over the Lao revolution have to be balanced, however, against the drawbacks. The extent of Vietnamese influence within the LPRP, as outlined above, is such as to preclude discussion of alternative policy options. LPRP cadres are constantly exhorted to cherish the Lao–Vietnamese special relationship and not to indulge in 'narrow nationalism'. But it is precisely a new sense of Lao nationalism that needs to be developed, so I have argued, if the present regime is to create the basis for a durable Lao state within present frontiers. Indochinese solidarity may be of central importance for the regional ambitions of the Vietnamese: it is far less so for the Lao.

Close identity of Lao with Vietnamese national interests within the Indochinese solidarity bloc has the unfortunate effect of leading other countries to link the two in their diplomacy and foreign policy. To the extent that Laos is perceived to be under Vietnamese domination, Thai, American or Chinese policies towards Laos tend to be influenced by their policies towards Vietnam. Opportunities for Laos to benefit from aid that might be made available to an impoverished Third World country which represents no threat to anyone are thus partially closed off because of Vietnam. Laos is therefore prevented from pursuing its own best national interests because its diplomacy is shaped by Vietnamese concerns.

Vietnamese involvement in the present phase of the Lao revolution is most obvious in the areas of foreign and defence policy. The presence of Vietnamese troops in Laos causes concern in Thailand and is a standing afront to China. But Vietnamese influence on Party political developments, and indeed on economic development, is just as pervasive. The LPRP is being deliberately shaped as a vehicle for the continuation of Vietnamese influence by including commitment to the 'special relationship' as a 'revolutionary qualification' for all Lao cadres, backed by the threat of re-education. At the same time the economic development of the LPDR is being increasingly linked to Vietnam through bilateral development projects (gypsum mining, a probable joint venture to exploit rich iron ore deposits) and through barter trade agreements (Vietnamese consumer goods and machinery for Lao timber and forest products). Such projects and agreements make economic sense given the present context of Lao development and are balanced to some extent by economic relations with Thailand (especially the sale of hydro-electricity, and likely future joint Mekong Valley projects). But Lao freedom of action in deciding the direction and priorities of the country's economic development would be compromised should the Lao economy become too dependent on Vietnam.

A recent confidential report to the World Bank stated that, in purely economic terms, 'prospects for Laos are quite positive in the time frame of 20–30 years', especially when compared with other impoverished Third World states. Much depends, however, on policies pursued, and on the ability of the Party to generate a sense of pride and commitment among the Lao people through permitting the broadest cross-section possible to contribute to shaping their own future. In other words, much depends on whether the LPRP leadership is prepared to pay more than lip service to the promotion of 'collective mastery', as the essence of socialist democracy. For so long as a semi-secret Party sees its primary task as maintaining its monopoly of political power through enforcement of a political orthodoxy tied to the interests of a foreign state, 'collective mastery' will remain a sham. With growing confidence and experience, however, it may be possible for the LPRP to free itself progressively from Vietnamese tutelage, and place its trust in 'the multi-ethnic Lao people'. On the extent that it is able to do this will depend the future of Laos as a continuing independent entity among the states of mainland Southeast Asia.

Bibliography

Adams, Nina S., & McCoy, Alfred W., 1970. *Laos: War and Revolution*. New York, Harper & Row.

Aijmer, Goran, 1979, 'Reconciling Power with Authority: An Aspect of Statecraft in Traditional Laos', *Man*, vol. 14, pp. 734–49.

Amnesty International, 1980. *Political Prisoners in the People's Democratic Republic of Laos*. London, Amnesty International (AI Index: ASA 26/02/80).

——, 1985. *Background Paper on the Democratic People's Republic of Laos (DPRL) Describing Current Amnesty International Concerns*. London, Amnesty International (AI Index: ASA 26/04/85).

——, 1986. *'Re-education' in Attopeu Province, the Democratic People's Republic of Laos*. London: Amnesty International (AI Index: 26/01/86).

Anon., 1982. *Laos: An outline of ancient and contemporary history*. Hanoi, Foreign Languages Publishing House.

——, 1980. *Pages historiques de la lutte héroique du peuple lao*. Vientiane, Éditions en Langues Etrangères.

Archaimbault, Charles, 1973. *Structures Religieuses Lao (Rites et Mythes)*. Vientiane, Vithagna.

Asian Almanac, 1983.

Asian Development Bank, 1980. *Economic Report on Lao People's Democratic Republic*. No. LAO: Ec-4, May.

Asian Survey, annual articles on Laos, 1975–1985 (by MacAlister Brown & Joseph J. Zasloff, Stanley S. Bedlington, Arthur Dommen, and Carlyle Thayer).

Barber, Martin John Philip, 1979. 'Migrants and Modernization: A Study of Change in Lao Society'. Doctoral dissertation, University of Hull.

Barbier, Jean-Pierre, 1975. 'Objectifs et résultats de l'aide économique au Laos: Une évaluation difficile', *Revue Tiers Monde*, vol. 16, no. 62, pp. 333–53.

Borosage, Robert L., & Marks, John, 1976. *The CIA File*. New York, Grossman Publishers.

Brown, MacAlister, & Zasloff, Joseph J., 1985. 'Laos: Gearing up for National Development', *Southeast Asian Affairs 1985*. Singapore, Institute of Southeast Asian Studies.

——, & ——, 1986. *Apprentice Revolutionaries: The Communist Movement in Laos, 1930–1985*. Stanford, Hoover Institution Press.

Cahour, Marcel, 1979. 'Classe ouvrière et paysannerie', *Approches Asie*, vol. 4, pp. 135–51.

Caply, Michel (Jean Deuve), 1966. *Guérilla au Laos*. Paris, Presses de la Cité.

Coèdes, G. 1968. *The Indianized States of Southeast Asia*. Ed. by Walter F. Vella. Translated by Susan Brown Cowing. Canberra, Australian National University Press.

de Berval, René (ed.), 1959. *Kingdom of Laos: The Land of the Million Elephants and the White Parasol.* Saigon, France-Asie.

Deuve, Jean, 1984. *La Royaume du Laos 1949-1965: Histoire événementielle de l'indépendance à la guerre americaine.* Paris, École Française d'Extrème Orient.

Dommen, Arthur J., 1971. *Conflict in Laos: The Politics of Neutralization.* Revised edition. New York, Praeger.

—, 1979. 'Laos: Vietnam's Satellite', *Current History*, vol. 77, pp. 201-2, 255.

—, 1985. *Laos: Keystone of Indochina.* Boulder, Co., Westview Press.

Documents du Congrès Nationale des Représentants du Peuple, 1976. Vientiane, Éditions 'Lao Hak Sat'.

Documents sur le 25ᵉ anniversaire de la fondation du Parti Populaire Révolutionaire Lao, 1980. Vientiane, Éditions en Langues Etrangères.

Doré, Amphay, 1980. *Le Partage du Mekong.* Paris, Encre.

Embassy of the LPDR, Canberra, 1980-1985. *Lao News Release.*

Embassy of the LPDR, Paris, 1985. *Nouvelles du Laos.*

Evans, Grant, 1983. *The Yellow Rainmakers: Are Chemical Weapons Being Used in Southeast Asia?* London, Verso.

Evans, Grant, & Rowley, Kelvin, 1984. *Red Brotherhood at War.* London, Verso.

Fall, Bernard B., 1969. *Anatomy of a Crisis: The Laos Crisis of 1961.* New York, Doubleday.

Far Eastern Economic Review, 1975-86.

Far Eastern Economic Review, *Asia Yearbooks*, 1975-85.

Front Lao d'Édification Nationale (FLEN), 1980. *Les Principaux Documents Importants du Congrès du Front.* Vientiane. Imprimerie du Comité Central du Front Lao d'Édification Nationale.

Gunn, Geoffrey C., 1980. 'Foreign Relations of the Lao People's Democratic Republic: The Ideological Imperative', *Asian Survey*, vol. 20, pp. 990-1007.

—, 1983. 'Resistance Coalitions in Laos', *Asian Survey*, vol. 23, pp. 316-40.

Halpern, Joel M., 1964. *Government, Politics, and Social Structure in Laos: A Study of Tradition and Innovation.* New Haven, Conn., Yale University Press.

International Monetary Fund Reports SM/79/219 (16 August 1979); SM/80/174 (22 July 1980); EBS/81/66 (20 March 1981); SM/84/38 (3 February 1984); and Staff Report dated January 1985. (Referred to as *IMF Report*, and then the year.)

International Institute for Strategic Studies, 1985. *The Military Balance, 1985-1986.* London: IISS.

Khan, Azizur Rahman, & Lee, Eddy, 1980. *Employment and Development in Laos: Some Problems and Policies.* Bangkok, ILO.

Khao San Pathet Lao, 1975-1986. *Bulletin Quotidien.*

Khao San Pathet Lao, 1985-1986. *News Bulletin.*

Kunstadter, Peter (ed.), 1967. *Southeast Asian Tribes, Minorities, and Nations.* Princeton, N.J., Princeton University Press.

La Banque Mondiale, 20 November 1978. *La Transformation Socialiste en République Démocratique Populaire Lao.* No. 2282-LA.

Langer, Paul F., & Zasloff, Joseph J., 1970. *North Vietnam and the Pathet Lao: Partners in the Struggle for Laos*. Cambridge, Mass., Harvard University Press.

Lao People's Democratic Republic, May 1983. *Report on the Economic and Social Situation, Development Strategy and Assistance Requirements*. Prepared for the Asian Pacific Round Table Meeting concerning the implementation of the Substantial New Programme of Action for the Least Developed Countries, Geneva. AP/RTM/83/Lao (referred to as *LDC Report*, 1983).

Laos Rides Out The Storms, 1980. Special Issue, *Southeast Asia Chronicle*, no. 73.

Larteguy, Jean & Dao, Yang, 1979. *La Fabuleuse Aventure du Peuple de l'Opium*. Paris, Presses de la Cité.

Le Boulanger, P., 1931. *Histoire du Laos français*. Paris, Plon.

LPDR Ministry of Foreign Affairs, October 1984. *The question of Thai aggression on June 6, 1984 against Lao territory before the Security Council of the United Nations*. Vientiane.

Lévy, Paul, 1974. *Histoire du Laos*. Paris, Presses Universitaires de France.

Luther, Hans V., 1982. 'Socialism in a Subsistence Economy: The Laotian Way', *Internationales Asienforum*, vol. 13, nos. 3/4, pp. 231–49.

Mikhéev, Youri, 1985. *Les debuts du socialisme au Laos*. Moscow, Éditions de l'Agence de presse Novosti.

Ministère des Affaires Étrangères de la République Démocratique Populaire Lao, 1975–1985. *Bulletin de Nouvelles*.

—, September 1984. *Livre Blanc: La vérité sur les relations Thailande-Laos*. n.p. (Referred to as *Livre Blanc*).

—, Département de Presse, 1983. *Documents de la Politique Extérieure Serié: Communiqués Conjoints et Traités d'Amitié et de Coopération (1976-1979)*. Vientiane.

Ngaosyvathn, Pheuiphanh, 1985. Thai–Lao Relations: A Lao View, *Asian Survey*, vol. 25, pp. 1242–59.

Norindr, Chou, 1980. 'Le Néolaohakxat ou le Front Patriotique Lao et la Révolution Laotienne'. Doctoral dissertation, Université Sorbonne Nouvelle, Paris.

Pasakhom, Uthit, 1985. 'Beyond a Soviet-Vietnamese Condominium: The Case of Laos', *Indochina Report*, no. 1.

Phomvihane, Kaysone, 1978. *Selected Speeches and Articles*. New Delhi, Embassy of the LPDR.

—, 1980. *La Révolution Lao*. Moscow, Éditions du Progrès.

Reynolds, Frank, 1969. 'Ritual and Social Hierarchy: An Aspect of Traditional Religion in Buddhist Laos, *History of Religions*, vol. 9, pp. 78–89.

Robequain, Charles, 1944. *The Economic Development of French Indo-China*. Translated by Isabel A. Ward. London, Oxford University Press.

Rochet, Charles, 1946. *Pays lao: le Laos dans la tourmente, 1939-1945*. Paris, Vigneau.

Southeast Asian Affairs, annual articles on Laos, 1980–1986.

Stuart-Fox, M., 1977a. 'The Lao Revolution: Leadership and Policy Differences', *Australian Outlook*, vol. 31, no. 2, pp. 279–88.

—, 1977b. 'The Lao Revolution: Errors and Achievements', *World Review*, vol. 16, no. 2, pp. 3–15.

Stuart-Fox, M., 1980a. 'Laos: The Vietnamese Connection', in Leo Suryadinata (ed.), *Southeast Asian Affairs 1980*. Singapore, Institute of Southeast Asian Studies/ Heinemann, pp. 191–209.

—, 1980b. 'The Initial Failure of Agricultural Cooperativization in Laos', *Asia Quarterly*, no. 4, pp. 273–99.

—, 1981a. 'Socialist Construction and National Security in Laos', *Bulletin of Concerned Scholars*, vol. 13, no. 1, pp. 61–71.

—, 1981b. 'Reflections on the Lao Revolution', *Contemporary Southeast Asia*, vol. 3, no. 1, pp. 41–57.

—, 1981c. 'Lao Foreign Policy: The View from Vientiane', *Journal of Contemporary Asia*, vol. 11, no. 3, pp. 351–66.

—, 1981d. 'Laos in China's Anti-Vietnam Strategy', *Asia Pacific Community*, no. 11, pp. 83–104.

—, 1982a. *Contemporary Laos: Studies in the Politics and Society of the Lao People's Democratic Republic*. St. Lucia, University of Queensland Press, and New York, St. Martin's Press.

—, 1982b. 'Laos 1981: Economic Prospects and Problems', in Huynh Kim Khanh (ed.), *Southeast Asian Affairs 1982*. Singapore, Institute of Southeast Asian Studies/ Heinemann, 1982, pp. 229–42.

—, 1983. 'Marxism and Theravada Buddhism: The Legitimation of Political Authority in Laos', *Pacific Affairs*, vol. 56, pp. 428–54.

—, 1984. 'Laos in 1983: A Time of Consolidation', in Pushpa Thambipillai (ed.), *Southeast Asian Affairs 1984*. Singapore, Institute of Southeast Asian Studies, pp. 179–94.

—, 1986a. 'The First Ten Years of Communist Rule in Laos: An Overview', *Asia Pacific Community*, pp. 55–81.

—, 1986b. 'Laos 1985: Time to Take Stock', in Lim Joo-Jock (ed.), *Southeast Asian Affairs 1986*. Singapore, Institute of Southeast Asian Studies, pp. 165–81.

—, 1986c. 'Relations Between the States of Indochina: the Lao–Vietnamese "Special Relationship" as a Model for Kampuchean–Vietnamese Relations'. Paper prepared for the 6th Biennial ASAA Conference, Sydney, May 1986.

— & Bucknell, R. S., 1982. 'Politicization of the Buddhist Sangha in Laos', *Journal of Southeast Asian Studies*, vol. 13, no. 1, pp. 60–80.

Szajkowski, Bogdan, 1981. *Marxist Governments: A World Survey, vol. 2: Cuba–Mongolia*. London, Macmillan.

Taillard, Christian, 1977. 'Le village lao de la région de Vientiane: un pouvoir local face au pouvoir étatique', *L'Homme*, vol. 17, nos 2–3, pp. 71–100.

—, 1983. 'Les transformations de quelques politiques agricoles socialistes en Asie entre 1978 et 1982' (Chine, Vietnam, Cambodge, et Laos), *Études rurales*, nos 89–90-91, pp. 111–43.

Tambiah, S. J., 1976. *World Conqueror and World Renouncer*. Cambridge, Cambridge University Press.

Terwiel, B. J., 1978. 'The Origin of the T'ai Peoples Reconsidered', *Oriens Extremus*, vol. 25, pp. 239–57.

Thee, Marek, 1973. *Notes of a Witness: Laos and the Second Indochinese War*. New York, Random House.

Toye, Hugh, 1968. *Laos: Buffer State or Battleground*. London: Oxford University Press.

UNDP, 1980. *Report on Development Co-operation Lao P.D.R.* Vientiane, UNDP.

—, 1984. *Summary of Foreign Aid to Laos, 1983*. Vientiane, UNDP.

—, 1985. *Draft Report submitted to the government of the LPDR in preparation for the country's second five-year plan*. Vientiane, UNDP, (cited as UNDP Draft Report, 1985).

UNHCR, 1985. *Refugees and Displaced Persons from Indo-China in UNHCR-Assisted Camps in Thailand (as of 30 June 1985)*. Bangkok, UNHCR. (cited as *UNHCR Report*, 1985).

Viraphol, Sarasin, 1985. 'Reflections on Thai-Lao Relations', *Asian Survey*, vol. 25, pp. 1260-78.

Vongvichit, Phoumi, 1968. *Le Laos et la lutte victorieuse du peuple lao contre le néo-colonialisme américain*. n.p., Éditions du Neo Lao Haksat.

Vo Thu Tinh, 1983. *Les Origines du Laos*. Paris, Sudestasie.

War Experiences Recapitulation Committee of the High-Level Military Institute, 1980. *Vietnam: The Anti-U.S. Resistance War for National Salvation 1954-1975: Military Events*. Hanoi, People's Army Publishing House. (Translated as JPRS 80968, 3 June 1982)

Westermeyer, Joseph, 1982. *Poppies, Pipes, and People: Opium and its Use in Laos*. Berkeley, University of California Press.

World Bank, 15 April 1983. *The Lao People's Democratic Republic: A Country Economic Memorandum*. No. 4125-LA.

Wyatt, David K. (ed.), 1975. *Lao Issara: The Memoires of Oun Sananikone*. Translated by John B. Murdoch. Ithaca, N.Y., Cornell Southeast Asia Program Data Paper no. 100.

— (ed.), 1978. *Iron Man of Laos: Prince Phetsareth Ratanavongsa*. Translated by John B. Murdoch. Ithaca, N.Y., Cornell Southeast Asia Program Data Paper no. 110.

—, 1984. *Thailand: A Short History*. New Haven, Yale University Press.

Zago, Marcel, 1972. *Rites et cérémonies en milieu Buddhiste Lao*. Rome, Universita Gregoriana Editrice.

Zasloff, Joseph J., 1973. *The Pathet Lao*. Lexington, Mass., D.C. Heath and Company.

—, 1981. 'Politics in the New Laos Part I: Leadership and Change; Part II: The Party, Political "Re-education" and Vietnamese Influence', *American Universities Field Staff Reports*, nos. 33 and 34.

—, 1981b. 'The Economy of the New Laos Part I: The Political Context; Part II: Plans and Performance', *American Universities Field Staff Reports*, nos. 44 and 45.

— & Brown, MacAlister (eds), 1975. *Communism in Indochina: New Perspectives*. Lexington, Mass., Lexington Books.

— & — (eds), 1978. *Communist Indochina and U.S. Foreign Policy: Postwar Realities*. Boulder, Col., Westview Press.

— & Goodman, Allen E. (eds), 1972. *Indochina in Conflict: A Political Assessment*. Lexington, Mass., D.C. Heath.

Index